# Growing Civil Society

## Philanthropic Studies

Albert B. Anderson. *Ethics for Fundraisers*

Karen J. Blair. *The Torchbearers:*
*Women and Their Amateur Arts Associations in America*

Eleanor Brilliant. *Private Charity and Public Inquiry:*
*A History of the Filer and Peterson Commissions*

Dwight F. Burlingame, editor. *The Responsibilities of Wealth*

Dwight F. Burlingame and Dennis Young, editors.
*Corporate Philanthropy at the Crossroads*

Charles T. Clotfelter and Thomas Ehrlich, editors.
*Philanthropy and the Nonprofit Sector in a Changing America*

Marcos Cueto, editor. *Missionaries of Science:*
*The Rockefeller Foundation and Latin America*

Gregory Eiselein. *Literature and Humanitarian Reform in the Civil War Era*

David C. Hammack, editor.
*Making the Nonprofit Sector in the United States: A Reader*

Jerome L. Himmelstein.
*Looking Good and Doing Good: Corporate Philanthropy and Corporate Power*

Warren F. Ilchman, Stanley N. Katz, and Edward L. Queen, II, editors.
*Philanthropy in the World's Traditions*

Thomas H. Jeavons. *When the Bottom Line Is Faithfulness:*
*Management of Christian Service Organizations*

Ellen Condliffe Lagemann, editor.
*Philanthropic Foundations: New Scholarship, New Possibilities*

Mike W. Martin. *Virtuous Giving: Philanthropy, Voluntary Service, and Caring*

Mary J. Oates. *The Catholic Philanthropic Tradition in America*

J. B. Schneewind, editor. *Giving: Western Ideas of Philanthropy*

Bradford Smith, Sylvia Shue, Jennifer Lisa Vest, and Joseph Villarreal.
*Philanthropy in Communities of Color*

David H. Smith. *Entrusted: The Moral Responsibilities of Trusteeship*

# Growing Civil Society

*From Nonprofit Sector to Third Space*

Jon Van Til

INDIANA
UNIVERSITY
PRESS
*Bloomington & Indianapolis*

This book is a publication of
Indiana University Press
601 North Morton Street
Bloomington, Indiana 47404-3797 USA

www.indiana.edu/~iupress

*Telephone orders*  800-842-6796
*Fax orders*  812-855-7931
*Orders by e-mail*  iuporder@indiana.edu

*The paper used in this publication meets the minimum
requirements of American National Standard for Information
Sciences—Permanence of Paper for Printed Library
Materials, ANSI Z39.48-1984.*

MANUFACTURED IN THE UNITED STATES OF AMERICA

**Library of Congress Cataloging-in-Publication Data**

Van Til, Jon.
Growing civil society : from nonprofit sector to third space / Jon Van Til.
p.   cm. — (Philanthropic studies)
Includes bibliographical references and index.
ISBN 0-253-33715-1 (cloth : alk. paper) — ISBN 0-253-21372-X (pbk. : alk. paper)
1. Nonprofit organizations—United States. 2. Charities—United States. 3.
Voluntarism—United States.   I. Title.   II. Series.

HD2769.2.U6 V36 2000
361.7′ 0973—dc21
99-054919

1  2  3  4  5    05  04  03  02  01  00

To William Van Til and Claire Heller Van Til,
each skilled in the understanding and uses
of society's third space.

# CONTENTS

## **Part Five** Searching for Meaning and Justice

## **Part Six** A Third Space

# PREFACE

For the past twelve years, I have had the privilege of writing an intermittent column, "On the Boundary," for the *NonProfit Times.* Themes raised in this column served as the basis for this book, which is intended to address questions about the world of voluntary, nonprofit, philanthropic activity that concern the intelligent citizen and general reader.

I am particularly grateful to the current editor of the *NonProfit Times,* Paul Clolery, for his support of my column over the past several years. Colleagues in the Association for Research on Nonprofit Organization and Voluntary Action (ARNOVA) have generously responded to my requests for comments on column drafts, and I am particularly grateful to Richard Bush, Roger Lohmann, and Arthur P. Williamson for their careful following and intelligent critique of these ongoing efforts.

William Van Til, always a careful reader and skilled editor, gave the manuscript a most useful reading and critique. I am grateful to him for this, and much else. Steven Ross behaved as a model doctoral student, and decorated a late draft I shared with him with hundreds of useful comments and queries arrayed on little yellow tags. Charles E. Gilbert, my longtime mentor in political affairs, offered useful comments on several chapters, as did a more recent colleague, Hillard Pouncy.

Rutgers University at Camden provided a most helpful sabbatical term in 1998 to permit the preparation of the manuscript. I particularly appreciate the support of my departmental chair, Michael Lang, and my dean, Margaret Marsh, in this regard.

Claire Van Til assisted in the preparation of the references, and served as a gracious hostess during a four-day residency at Mary Washington College, where I presented Chapter 13 in a public lecture in the fall of 1998. During that visit, Claire also treated her dad to the sublime experience of seeing her score the winning goal for the Mary Washington field hockey team in a game that sent her team to the finals of their conference championship. She, like her grandfather, are gratefully acknowledged in the dedication of this book.

# INTRODUCTION:
## THIRD SECTOR, THIRD SPACE

It is a Sunday afternoon, and a child's parents discover that she has a medical problem that appears to require immediate attention. A choice presents itself among four options: 1) head to the emergency room of a for-profit hospital or emergency care center; 2) go to a public hospital or health center; 3) choose a church- or university-related nonprofit hospital as the place of care and treatment; or 4) observe the child at home, asking a neighbor or relative to join in the provision of observation and care.

Four choices: 1) first, to call upon the services of a business firm; 2) second, to seek assistance from a governmental agency; 3) third, to find the service required as delivered by a voluntary, or nonprofit organization; or 4) fourth, to provide what is needed with the aid of extended kin, neighbors, and other resources found in the immediate community.

Each of these choices involves the use of organizations that are located within what scholars have come to call organizational "sectors" in society. The first, because it is the largest in financial terms, is known as the "private," "business," or "for-profit" sector. The second, with the power to wage war and raise taxes, is the "public" or "governmental" sector. The third, less easy to identify but nonetheless significant, is known as the "voluntary," "nonprofit," or "third" sector. The fourth, and most important to the largest number of people, is the "informal" sector of family, kin, neighborhood, and community.

Choices between the use of these four sectors confront each of us on an everyday basis. Let us say we do not mow a thistle weed from our front yard when it emerges from the turf, but rather let it grow in the hope that it will blossom with a dazzling array of desert flowers. Within weeks the thistle plant assumes the size of a small tree, and arouses the distress of our neighbor, who worries that the plant will soon disperse its seeds more widely, and requests its removal.

Again, we face a four-sector choice. We can involve our lawyer (first sector) to investigate the borough's laws (second sector); we can call the local horticultural society (third sector) to ask about the decorative uses of the thistle bush; or we could speak further with our neighbor and others in the community (fourth sector) to explain our desire to see, once more, the desert blooms we enjoyed in a Colorado childhood. If we changed our mind on things, we could even call a tree-removal service (first sector) to extricate the spreading weed from our front yard.

Examples might spread as quickly as the thistle bush grows, and need not be proliferated here. The point is that, in everyday life, we often do choose between the solutions to problems offered by the four institutional sectors. The question that this book seeks to answer has to do with why such choices make any difference, either to us or to society at large. In particular, the question is addressed: What is it about the choices offered by the third of these sectors—consisting of its wide variety of clubs, associations, and organizations—that makes real differences to the quality of our lives, both as individuals and members of society?

## How the Third Sector Relates to the Rest of Society

A simple way to understand what forces are at play in society is provided by what I call the PECTS schema. Based on an almost totally incomprehensible system developed some years back by the Harvard sociologist Talcott Parsons (1966), this way of categorizing society's workings suggests to us that every social organization, whether a family or a town or a nation, has to solve four problems if it is to thrive, or even survive. These problems include setting goals, attracting resources, sharing meaning, and sticking together.

Every society has to solve these problems, too, and that is where the PECTS come in. We tend to develop a set of institutions around each of these needs, as follows:

P = Politics (or Government): how decisions are made about basic problems we face in our communities. In a country like our own, this is done by a system we call "constitutional democracy."

E = The Economy: how work is organized in order to make our livings, produce goods and services, and create wealth. In a country like our own, this is done by a system we call "mixed capitalism."

C = Culture: how meaning is made of life through language, ethnic identity, and religion. In a country like our own, this is done by structures we call families, neighborhoods, and communities.

TS = The Third Sector (sometimes called the voluntary or nonprofit sector): how fellowship or common cause is created by joining with others in voluntary association. In our society, this is done by means of some million and a half tax-exempt organizations and many more clubs, groups, and voluntary associations.

An important use of the PECTS system is that it reminds us that society's major institutions are always in interaction with each other, and that transactions continually flow between one sector and another.

From the point of view of the individual in society, the activities of third-sector organizations affect everyday life in a number of ways. We may choose to receive medical care from a third-sector hospital; we may turn to third-sector associations for information on thistles and other growing things. Additionally, we will find ourselves called upon (sometimes by phone at inconvenient times) to support third-sector organizations through individual solicitations or by participating in the United Way. And in our community life, we will find that various nonprofit athletic, social, civic, business, and religious organizations often merit our interest, participation, and support. Indeed, the nearly one and one-half million formally certified nonprofit organizations within the United States, not to mention the almost ten million other voluntary associations, are inescapable parts of our daily lives.

From a society-wide perspective, the role of the third sector is not only important because it concerns individuals, it is also important because the third sector has become a major player in modern institutional life. Potential presidential candidates like Colin Powell, Lamar Alexander, Elizabeth Dole, and Bill Bradley assume leadership roles in third-sector organizations while they await the nation's call to higher leadership. The policy recommendations of nonprofit think tanks like the Brookings Institution or the Heritage Foundation are attended with interest by both media and governmental leaders. And the services provided by a myriad of agencies provide many millions of Americans with the necessities of food, shelter, clothing, and personal support they require if they are to survive in a land of limited opportunities to achieve adequate levels of work, income, and personal wealth.

Third-sector organizations provide a full 7 percent of all paid employment in society; when the work of volunteers is included, this total rises to 9 percent. These organizations work for a myriad of purposes, and often oppose each other in the aims that they seek. They enjoy close relations with businesses and governmental organizations: there are many revolving doors and quiet lunches in this world.

The third sector is hardly a realm of virtue unalloyed, in the United States or anywhere else. Novelist Robert Stone puts it dramatically in his best-seller *Damascus Gate* (1998: 351), describing the mix of governmental and non-governmental organizations in contemporary Jerusalem:

Organs that were not in fact of the state represented themselves as being so. State organs pretended to be non-state, or anti-state, or the organs of other states, including enemy ones. . . . Some people worked simply for fun or money. Then there were the pious and the patriots. . . .

## From Sector to Space

Many books have been written that extol the virtues of one institutional sector or another in American life. Social theorists have searched throughout the ages for the proper balance between market, state, and society, and that search continues until the very present, as a recent title, *Beyond Prince and Merchant: Citizen Participation and the Rise of Civil Society* (Burbidge, 1998), indicates.

Each institutional sector has its intellectual boosters, who assert that they have located the key to the right ordering of society's structure. Economists from Karl Marx to Milton Friedman have preached the primacy of a right ordering of economic forces, whether socialist or capitalist. Their intellectual descendants, from linguist Zellig Harris (1997) to writer George Gilder (1981), rehearse the various materialist arguments that underlie economic determinism.

Political theorists from Hobbes to Rousseau have located the key to society's right ordering in the governmental arena, and prescribed a variety of political arrangements from absolute monarchy to participatory democracy. Their intellectual followers in the field of political theory, like Theodore Lowi (1979) and Benjamin Barber (1984, 1998), develop their arguments for the primacy of political arrangements in securing the benefits of life, liberty, and happiness.

Associational theorists from Tocqueville to Durkheim have located the key to society's right ordering in the degree to which it engenders a flourishing third sector. Their intellectual descendants, from stock exchange executive Theodore Levitt (1973) to social theorists Paul Hirst (1994) and Jeremy Rifkin (1995), find in a varying mix of service and advocacy a best means to secure the blessings of contemporary life.

Even the informal sector has its intellectual defenders and critics. Lawyer Stephen Carter finds the keys to social reform in *Civility: Manners, Morals, and the Etiquette of Democracy* (1998), and Israeli social scientist Avishai Margalit seeks to develop a theory of *The Decent Society* (1996). Worrying that family and community will not be enough, literary critic Benjamin DeMott warns of *The Trouble with Friendship* (1995).

One doesn't have to be a pedigreed author and social theorist to pick a favorite among society's major institutional sectors. For instance, a recent *New York Times* story reported:

> "We have a different vision," said Representative John R. Kasich of Ohio, the budget committee chairman, who is considered a possible presidential candidate in 2000. "Our vision is that the Federal Government ought to be less important. The family and the individual ought to be more important." (May 21, 1998, p. A22)

There is a formula to the writing of many of the books I have just mentioned. I call it "sector chauvinism." The author of such a work identifies a favored institutional sector, describes a particular way in which its forces might be reconfigured, and proceeds to explain why a course of action based on the favored sector will prove productive, while the paths to change prescribed by devotees of the other sectors will prove fruitless and deceptive. What emerges is a scholarly literature of institutional boosterism, which often simply becomes an argument of titles: Is *Civility* enough? Can *Strong Democracy* assure *The Decent Society?* What lies *Beyond Prince and Merchant?*

This book tries to be different. I do not intend in developing its argument to take sides in the wars between the sectors. Rather, I begin with the recognition that ours is a four-sector society, and that it seems quite reasonable to assume that each major institutional sector will have to work productively if society is to cohere and thrive. Answers abound in the modern world, but it may be only when they are bound together in a coherent four-sector vision that they become real solutions to our pressing needs. Working in partnership, the institutions of government, businesses, families, and third-sector groups might be able to achieve understandings and efficiencies sufficient to sustain lives of good quality for most people in the years ahead. Working at cross-purposes and with the sense that only one way is truly right and productive would seem only a path to intellectual, political, and social conflict, cacophony, and immobilization.

The third sector is itself, as we shall see, a house of many mansions. This book examines its realm by means of a series of visits to its rooms. The cases it presents reveal the third sector in some of its glories and many of its limitations. In some cases, third-sector organizations seem like any other: fallible tools of human organization providing services that might as easily issue from a business corporation or a governmental agency. In others, particular organizations, individuals, and actions take on a more significant role in the working of society. This book is both about what is trivial and ordinary about this realm of human endeavor, and what is special and invaluable in some of its work.

The third sector, or at least an important part of it, as I will seek to show in this book, occupies a particularly important space in society, a space that includes a myriad of places in which individuals and groups daily create some of society's most important products. These products include expressions of caring and humanity, services to persons in need, and calls to action aimed at righting a wide range of problems and injustices. This "third space," as I will call it, may well be not only important in resolving many human problems, but it also has the potential to be a source for the reconstruction for a troubled society in an age of rapid change and turbulence.

## A Note to Readers

In this post-modern era, rare is the reader who devours a book from cover to cover. This book has been written for a general reader interested in the role of voluntary action and nonprofit organization in society. Chapters have been placed in six separate parts of the book: Part One provides an introduction to concepts and maps of the third sector. Parts Two, Three, and Four consider the interrelations between the third sector and the other major sectors of society: government, business, and culture. Part Five considers the role of the third space, to which third-sector organizations may importantly contribute in the quest for meaning and justice in social life. And Part Six presents a way of looking at building a truly civil society by means of individual and organizational action. The concept of "third space," I conclude, provides an important tool for that construction.

Colleagues in the study of the third sector might want to turn directly to Chapters 8 and 14, where the elements of a fresh perspective on the field have been placed, and then review other chapters that may address their particular interests. General readers might want to skim over the text of Chapter 2, which reviews theoretical conceptions with details that may exceed their interest, while attending to the maps of the sector there presented. Those with a particular interest in specific boundaries of the sectors might want to start where their own interests are particularly found. All are invited now to turn the page and consider the life of Florence Alberta MacLean, and reflect on what may happen when third sector and third space are but weakly developed.

# Part One

*The Uses of the Third Sector*

# 1

# Building Blocks
# for the Third Sector

When I think of what the third sector really means in our communities, I recall the experience of Florence Alberta MacLean of Gananoque, Ontario. Florence was the daughter of a brave young woman, Susannah Rex Perry, who chose to marry the son of a dour English Presbyterian minister. Daniel Grant MacLean earned the wrath of his father when he "married too young." And so he and his young wife decided to build their life in Canada, where they began to raise a family of five children. Daniel abandoned his dreams of becoming a physician and selected instead the career of veterinarian.

Daniel, alas, succumbed to an occupational hazard in 1885—yes, he was kicked in the head by a horse he was treating—and his family was left penniless and without support on his subsequent death. The generosity of the local community did not suffice, and the brave family eventually made its way to New York City, where the meager incomes made by Susannah and her brood sufficed to assure the survival of its members into the 20th century. Florence married a steamfitter, and their son, William Van Til, went on to become one of America's most eminent educators of the 20th century.

From that same William Van Til, my father—for yes, that daughter of Gananoque I have been telling you about was my paternal grandmother—I learned that experiential education was the best kind, and that service often provided the basis for both experience and learning. As a young high school teacher, William Van Til frequently involved his students in creating a loop of youth hostels in Ohio, and sponsored trips involving social travel to cities as disparate as Detroit and Washington, D.C.[1]

As I came of intellectual age, I became intrigued with the work of what I later learned to call the "third sector"—that vast network of persons and groups engaged in service, philanthropy, and participation—the network my grandmother's family had not found when they needed it in Gananoque, and which, indeed, was not much more fully developed in New York when they arrived there. My doctoral dissertation explored the ways in which groups of women welfare recipients in Pennsylvania, both white and black, joined in associations like the Welfare Rights Organization in a determined effort to advance their own needs for both income and self-respect. Later, I examined the roots of voluntarism, the practice of philanthropy, and the workings of nonprofit organization.

My concern in this chapter is to develop a number of ideas regarding the third sector that have become prominent in public thought in recent years. Seven such ideas will be introduced, and then looked at in relationship to each other in the remainder of this book. These building blocks for the third sector are:

1. Social Capital
2. Socio-Political Pluralism/Associationalism
3. Communitarianism
4. The Farewell State
5. The End of Work
6. Social Economy/Social Entrepreneurship
7. Civil Society

## Social Capital as a Product of Citizen Participation

The concept of "social capital" was introduced in 1990 by University of Chicago sociologist James S. Coleman in his massive treatise, *Foundations of Social Theory*, and used to very good advantage by Harvard political scientist Robert Putnam in his widely admired study of democracy in Italy, *Making Democracy Work*.

Social capital, Putnam (1993: 167) advises, "refers to features of social organization, such as trust, norms, and networks, that can improve the efficiency of society by facilitating coordinated actions." It is an idea parallel to the "physical capital" formed by machines and the "human capital" represented by an educated workforce. Social capital is that fund of valued interaction that results in a confidence that new problems can be tackled and resolved by groups of neighbors or citizens or fellow workers.

Putnam studied the "civic communities" in the Italian regions of

Emilia-Romagna and Tuscany. There he found values of solidarity, civic participation, and integrity to be strong, and institutions of democracy flourishing. Putnam describes the roots of these structures to be "astonishingly deep." At their core he identified rich "networks of civic engagement"—"neighborhood associations, choral societies, cooperatives, sports clubs, and mass-based parties" (1993: 173).

In later articles (the so-called "bowling alone" series), Putnam probes what he calls "the strange disappearance of civic America" (Putnam, forthcoming). He pursues the issue like a persistent detective, wondering why Americans are increasingly unlikely to participate in all sorts of group activities, ranging from bowling leagues to neighborhood socializing to attending church to voting in elections. The answer, he suggests, is to be found in the delivery of Americans, over the past thirty years, to the thrall of the almighty television tube, and their substitution of its easy pleasures for the more rigorous discipline of social interaction.

The steady depletion of social capital in modern society, Putnam asserts, provides a major challenge. His work illustrates that social capital is a public good, one that markets and their private agents alone cannot provide. Third-sector organizations, on the other hand, can play a crucial role in its amassing.

Putnam concludes his careful study with the observation (1993: 185), "Building social capital will not be easy, but it is the key to making democracy work." Where social capital exists, people can come together to understand what needs to be done and work to accomplish needed tasks. Where it is absent, they will stay home and let the TV set explain that much is going wrong in the world around them but there is not much that anybody can do about it.

## Socio-Political Pluralism/Associationalism

The idea of socio-political pluralism emerges from classical political and social thought, closely connected to concepts of separation of powers and relative autonomy of institutional activity in society. The pluralist vision involves a multi-institutional structure for society, in which political, economic, cultural, and associational forces are able to organize themselves, in relative independence from each other, to advance the distinct purposes they each embody.

Political theorist Paul Hirst presents a major statement of contemporary pluralist thought in his book *Associative Democracy*. Hirst (1994: 15) notes that associationalism "is not a new idea. It developed in the nineteenth century as an alternative to both liberal individualism and socialist collectivism. . . . Associationalism had two characteristic features. . . . The first was the advocacy of a decentralized economy based on the non-capitalistic principles of cooperation and mutuality. The second was the criticism of the centralized and sovereign state, with radical federalist and political pluralist ideas advanced as a substitute. The associationalists believed in voluntarism and self-government, not collectivism and state compulsion."[2]

In Hirst's conception, society is best organized if voluntary organizations are numerous, effective, and "thick" in meaning. A basic role of government is to assure a level playing field for these associations to grow, act, and contest with each other. Associations not only address social aims, but also serve as means for economic organization and cooperation.

Two fundamental principles guide the associationalist view of politics, economics, and society, Hirst asserts (1994: 51):

> 1. that associations must be justified in terms of their benefits for individuals . . .
> 2. that all associations should be communities of choice and not of fate, and that compulsion in an associational commonwealth is only justified in order to preserve the condition in which individuals can freely choose associations and enjoy the benefits of cooperating with others.

The pluralist position emerged prominently in the sociology and political science of the 1950s as a counterpoint to theories of democratic elitism, which contended that a small "power elite" tended to control decision making in American communities, from the small town to the national level. Many social scientists, like C. Wright Mills and William Domhoff, whose studies identified the prominence of the elite pattern in American life, were dismayed with what they found. Others, like a group of political scientists at Yale led by Robert Dahl, tended to find strengths in the pattern, and accommodated their pluralism to realities of limited participation. Recalling the work of political economist Joseph Schumpeter, these observers warned of a political system that might become "overheated" by excessive participation, and identified positive functions to such non-participatory actions as not voting, trusting in one's representatives, and even being "functionally" apathetic.

In the 1960s, the pluralists' effort to secure a position more accommodative to values of participation and equality was swamped by the rise of conceptions of more highly "participatory democracy." These ideas were much more akin to those of direct democratic decision making, and became the mantra of a variety of "new left" and "movement" organizations whose impact was felt both within the social politics of the age and the academic theories of the day. Increasingly, the pluralist approach was painted as just one more conservative, status quo–oriented theory.

What the pluralists had neglected, noted their critics from the left, was an observation made early in the debate by Schattschneider (1960: 35): "The flaw in the pluralist heaven is that the heavenly chorus sings with a strong upper-class accent." But rather than efforts to correct inequalities by incremental policies, visions of dramatic transformations, or even revolutions, increasingly came to characterize progressive political thought. It was not seen as sufficient to rely on the outcomes produced by an independent set of institutional spheres: the powers of economic control needed to be harnessed more directly to serve the good of a reformed society.

Ultimately, of course, the revolution did not occur, and the wealth and power of those who controlled America's great organizational empires, whether economic, political, or nonprofit, lay largely undisturbed. Taxes were dramatically reduced for those at the highest incomes; the spread in income and wealth between those at the top of the heap and those of moderate or even lesser means became a yawning gap; and the operational ideology of the era became that of "democratic capitalism," with the emphasis on the noun.

By the 1990s the theory of pluralism exhibited an increasing concern for the importance of economic redistribution. An early critic of the perspective, William Connolly, presented a set of essays dedicated to the proposition that pluralism was an important socio-political structure, and that it required both a tolerance of difference and a provision of at least a modicum of socio-economic equality. Connolly's argument for equality is both eloquent and notable for the degree to which it was ignored by the communitarians who carried the pluralist argument into the 1980s and beyond (1995: 81):

> Two goals, then: first, to establish a floor below which no one is compelled to fall, because such a floor enables anyone and everyone to participate in the common life if he or she is inclined to do so; second, to establish a glass ceiling that is difficult to break through. Such a ceiling would impede economically privileged minorities from constructing private escapes from the general conditions of education, crime, military service, and the environment, and it would encourage formation of political coalitions to forge affirmative public responses to the collective damage and suffering engendered by the history of private escapes.

## Communitarianism and the Search for Responsible Voluntarism

"Communitarianism," an awkward term coined by sociologist-reformer Amitai Etzioni, sought to combine liberal pluralist themes with conservative themes of individual responsibility. Adherents of this social theory, such as political theorist William Galston, were influential within President Clinton's administration, and Clinton himself often articulated tenets of this theory.

Communitarianism, granted, is a name that markets poorly, but its efforts to link the liberal tradition of individual rights with the conservative focus on individual responsibility represents an intriguing attempt to create a synthesizing intellectual perspective. In his inaugural State of the Union Address, William Jefferson Clinton struck strong communitarian themes, saying:

> It is time to break the bad habit of expecting something for nothing from our Government or from each other. Let us all take more responsibility not only for ourselves and our families, but also for our communities and our country. . . .

> I challenge a new generation of young Americans to a season of service; to act on your idealism by helping troubled children, keeping company with those in need, reconnecting our torn communities. There is so much to be done. Enough, indeed, for millions of others who are still young in spirit to give of themselves in service, too.

> In serving, we recognize a simple but powerful truth: We need each other and we must care for each other.

The key policy statement developed by communitarians is called the Responsive Communitarian Platform. Central to its vision is the recognition that all citizens are members of many communities, and "the rights that we cherish can only be sustained in the context of these communities." The Communitarian Platform states (Etzioni, 1993: 253–67):

> A Communitarian perspective recognizes both individual human dignity and the social dimension of human existence.

> A Communitarian perspective recognizes that the preservation of individual liberty depends on the active maintenance of the institutions of civil society. . . .

> A Communitarian perspective recognizes that communities and polities, too, have obligations—including the duty to be responsive to their members and to foster participation and deliberation in social and political life.[3]

The Responsive Communitarian Platform recognizes the pervasive character of voluntary action in American society. On the one hand, its drafters value the "bright side" of the voluntary tradition, noting the values of community problem solving through the working of "innumerable social, religious, ethnic, work place, and professional associations." Communitarians extend this tradition when they express the value of "some measure of caring, sharing, and being our brother's and sister's keeper" (Etzioni, 1993: 253–67).

The voluntary tradition, like the communitarian perspective, also values a locality-centered approach to problem solving. As the Responsive Communitarian Platform expresses it, problems should be dealt with as close to the community as possible. "This principle holds for duties of attending to the sick, troubled, delinquent, homeless, and new immigrants. . . . Moreover, partnerships are important in both the communitarian and voluntary traditions, and such policy initiatives as national service are valued by both."

Communitarians, on the other hand, are also aware of the "dark side" of the voluntary tradition. Regarding voluntary associations, they "ask how 'private governments,' whether corporations, labor unions, or voluntary associations, can become more responsible to their members and to the needs of the community" (Etzioni, 1993: 253–67).

As Amitai Etzioni, the founder of the contemporary communitarian movement, envisions it, a communitarian society carries out a "multilogue," or national town meeting, which is itself inspired by third-sector social movements. "In it, millions of citizens—over beers in bowling alleys, at water coolers at work, and over coffee and at cocktail parties—discuss and debate the issues flagged by sit-ins, demonstrations, boycotts, and other such dramatizations. The multilogue is further extended in radio call-in shows, letters to the editor, sermons in churches and synagogues. Gradually a new consensus emerges" (Etzioni, 1993: 230–31).

What the third sector might particularly provide to such a multilogue is a commitment to "responsible voluntarism" (Van Til, 1994). Such activity might take the form of a particular dedication to work, or "whistleblowing" within a governmental or corporate bureaucracy, or working with neighbors to care for elders, install a stop sign, or restrain illicit drug sales within a neighborhood.

Voluntary and nonprofit associations form one important set of institutions in the organizational world of contemporary society. From Tocqueville to the present, students of society have found in the intermediate association a source of participation, political competence, and legitimation. But real associations need to be held to tests of effectiveness and responsibility.

After all, if voluntarism is a force that includes the helping act of the altruist, the workings of the Red Cross organization to assure disaster relief, and the terrorist tactics of the Ku Klux Klan, it would certainly seem appropriate to be able to distinguish between "responsible" and "irresponsible" forms of civic participation.

Responsible voluntarism, from a communitarian perspective, is an active, spontaneous, and challenging force in society. Its development might serve, therefore, as an organizing principle for the development of an active democracy in an era better known for its complacency.

Communitarian thinkers have yet to develop, however, a way of bringing the power of economic corporations to the production of such necessary outcomes as sufficient employment, adequate incomes, and a proper respect for the natural environment. Thus the next two forces discussed in this chapter identify several serious challenges that beset the path of achieving these basic goals of social and economic justice.

## The Farewell State

Jacquelyn Thayer Scott, president of the University College of Cape Breton (Canada), has noted the rise of the "farewell state" in her country and the United States in a brilliant doctoral dissertation, "Voluntary Sector in Crisis." The farewell state, it may be observed, offers us a view from the rear of a disappearing welfare state.

The farewell state was simultaneously introduced in the United States by Ronald Reagan and in Britain by Margaret Thatcher. Its contemporary adherents in the U.S. Congress, led by former House Speaker Gingrich and his allies, often make Reagan and Thatcher look like timid liberals in comparison to the proposals they continue to advance.

The tenets of the farewell state are clear and unambiguous:

- The basic function of government is to provide for order in society (what Hobbes called the "watchman state"). Police and defense should grow; all other governmental programs should be drastically reduced.

- The business of a nation is business (as Ronald Reagan's favorite predecessor, Calvin Coolidge, put it). If taxes can be sufficiently reduced, those who own a country's corporations can be counted on to provide employment to all its workers; a rising economic tide will lift all boats.

- The family is society's basic institution. If children will only say no and parents will only stay together, the need for most social programs will be largely reduced.

- If any societal problems remain, the spirit of voluntarism can be relied upon to relieve suffering and to provide hope to those in need.

The critics of the farewell state identify a subtext to this chant. They see the rise of unprecedented corporate power and increasing levels of social and economic inequality; they see the domination of politics by the voting power of the rich and fearful; they see a reign of morality inappropriate to the increasingly desperate lives of the poor and desperate; and they see a third sector overwhelmed by societal need itself seeking to cope with the loss of governmental and philanthropic support.

The farewell state emerges to replace the welfare state, a creation of four centuries in the Anglo-American experience. The Welfare State itself may be traced to the Poor Laws of 1601 in Britain, when Parliament offered support to children whose parents were unable to provide for their support. Before that time, Catholic Britain provided such care through the parish and the local community. But as need and mobility increased in society, the local community yielded to the impersonality and rigors of the industrial-urban society.

The Welfare State became regularly, if inelegantly, extended throughout British and American history, its milestones marked by the development of a wide range of social insurance programs in the early 1900s, the passage of the Social Security Act in 1935, and the many programs developed during the War on Poverty of the 1960s. The high water mark of the Welfare State, however, was reached in Britain in 1948 with the establishment of socialized medicine and universal access to higher education.

As the farewell state takes its place, it is with a friendly admonition to do the right thing and the hearty wish that all will be for the best in this best of all possible worlds. Words, and not deeds, are the farewell state's strong suit.

Nonprofit organizations have come in for some unpleasant surprises in the farewell state. As efforts continue to balance budgets while at the same time cutting taxes, increasingly deep cuts have been anticipated in governmental support for nonprofit organizations. Nonprofits in the United States at present secure almost a third of their financial resources from government, an annual sum of approximately $100 billion. Lester Salamon, the leading expert on governmental-nonprofit relations, notes that the 1997 budget resolution passed by Congress in 1996 would have cut a "cumulative total of close to $90 billion in Federal support over the 1997–2002 period" (1997: 19).

Can the third sector invent ways to meet increasing human needs while its budgets are being ravaged by declines in public support? This is a vital question in our neo-conservative age. Unless we resolve it, the coming of the 21st century may find society torn by conflicts between the wealthy and the desperate, the complacent and the needy. We may yet come to miss the Welfare State, and to realize that it must be reinvented.

# The End of Work

The concept of "the end of work" was developed by economist and policy analyst Jeremy Rifkin in a book of the same title. Most of the book is about work, and why it has become so hard to find in recent years.[4] In writing both clear and detailed, Rifkin documents the impact of the new technology revolution brought by automation and microchip-based information processing. This revolution offers a choice between liberation from long work hours, on the one hand, and an increasing social division between the over- and the underemployed, on the other.

Rifkin believes that we are in the process of making the wrong choice, and that future generations will be faced with dwindling prospects for steady employment of any sort. While fortunes are being made by those who own the patents on technological innovations, most members of the middle classes are on their way to dwindling incomes, threats to whatever jobs they are able to secure, and an inadequate financial base to assure a comfortable retirement.

Society provides its members with only four institutional means of solving its problems: government, business, the third sector, and the informal sector (family and neighborhood). If government is bowing out at the same time that corporations radically cut back their offers of work, what is left for us? Can the family replace the need for income and social service? Can the third sector?

So where does this leave us? Rifkin, having painted us into a corner, is not without hope. He sees two ways of dealing with the potential crisis of uneven employment: 1) by developing public policies that share the available work by shortening the work week and thereby redistributing income; and 2) by developing governmental programs to provide alternative employment in the third sector—"the social economy"—for those whose labor is no longer required in the marketplace.

## Social Economy/Social Entrepreneurship

The concept of "social economy" ("economie sociale" as widely used in France in the 1970s, and introduced to American audiences by the present writer in his *Mapping the Third Sector* in 1988, and then to a wider public by Jeremy Rifkin in his book *The End of Work* in 1995) depicts a society that meets many of its economic needs through the provision of cooperative economic activity. Rifkin (1995: 242) notes that the "French economist Thierry Jeantet says that the social economy is not 'measured the way one measures capitalism, in terms of salaries, revenues, etc., but its outputs integrate social results with indirect economic gains, for example the number of handicapped persons well cared for at home and not in hospitals; the degree of solidarity between persons of different age groups in a neighborhood.'"

The idea of "social entrepreneurship" also seeks to integrate the third sector into economic life. As columnist Thomas McLaughlin (1999: 18) sees it, social entrepreneurs blend "business and traditional social service" by themselves generating some of the wealth that they use. They seek to make money while providing service, and deploy their profits to expand the services they provide. An example of social entrepreneurship McLaughlin presents is "Road to Responsibility, a Marshfield, Mass., provider of services to mentally retarded and developmentally disabled individuals, which bought a motel in bankruptcy, reorganized it and currently operates it by employing its own clients."

Programs based on ideas of social economy and social enterprise respond to the provision of economic goals in an era of declining public and private employment. The social economy allows individuals to pool their producing and buying power in a voluntary way, to develop voluntary work-sharing schemes as those involving the use of "time dollars" (as developed by lawyers Jean and Edgar Cahn), and to otherwise participate in the building and maintenance of productive communities.[5] The concept may seem too French to succeed in this Anglo culture, but its ideas are well defined and powerful. They suggest that an important task of the third sector is not simply to offer "service" and "participation," but also to meet the more basic human needs for economic security, support, and productivity.

Americans tend to talk less about "social economy" and more about "social entrepreneurship." Entrepreneurs (the word is French, and means the middle person who takes from both sides) have been treated with reverence by social scientists since Joseph Schumpeter envisioned their role as that of the "risk-taker" in his classic study, *Capitalism, Socialism, and Democracy* (1947).

According to Jerr Boschee, president of The National Center for Social Entrepreneurs,[6] "Social entrepreneurs are nonprofit executives who pay increasing attention to market forces without losing sight of their underlying missions—and that balancing act is the heart and soul of a movement that is rapidly accelerating throughout the sector." The concept has been advanced in important statements by psychiatrist Leonard Duhl (1990) and foundation leaders Robert Long and Joel Orosz (1997), and has become a fashionable term in the contemporary lexicon of nonprofit organization leadership.

Duhl observes that social entrepreneurs or planners must direct their loyalty "outside of particular organizations and specific goals." He identifies the social entrepreneur as one who has developed substantial "map-making skills" and can navigate the "cracks between systems" (Duhl, 1990: 113). The social entrepreneur is an effective boundary spanner, an individual experienced in the arts of community and organizational collaboration (cf. Lippitt and Van Til, 1980).

Social entrepreneurism represents the capitalist version of the more cooperative, or socialistic, conception of social economy. Both perspectives seek to use the language and skills of the business world to advance the material well-being of their members/clients. And both give rise to the important boundary issue of just how distinct the nonprofit world is from the world of business organization and practice.

## Civil Society

The idea of "civil society" has become the most fashionable of contemporary third-sector concepts. It is a very old and very slippery concept. The civil society concept has become the master theme in contemporary thought about the third sector. Scarcely a week goes by without a major new publication with the term in its title, and still its meaning and implications remain difficult to grasp.[7]

Classical political economists like John Stuart Mill and Adam Smith viewed civil society as a realm of virtuous freedom, both economic and personal, and contrasted it with the evils of the state. Hegel, on the other hand, used it to explain how government could find its niche in a market-driven society by nurturing cooperation in the face of economic and social conflict.

Marx expanded Hegel's argument, and delineated the terrain of civil society as one of "exploitation, alienation and social injustice" (Abdelramen, 1998: 6). Neo-Marxist Antonio Gramsci saw civil society as the "place where the state operates to enforce invisible, intangible and subtle forms of power, through educational, cultural and religious systems and other institutions" (Abdelramen, 1998: 7).

The idea of civil society was rescued from the dustbin of history by its seeming fit to the needs of emerging democracies in Eastern Europe following the evaporation of communist structures in 1989 and thereafter. But, as Ralf Dahrendorf (1997: 3, 12) has observed, it is "clearly far too early to pronounce with any degree of certainty on whether the revolution of 1989 has succeeded or not. . . . The revolution of 1989, like other revolutions before it, was bound to disappoint those who entered it with extravagant hopes for a new world of unconstrained discourse, equality and fundamental democracy." And yet, Dahrendorf (1997: 60) observes with greater hope, "citizenship and civil society go one important step further than elections and markets. They are goals to strive for rather than dangers to avoid."

In its current incarnation, civil society continues to mean many

Figure 1. The Many Faces of Civil Society (Adapted from Hyden, 1997)

STATE AND CIVIL SOCIETY ARE LINKED

| ECONOMIC INTERESTS DOMINATE | ASSOCIATIONAL LIFE MOST CENTRAL |
|---|---|
| POST-MARXIST <br><br> (Hegel, Gramsci) | LIBERAL (or Strong Democratic) <br><br> (Locke, Barber) |
| LIBERTARIAN <br><br> (Paine, Shils) | ASSOCIATIONAL (or Communitarian or Strong Cultural) <br><br> (Tocqueville, Eberly) |

STATE AND CIVIL SOCIETY ARE SEPARATE

things to many people. To a liberal like Dahrendorf (1997: 77–78) it is "created by grass-root initiatives" and association. To another liberal, former Senator Bill Bradley (1996), civil society forms the "third leg" of a societal stool in which both government and the marketplace are seen to have their limitations. Bradley includes the nonprofit sector in this vision, but also the family, neighborhood, and community.

To conservatives like presidential hopeful George W. Bush, as well as William Bennett and Senator Dan Coats, the issue is how to nurture civil society as a replacement for much of what government has previously done. Aware of the frenzy among their fellow Republicans to eliminate government from nearly every corner of American life, theirs is a voice of moderation asserting the need for government itself to play a major role in the reconstruction of civil society. This approach aims to subsidize charitable giving and a variety of sociable behaviors and organizations.

As a concept, civil society comes perilously close to being the "play-dough" of the social sciences, capable of being formed into nearly whatever shape the theorist chooses. Political scientist Goran Hyden composes a four-cell table that accommodates Marxist, liberal, associational, and libertarian renditions of the concept, as depicted in Figure 1.

Political theorist Benjamin Barber focuses on three of these traditions, omitting only the post-Marxist view, in his recent book, *A Place for Us: How to Make Society Civil and Democracy Strong*. Barber calls Hyden's associational variant "communitarian," and identifies the liberal version of the theory, the one he prefers, as "strong democratic," recalling his development of that concept in his influential earlier study of democratic theory (1984). Barber sees civil society as a voluntary realm "devoted to public goods"—the "true domain" of "church, family, and voluntary association" (1998: 44).

Policy analyst Don E. Eberly develops a theory of "civil society plus" in his recent book, *America's Promise: Civil Society and the Renewal of American Culture* (1998). Like Barber, Eberly rejects economic versions of the theory, and strongly prefers the "civic republican" variant. But his theory partakes far more of the "associational" and "communitarian" than Barber's. For Eberly, civil society cannot simply be created by participation; rather, it must rest on a cultural basis of shared values and beliefs. Such a "strong culture," he asserts, best rests on a "transcendent proposition":

> That our democracy has a soul, that our nation has a creed, that our institutions must possess moral cohesion, and that American renewal draws its inspiration and power from our country's venerable heritage of religious faith. (Eberly, 1998: 198)

An appealing aspect of the civil society concept may be found in the linguistic root it shares with the concept of "civility." Sociologist Edward Shils, who used the concept often, sought to establish links between the theory of civil society and "civility" in behavior. Like Hegel, Shils tended to see civil society as highly interrelated with a market economy. Shils (1997: 91) was concerned that civil society was declining in American life, citing its decline within universities, churches, persons of wealth, labor unions, rural communities, and among the "rather large unemployed *Lumpenproletariat* and the criminal and delinquent class." Shils, who died in 1995, was frankly puzzled as to whether civil society was in decline or growth:

> Against this background of incivility among the various classes and major institutions of present-day liberal democratic societies, the prospects of civility do not seem to be dazzlingly bright. . . . Civility has become somewhat stronger in the United States after a low ebb during the war in South East Asia and in the decade which followed it, but it is still under siege. (Shils, 1997: 93)

No small part of the appeal of the concept of civil society lies in this apparent ability to grow while in decline. In later chapters, we will see how the leadership of national commissions strike similar themes in their reports. Civil society appeals to us because of its many implications: it sounds better to be "civil" to each other than to be uncivil; things civil also seem rather less regimented than what is militarized or bureaucratic; and, of course, a civil society has a welcome ring to it in a time of uncertainty and social turbulence.

But a wholesome sound goes only so far in social theory. The fact remains that the concept of civil society will have to be more solidly defined and constructed if it is to play a role in the reconstruction of modern society. In this book, I will make an effort to provide that grounding, eventually coming to the conclusion that civil society is best understood as a very special space within and between the major institutions of society.

## Conclusion

As we experience the depletion of the *social capital* of our post-modern consumer societies, we hear many voices calling for the reconstruction of *civil society*. This task is complicated by the coming of the *farewell state,* which limits governmental action, and the simultaneous *end of work,* which limits employment prospects. How can we create a *pluralist* or *communitarian* society, which balances rights and responsibilities, when the very bases of public support for the needy and corporate employment of the well trained are being so dramatically eroded? Surely, the new realities of our *social economy* will need to be understood, with the limits it places on traditional economic advancement, and the opportunities it offers for those who learn to work together in communities.

New skills of *social entrepreneurship* will be required of many in this new configuration of society. Among the literacies of the new age will be the ability to navigate within society's third sector, a vast network of organizations within which many group and individual needs will be met throughout the coming years. It is a major task of that sector to see that social capital is built, and steps are taken to assure that fewer of our fellow citizens, like my grandmother's family in Gananoque a century ago, are left to suffer alone when life conspires to deprive them of the supports we all so desperately need and richly deserve. Vital steps can and should be taken to assure the development of spaces within our society where such need for support and solidarity can be met.

# 2

# Mapping the Boundaries

In the scholarly literature, the boundaries between the major institutional sectors are usually spoken of as being "blurred," "overlapping," or "indistinct." Perhaps the best way to get a grip on these boundary relations is to review some of the most influential maps that have been drawn suggesting how the major institutional sectors in society relate to each other. Such maps have recently been drawn showing three (Mertens, 1998), four (Van Til, 1988), five (Smith, 1991), six (Paton, 1991), and even seven sectors (Schuppert, 1991).

## Two-Sector Maps

The concept of "sector" provides a useful way of visualizing society's institutions. The traditional map of society's key institutions simply distinguishes between market and state. It is clearly inadequate to the realities of our times because it ignores the vast organizational terrain of society's third sector, as well as the important core institutions of family, kin, and neighborhood.[1]

## Three-Sector Maps

Three-sector models are increasingly being used by scholars whose work focuses on voluntarism and nonprofit organizations. In such conceptions, business usually takes its place as the first sector (because it is largest); government is the second sector; and the voluntary nonprofit is the third sector.[2] Much of the scholarship of the nonprofit field uses this tripartite model. Seeing the third sector as composed of a special category of organizations, those that are both non-state and non-capitalist, is the basic insight of those who construct three-sector maps of society. Increasingly, contemporary social theorists refer to the distinctive nature of each of three sectors (government, business, voluntary) when they seek to represent the structure of a modern society.

Among the most compelling of the three-sector conceptions are two that developed in the shadows of the spreading fascism, communism, and militarism of their times. The central European social theorists Karl Polanyi (1944) and Karl Mannheim (1940) sought in their work to understand the ways in which business, government, and social institutions related to each other. Both aimed to develop a theory of the proper relation between the sectors, hoping thereby to contribute to a world in which the maladies of their era could be permanently banished.

To Polanyi, the key to peaceful development involved the creation of a balanced role for the three sectors of market, state, and society. The danger he saw was that the market would come to be seen as the essential institution, and its basis in contract would give rise to a misleading and incomplete vision of human freedom. There are limits to what such "free" enterprise can provide, he argued: markets fragment human relations and render important social relations invisible. They also tend to relegate the state to a position of insignificance.

In Polanyi's view, it is only when we come to recognize that the free market alone will not solve our problems that we come face to face with how freedom can be maintained in society. A line dividing liberalism, on the one hand, from fascism and communism, on the other, begins to appear. And we also begin to see that the difference between freedom and oppression is not primarily economic, but is rather moral and religious (1957: 258; cf. also Wolch, 1990). Polanyi's work suggests a vital role for what would later be called the "third sector": to play a leading role in the struggle for justice and freedom.

To Mannheim, the key to social reconstruction was to be found in applying knowledge to the resolution of problems and in learning how to do social planning. He introduced powerful distinctions between ideology (the interest of the status quo) and utopia (the vision of what ought to be), and between functional (what appears to work, however misguided it may be) and substantive rationality (what undergirds the resolution of genuine human needs).

Mannheim observed that modern "society is faced, not with brief unrest, but with a radical change of structure; . . . this realization is the only guarantee of preventive measures. Only if we know why Western society in the crisis zone is passing through a phase of disintegration is there any hope that the countries which still enjoy comparative peace will learn to control the future trend of events by democratic planning, and so to avoid the negative aspects of the process: dictatorship, conformity, and barbarism" (1940: 6).

Planner John Friedmann extended Mannheim's vision in the development of a full-blown social theory. Friedmann developed Mannheim's concern that we learn to plan for an increasingly democratic and interdependent world. Friedmann identifies productive roles for civil society (or voluntary sector) to play in modern society (1987: 355–56). The world, he observed, is best seen as a "common" (p. 383; cf. also Lohmann, 1992) in which varying institutional interests meet and contest with each other. Third-sector organizations, Friedmann asserts, play important roles in helping individuals and groups build societies that will meet their needs to work together productively.

## Four-Sector Maps

In an earlier book I authored, *Mapping the Third Sector* (1988), a four-sector model of society is presented. The household, or informal sector, is added to the conventional three of business, government, and nonprofit sectors. A dynamic aspect is added to the model by a description of sector interdependence, with the household sector serving as the keystone. Households (or individual members of households) earn money and buy products and services in the business sector, form foundations, volunteer, and become members of associations in the nonprofit sector, and support government through voting and paying taxes.

In *Mapping the Third Sector,* I contended that each of the major sectors conduct transactions with each other across the various boundaries between them, and I showed how these transactions affect the third sector. Government, for example, both "legitimizes" and regulates third-sector organizations when it awards IRS certification of "501(c)" standing. Business provides resources through donations and the support of employee volunteering, while government reduces the tax burden of individual donors who support appropriately certified organizations. Figure 2 illustrates how the four major sectors routinely interact with each other.

*Mapping the Third Sector* sought to develop theoretical maps to aid in the understanding of the role of voluntarism in modern life. One map was metaphorical, the other conceptual.

The metaphorical map identified factors as pertaining to "climate," "topography," and deep "tectonic" structures. Climatic factors were depicted as dominant values in society: self-absorbed privatism and voluntaristic concern for others. Topographic factors were the familiar four sectors: private economic, government, voluntary, and in-

Figure 2. Transactions between the Sectors

| | |
|---|---|
| GOVERNMENT regulates, subsidizes, and contracts with voluntary sector organizations. | BUSINESS provides philanthropy (through federated giving, corporate giving, and the establishment of foundations) and encourages worker volunteering. |
| (Some) THIRD-SECTOR organizations are certified by GOVERNMENT as eligible for tax-deductible contributions of income earned in BUSINESS, provide services contracted by GOVERNMENT, employ volunteer time and effort donated from the INFORMAL SECTOR. | INFORMAL organizations (family and neighborhood) provide many services as volunteers, often coordinated by THIRD-SECTOR organizations. |

formal. Underlying tectonic factors were linked to the key problems identified by major social theorists: the problem of solidarity of association identified by Alexis de Tocqueville and Emile Durkheim, the problem of bureaucratic control centrally addressed by Max Weber, the problem of economic hegemony that preoccupied Karl Marx, and the problem of oligarchical control posed by Robert Michels. My argument was that each level of analysis—values, institutional form, and deep social structure—had to be taken into account in understanding the role of the third sector in modern life.

Finally, *Mapping the Third Sector* distinguished between five principal theoretical approaches taken by scholars in their attempt to understand voluntary action and nonprofit organizations in modern society. These models were identified as being either "essentially" derivative, sectoral, or action oriented. Jacquelyn Thayer Scott (1992) built on this theory to make room for communitarian theory. Scott notes that third-sector organizations can play a critical role in building and supporting community at all levels of modern society (Figure 3).

## More Than Four Sectors

David Horton Smith (1991) subdivides the third sector into two, distinguishing a "public benefit" from a "private benefit" third sector. But like Mannheim and Friedmann, Smith sees both variants of the third sector as manifesting society's "fundamental value-based concerns."

A more functional model has been developed by the British educator Rob Paton (1992), who focuses on two major dimensions: the

Figure 3.  Van Til's Map of Models, Extended by Scott

| DERIVATIVE MODELS | SECTORAL MODELS | ACTION MODELS |
|---|---|---|
| Neo-corporatist (economic) | Pluralist (organizational) | Populist (direct action) |
| Social democratic (political) | Communitarian | Idealist (informed action) |

formality-informality of organization and the social or economic nature of goals sought. Paton's model (Figure 4) identifies a range of economic styles of organization, and clusters them in sectors.

Finally, a seven-sector map has been presented by German legal scholar G. F. Schuppert (1991). The sectors he identifies are:

1. Market
2. State
3. Self-administered organizations
4. Self-organized groups
5. Associations
6. Organized interests
7. Private governmental organizations

What Schuppert essentially does in his representation is divide the third sector into five constituent parts, continuing the sub-structuring of this diverse societal arena that Smith began by dividing into two.

Of the drawing of social maps there will surely be no end. But a number of recent representations have introduced a more dynamic set of conceptions of size, scale, and boundary. They seek to depict the sectors in vital interaction with each other.

## Interacting Sectors

Interactive sectoral models have been developed by several prominent European scholars of the third sector. Building on the observations of earlier writers that sectoral boundaries are themselves blurred, David Billis, Victor Pestoff, and Rudolph Bauer have presented models that combine multiple dimensions into fruitful representations.[3] Pestoff's triangle (1991), later elaborated by Evers and Svetlik, offers a compelling representation which places the third sector at the core of interactions anchored by market, state, and family (Figure 5).

Figure 4. Paton's Map of the Organizational World

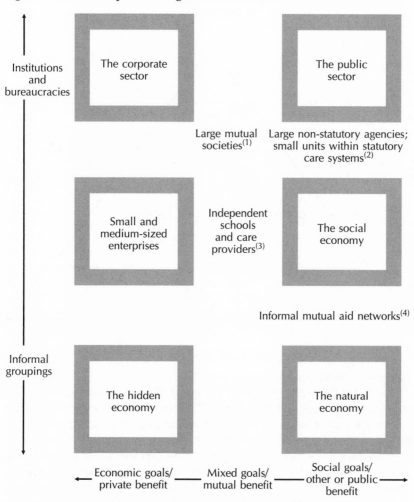

Notes

(1) for example, building societies, retail co-ops, the Automobile Association
(2) for example, large housing associations, local authority family
    centres, cottage hospitals
(3) for example, charitable public schools, nursing homes (private but
    professionally run)
(4) for example, baby-sitting circles, mother and toddler clubs

Figure 5.  Pestoff's Triangle

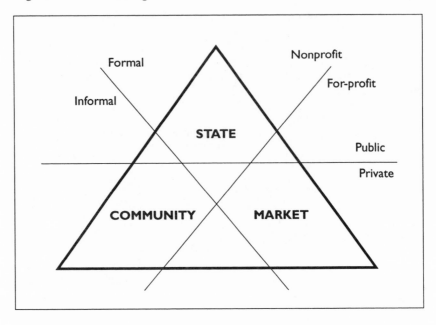

British organizational scholar Billis (1993) focuses on the blurring of the sectors (Figure 6).

In several far-reaching recent presentations, German social policy specialist Rudolph Bauer (1993, 1998) extends Billis's point that the nonprofit sector takes on major characteristics of the other sectors. Bauer suggests that volunteers tend to treat nonprofit organizations as though they were providers of charitable service, while board members tend to see them as though they were political organizations. Meanwhile, staff behaves as though the same organization is a business. In this way, Bauer observes, a third-sector organization tends to take on the coloration of business (first sector), politics (second sector), and community (fourth sector). Figure 7 shows this representation.

Bauer (1998) sees the third sector as an intermediate realm between the market, state, and informal networks—a realm composed of a variety of different organizational types. Closest in structure and interest to market organizations are cooperatives and "communal economic corporations." Closest in interest to the state are "public benefit organizations," "federations," and "associations." Closest to informal networks are "societies," "self-help groups," and "small co-operatives."

Bauer's theory of the third sector goes a long way to advance un-

Figure 6. Billis's View of the Blurring of the Sectors

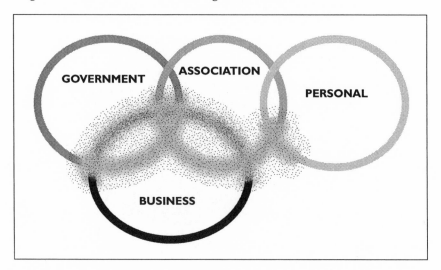

derstanding of why organizations in this category so often resemble governmental agencies, business corporations, or informal groups. Third-sector organizations take on the coloration of the other sectors, he indicates, and themselves contain organizational themes that closely resemble those of the other sectors.

If the third-sector is seen as an intermediary social construction, it follows that it can play a crucial bridging role in society. The linking potential of the third sector is one that is increasingly recognized in modern life, and the exploration of its expansion forms a central theme of this book.

## An Alternative View: Action Rather Than Sector

An alternative approach tends not to begin with the identification of sectors, but rather with a distinction between public and private action (cf. Dewey, 1927). This dichotomous approach introduces tension between the two forms of action, implicitly introducing a relationship of power or exchange into the discussion. Gamwell (1984), for instance, uses a two-sector model, distinguishing between governmental and non-governmental organizations and then dividing the latter into "private-regarding and public-regarding" agencies. "Public-regarding" agencies are further split on the basis of exclusivity into "less inclusive" and "more inclusive" groupings, which latter are then divided into "nonpolitical regarding" and "political regarding." Sumariwalla (1983) visualizes two principal sectoral divisions also, and

Figure 7.  Rudolph Bauer's View of the Third Sector as a Coat of Many Colors

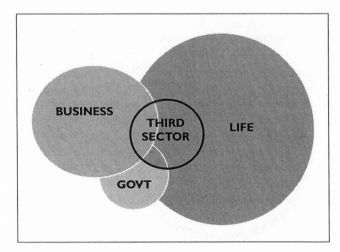

classifies nonprofit organizations as private-sector "non-business" entities, operating either in the public interest or as part of an "all other" sub-category.

An important contribution of these simple two sector models is that they focus less on boundaries (what fits inside) and more on relations across boundaries. As was discovered by Lord Beveridge (1948) in his pioneering study of voluntary action in Britain, the state and voluntary associations are partners in cooperation for social advance. As Ostrander, Langton, and Van Til (1987) would later demonstrate, the government, voluntary association, and business are more often interdependent with each other than independent of each other.

In much the same way, Kramer (1984) focuses his three-sector model on relationships for the delivery of personal and social services. He adds the element of power relationships, laying the foundation for a fuller understanding of nonprofits. In looking at the interrelationships among profit-making, governmental, and voluntary organizations, he examines the activities involved and identifies the five possible relationships among sectors as reprivatization, empowerment, pragmatic partnership, governmental operation, and nationalization.

Even our manner of naming the sectors (first, second, third) implies a power order. To gain perspective on this implied order it is helpful to look at the work of Peter Dobkin Hall (1992). Hall's historical analyses invite an interesting exercise about naming the order of the sectors. The nonprofit sector is, as we have seen, most often identified as the third sector. However, at any point in history, if we were to stop and try to put order to the sectors as we viewed them from the perspective of that time and place, we might call our first, second, and third sectors differently (cf. also Young, 1988). For example, why not call the family the first sector? It was here first. Would voluntary organizations, or government, be the second in order of time? The labels become very dependent on where one stands to do the labeling.

Part of the problem with understanding the sector issue comes from jumping into the parade in the middle of it. Salamon and Anheier (1992: 126) have noted that discussion of sectors is a relatively recent academic discovery. "[T]he emergence of the large-scale profit-making form and of public administration represented the major institutional innovations of the eighteenth and nineteenth centuries, and the results have been institutional complexes of enormous social and economic power." The nonprofit sector, as Hall (1992) indicates, is an even more recent invention, emerging only over the last twenty years in academic discourse.

Smith (1997) and Kramer (1998) take the critique of sector further in recent work. Like Hall, they view the concept of sector with suspicion, noting the vast diversity of purposes and structures contained within the third sector, and the lack of solidarity among its many varied participants. These themes will figure strongly in the argument of the present volume as well.

## Beyond Prince and Merchant

A recent reader on third-sector organizations sports the intriguing title, *Beyond Prince and Merchant*. The realms of prince and merchant have traditionally been explored from separate disciplinary perspectives, with their interactions primarily concerning historians and social theorists. With the rise of a distinctive scholarship of voluntarism and nonprofit organization, the space between the two has begun to be filled.

Voluntary action has been described as "private action for the public good" (Payton, 1984) and "private organization serving a public purpose" (O'Neill, 1989). Voluntary action fulfills a variety of societal roles: 1) supporting society's ability to act for the common good (the communitarian model, a social role); 2) partnering with government to provide collective goods and services (the shadow state model, an economic role); 3) speaking for the minorities and serving as an advocate for pluralism and diversity (the loyal opposition model, a political role).

These perspectives each give rise to their own approaches to understanding what has been called the "third-sector elephant" (recalling the old story of the manifold observations of blindfolded experts trying to identify an elephant by touch). The economic approach argues that providing public goods which cannot be provided profitably in the market is a major task for voluntary action.[4] The political ap-

Figure 8.  Comparing the Lohmann and Salamon Definitions

| LOHMANN | SALAMON |
|---|---|
| PARTICIPATION IS UNCOERCED | VOLUNTARY |
| PURPOSE IS TO ADVANCE COMMON GOOD | PRIVATE (NON-GOVERNMENTAL) |
| RESOURCES ARE COMMON | NONPROFIT DISTRIBUTING |
| PARTICIPATION INVOLVES MUTUALITY | SELF-GOVERNING |
| SOCIAL RELATIONS ARE FAIR | FORMAL |

proach argues that voluntary organizations should advocate minority opinions, argue for change, and serve as a watchdog for government.[5] The communitarian approach argues that voluntary action provides a vehicle for individuals to join in common action for the common good. Additionally, legal[6] and organizational[7] perspectives have been developed and elaborated for third-sector definitions and organizations.

## Two Influential Definitions

Two of the most influential and thoughtful definitions of the third sector have been offered by Lester M. Salamon and Helmut K. Anheier (1992) and Roger Lohmann (1992: 58–60), respectively. The definition provided by Salamon and Anheier is formal and operational, providing a way to distinguish nonprofit from other organizations in society. The defining structural/functional characteristics of third-sector organizations, Salamon and Anheier assert, are that they are formal, private, non-profit-distributing, self-governing, and voluntary (1992: 6). Lohmann, on the other hand, focuses in his definition on the processes and purposes common to third-sector organizations (Figure 8).

In another effort, Salamon (1992) moves closer to Lohmann's definition; there he adds the point that the purpose of a nonprofit organization must address the building of a public good. As such, he recognizes the greatest strength of Lohmann's definition: its ability to capture the sense that a great aim of many third-sector organizations is the building of something distinctive from the collective action of many, gathered in a variety of places that allow for creation and construction.

# Part Two

---

*On the Boundary between
Government and the
Third Sector*

# 3

# The Third Sector
# as a Political Force

The major national organization that represents the interests of non-profit organizations is called Independent Sector. But the third sector is hardly independent of other major institutions in society, as it is frequently the subject of governmental pressure and regulation, corporate influence and control, and community direction and organization. At the same time, third-sector organizations influence government policy, constrain corporate activity, and shape the direction of community development. The third sector, in short, is an important player in the social and political conflicts of our age.

The third sector has served as a training ground for Presidents Wilson (president of Princeton University) and Eisenhower (president of Columbia University). It is where the greatest accomplishments of Jimmy Carter were achieved, after the termination of his presidency. It provides a place to await the call to higher office for a Colin Powell, or Lamar Alexander, or Elizabeth Dole, or Bill Bradley.

As with government, the third sector is frequently the locus of ideological disputes. The coming to power of a Republican Congress in 1994, to take an important recent example, has led to a repeated congressional effort to restrain nonprofit advocacy and to enhance the role of certain community- and faith-based social service organizations. Recognizing this new politics of voluntarism and philanthropy is crucial to understanding the nature of modern political conflict. This chapter, therefore, deals with the emerging conflicts over the third sector as they figure in contemporary American political life. Three separate "boundary wars" are identified and examined in this chapter.

## Boundary War 1: Congress and Nonprofit Advocacy

The idea that organizations within the four sectors should work together smoothly and productively to advance societal goals often proves utopian. Skirmishes are regularly conducted on the boundaries of each sector between and among each of these major institutional forces. In the case of government and the third sector, the major area of conflict regards the advocacy activities of nonprofit organizations.

In the Reagan era of the 1980s, the federal government actively sought to dissuade nonprofit organizations from advocating social change. The role of the third sector, it was held by a wide range of Republican leadership, was appropriately to provide social services to needy persons in society. That, and nothing more.

This preference for service, rather than advocacy, represented a prudent Republican reaction to what was perceived as the excesses of advocacy in the 1960s. In that turbulent decade, a wide range of third-sector organizations spearheaded a set of social movements that shook a good many institutional pillars, from commercial facilities to classrooms, from personnel offices to Pentagon decision rooms.

Among the legacies of the 1960s was the legitimacy of providing governmental support for social service programs offered by nonprofit organizations. Such organizations might be affiliated with religious institutions and/or they might engage, as part of their effort, in programs advocating legislative policy or broader social change. These issues had been resolved in the 1960s through such struggles as the one involved in regulating the Community Action Programs of the Office of Economic Opportunity (OEO) in Mississippi. There community action employees whose salaries were funded by OEO were permitted to volunteer as activists in the civil rights struggle, providing they were clearly acting as citizens on their own time, and not as OEO employees.

Nonprofit law began to draw an accepted distinction: federal funds could not be used to support advocacy, but funding could be received by nonprofits which engaged in advocacy, provided that the federal funds clearly went to the support of service. It was a matter of policy and good accounting: Advocacy *required* the sole support of the organization and its voluntary sources; service *could* be supported by governmental funds.

The election of Ronald Reagan to the presidency in 1980 signaled a change in this understanding. Aggressive steps were taken within the new administration to assure that nonprofit organizations which advocated changes unpalatable to the administration would not be given the chance to solicit funds from federal employees in their combined charitable appeal. These efforts had limited success, but were met by an aggressive effort to counter their impact, led by the National Committee for Responsive Philanthropy, itself a leading advocacy organization within the third sector.

When Democrat Bill Clinton assumed the presidency in 1992, he found his major domestic initiative, national service, confronted by the insistence of many of its young participants to engage in action during what was billed as an initial "Summer of Service." When Clinton persisted in advancing this program under its new name, Ameri-Corps, he found that program continually opposed by congressional Republicans, who, in 1994, assumed control of both the Senate and the House of Representatives. A major theme in this opposition continued to be the argument that third-sector advocacy of social change must be thoroughly insulated from the delivery of subsidized service.

The coming of what the National Committee for Responsive Philanthropy called "The Newt Era" gave rise to what the same organization, in the fullest coverage of the effort, identified as an all-out "War on Nonprofits." Nurtured in think tanks close to Republican strategists, this campaign was led by Congressman Ernest Istook (R-OK), with strong support from his colleagues McIntosh of Indiana and Ehrlich of Maryland. In a series of legislative skirmishes, Istook and his colleagues sought to curtail, if not outright end, the lobbying activities of nonprofit organizations that receive federal funds. Each time an "Istook-type" amendment was introduced, it was faced with vigorous opposition from the community of nonprofit organizations. The Senate consistently rejected House bills that carried Istook amendments with them.

The campaign against nonprofit advocacy was conducted on several other fronts as well:

- Senator Alan Simpson's (R-WY) efforts to get the Senate to approve legislation denying federal grants to social welfare organizations engaging in advocacy

- Congressman Gerald Solomon's (R-NY) attempt to deny grants to universities that allowed student organizations to use mandatory student activity fees to influence public policy

- legislation supported by Senators Sam Nunn (D-GA) and Pete Domenici (R-NM) to deny federal tax exemption to any educational organization that spent substantial time and money on activities such as conducting research to educate the public or Congress on public policy issues

- Congressman John Mica's (R-FL) threat to eliminate advocacy groups from the Combined Federal Campaign (the government's "United Way")

The Istook-sponsored "gag rule" would have allowed governmental officers to require all citizens and organizations with a financial connection to government, whether as recipient of aid or contractor of service, to report annually the nature and degree of their "lobbying" or "seeking to influence" public policy or political campaigns. If such activity were found to amount to more than 5 percent of their total income, they would be subject to fines and loss of government funding.

Such efforts to throttle the advocacy and lobbying role of nonprofit organizations and their citizen members reflected conservative perceptions that groups with generally "progressive" social agendas (liberal or "left-wing," oriented to social justice and income redistribution) are more likely to be dependent upon federal government funding than groups advancing a "conservative" agenda ("right-wing," supportive of free markets and the "farewell state"), which groups are seen as deriving their support from the firmer base of individual and corporate giving.

In their quest to create a society dominated by values of limited governmental spending and acquiescence to market power, Istook and his colleagues targeted nonprofits as a particularly subversive force. The third sector, after all, was the cradle from which emerged such dangerous policy ideas as affirmative action, the extension of health care, and a guaranteed income for all Americans.

To be sure, many of these "legislative initiatives" amounted to little more than puffery and posturing, mere efforts to build a campaign resume for the next election. The most extreme of these measures had little chance of prevailing against the cooler judgment of the Senate, or of surviving a presidential veto. They were symbolic shots fired in the cultural wars of our era, warnings to students and faculty and women and blacks and working folk and the unemployed that a rebirth of social movements '60s style would not be without its consequences.

The Istook challenge, it may be argued, was fundamentally flawed by its ignorance of the role of the third sector in sustaining American democracy. By denying members of associations basic rights of citizenship simply because they receive federal support, and subjecting them to congressional regulation, Istook ignored 200 years of American history, and the long interdependent relationship between third-sector and governmental organizations.[1] His approach also denies the role of third-sector organizations as watchdogs on business and government, as partners in the resolution of problems, and as voices articulating the interests of those who have been left behind in the always perilous struggle to achieve the American dream.

The legislation proposed by Congressman Istook and his colleagues was defeated, as was the legislation proposed by Congressman Solomon and the measure backed by Congressman Mica. The Nunn-Domenici legislation died without action. Senator Simpson's legislation passed, but had virtually no negative impact on social welfare associations because those organizations are permitted to set up tax-exempt organizations under IRS Section 501(c)3 which could receive federal grants. In summary, nonprofits won in a "clean sweep," and subsequent efforts to raise initiatives of the Istook variety have been turned aside with relative ease.

The efforts of Istook and his colleagues were met with strong opposition led by Congressman Skaggs (D-CO), Congresswoman Slaughter (D-NY), Senator Jeffords (R-VT), and Senator Specter (R-PA), who opposed the initiatives to curtail lobbying by organizations that receive federal funds. Within the community of nonprofit organizations, Independent Sector, the National Committee for Responsive Philanthropy, OMB Watch, and the Alliance for Justice were particularly effective in opposing the measures. By the middle of Clinton's second term, it became clear that the House Republican leadership was no longer interested in supporting any major new initiatives along the original Istook lines, and Istook himself had turned his attention toward efforts to extend the practice of school prayer.

The defeat of the Istook effort stands as an important defining moment in the boundary war over nonprofit organizational advocacy. The forces represented by Istook, however, continue to wield power in American political life. California Proposition 226, proposed in 1998 to negatively affect giving through payroll deductions for support of ballot initiatives, may be seen as symptomatic of a continuing effort to achieve Istook-type initiatives at the state level.

On yet another front, budget writers within the new Republican congressional majority proposed, in 1995 and 1996, huge impending cuts in the funding of social programs. The actual cuts were not nearly as severe as first proposed, again indicating that the message did get through to Congress that third-sector organizations play an important role in both the delivery of service and the representation of an independent, and sometimes critical, citizen voice.[2]

The War on Nonprofits raises thorny questions about the government's right to regulate the ability of nonprofits to advocate for social causes and policy changes. Four major positions have emerged in this controversy:

- Some assert that the government has no right to regulate the lawful actions of nonprofits, and that the independent sector should be free to follow the wishes of its members. These "independistas" hold the belief that voluntary action and nonprofit organization are usually more humane, effective, and valuable than governmental efforts. Defenders of this view tend to extol the virtues of a "civil society" in which individuals freely organize themselves into groups to solve mutual problems, and in which the role of government is greatly minimized.

- Others claim that only organizations out of synch with the prevailing values of society should be regulated. These "conformists" fear that deviant or radical ideas will corrupt the loyalty and virtue of right-thinking citizens (by which they usually mean people like themselves), and they typically urge that nonprofits direct their attention to the provision of services to worthy persons in some state of need. A case in point are those who, once they achieve elected office, try to restrain the efforts of their defeated opponents to advance their interests through the vehicles of nonprofit organizations.

- A third position, directly opposed to the second, sees advocacy as the primary, if not the exclusive, role of those who set themselves up to challenge prevailing values and institutions in society. Such "oppositionists" see the advocacy of nonprofit organization as the basic way in which radical changes are introduced into the policy arena. A case in point are those movements, like the black, or women's, or gay rights, which address issues that might otherwise have languished in the give and take of everyday life.

- A fourth position finds the right to constrain associations well within the role of a democratic government. These "interdependents" note that nonprofit organizations are sometimes created to advance the special interests of the few, and can be used to prevent overwhelming majorities from achieving policies that they clearly desire. A case in point here involves the power of the National Rifle Association to neutralize the massive majorities that disagree with their position on the easy availability of firearms. Interdependents are willing to explore the complexities of the interrelationship between government and nonprofit organizations.

While one's choice of a position depends on both ideology and one's view of the nonprofit sector, and is clearly a matter of personal preference, it may be useful in contemplating the options to think a bit about the actual experience of advocacy organizations. Research by

University of Texas social work professor Richard Hoefer is helpful to review. Hoefer reported on a study of 249 Washington-based non-profits whose work primarily involves the advocacy of some sort of change in government policy.

On the whole, Hoefer finds that the executives of these advocacy organizations do not view their relationship with government as an adversarial one. Rather, they see themselves seeking to develop collaborative relations with government, and they report an experience of increasing cooperation. Moreover, they see themselves as less likely than they previously were to urge an increasing federal role in problem solving. And they report that, in general, they are satisfied with the effects of their work.

Hoefer's findings indicate that advocacy organizations are comfortable in working on the blurred boundaries that exist between today's nonprofit organizations and government. Clearly they see themselves as "interdependents" rather than "independistas," "oppositionists," or "conformists."

As interdependents, contemporary nonprofits have found a niche for themselves in the world of policy development and implementation. It is not, therefore, surprising that some in the governmental world should find them seeking to establish a relationship that is inappropriately close. From the governmental point of view, it is the political process—the fruit of elections—that is primary in a democracy. For "private" associations and organizations to try to crawl into the policy-making bed understandably gives rise to some discomfort, especially if these organizations are seen to represent hostile political interests.

For Republicans, the answer to this dilemma has been found in creating greater distance; for Democrats, efforts have focused on moving closer. This dance continues without evident resolution, and it will apparently remain primary among the political conflicts occasioned by third-sector organizations.

## Boundary War 2: Financing Social Services

A second boundary issue regarding government and nonprofits is found in the area of taxation. Hartford, Connecticut, has sought to limit the creation of new tax-exempt organizations. Pennsylvania, my home state, has become the center of an important struggle between local governments and nonprofits. Local governments, desperate to sustain services in an era of tax limitation and slow economic growth, have turned toward the taxation of nonprofits as a new source of revenue. And nonprofits, faced with their own fiscal crises, are responding with fear and anger to this perceived incursion on their rights to tax-exemption.

As pioneering research by Pamela Leland of Seton Hall University (1996) indicates, a number of Pennsylvania's local governments have been inspired by a 1985 court ruling to apply the five-point HUP (*Hospital Utilization Project v. Commonwealth of Pennsylvania*) test to nonprofits within their boundaries. The HUP test requires a nonprofit to prove that it meets five criteria: 1) it advances a charitable purpose; 2) it donates or renders freely a substantial portion of its services; 3) it benefits a substantial class of persons who are legitimate subjects of charity; 4) it relieves the government of some of its burdens; and 5) it operates entirely free from a private profit motive.

Two important cases have seen the county decisions overruled in favor of a challenged nonprofit. In 1994 the Pennsylvania Supreme Court ruled that St. Margaret Seneca Place, a nursing home, fully met the HUP criteria. And in 1995, the Commonwealth ruled that Washington and Jefferson College, a liberal arts college, was similarly qualified.

These court reversals have not discouraged local taxing bodies in Pennsylvania from continuing their efforts to collect property taxes from nonprofits within their boundaries. Philadelphia has vigorously pursued the collection of payments in lieu of taxes (PILOTs), assessed in the form of suggested contributions from a wide variety of nonprofits. Even churches and monasteries have been told that the portions of their property not directly used for religious purposes are fair game for either taxation or a surrogate "contribution."

Recently, my own school district (Wallingford-Swarthmore) undertook an effort to tax a variety of religious and educational institutions within its bounds, including Swarthmore College. Rebuffed at every turn by the county office of assessment, the board has nonetheless persisted with two of its claims, bringing them on appeal to the Commonwealth Court. One of these claims, that the Quaker center for study and contemplation, Pendle Hill, should pay property taxes, illustrates the complexities involved in the current fiscal struggle.

Pendle Hill was founded in 1930 by the Religious Society of Friends, and has provided a variety of adult education programs over this 65-year period. Its 14-acre campus occupies a lovely wooded site in suburban Philadelphia.

Pendle Hill is governed by an independent board of directors, all of whom must be members of the Society of Friends. Its educational mission is rooted in the four basic social testimonies espoused by Quakers: equality of opportunity, simplicity of environment, harmony of action, and community in daily life.

Pendle Hill's annual income amounts to some $1.4 million. About

40 percent of its support issues from gifts, and the remaining 60 percent results from tuitions and book sales. On a voluntary basis, Pendle Hill provides an annual contribution of $12,000 to local taxing authorities to compensate for the use its residents make of local services. The school board staked a claim for an additional $40,000 in taxes, claiming the full value that the land would yield were it used for private housing.

From a nonprofit organization perspective, the case seemed open and closed. A greedy political body acts with reckless abandon to tax a worthy institution, seemingly protected from taxation by its double standing in the religious and educational worlds. But life, of course, is never so simple.

First of all arises the issue of the HUP test. If it is a legitimate one to apply to nonprofits (and that contention may itself be debated), then is it clear, as the school district claims it is not, that Pendle Hill meets the criterion of relieving the government of a burden? Does, in other words, government have an obligation to favor the religious education of adults?

Second, the issue of how to reckon payments in lieu of taxes presents itself. Pendle Hill not only receives the protection of local police and fire services, it also sends a number of children of its resident staff and students to the Wallingford-Swarthmore public schools. The annual cost of a year's schooling in the district amounts to over $7,000, and out-of-district students are charged a tuition of $6,900 per year to attend public school within the district. Who should pay for the schooling of these children who reside in nonprofit space? The citizens of the community? Their parents? Or the nonprofit itself?

Third arises the issue of process. The school board enters the fray firmly defended by its lawyers, and the fact that claims are in litigation removes the issue from public consideration. In response, the nonprofit, even if one informed by Quaker values of community, is itself pushed into a defensive, litigious, and even adversarial mode. How might a "win-win" outcome even be hoped to emerge from such a conflictual process? Indeed, who wins from such a process except the lawyers?

The issue of governmental burden is a thorny one. Certainly it can persuasively be argued that religion is not only tolerated, but is indeed highly valued, in the American experience. But to extend that argument to assert that without independent religious institutions, government would have to create a "civil religion" to provide the requisite meaning, values, and community life religious institutions currently provide, surely extends the realm of legal argument further than any court would be willing to go. Not only would the First Amendment directly condition such considerations, but the concept of civil religion, as discussion in Chapter 13 will indicate, does not necessarily involve state direction and control.

The second issue, paying for services that are used, raises starkly the problem of "free riding" by nonprofit organizations. The church or the college may deserve its exemption from property tax, but on what grounds can it justify sending the children of its resident ministry or faculty to local schools in the absence of a financial contribution? There is certainly a case to be made that nonprofits pay directly for services received by persons housed on tax-exempt property.

Finally, the quest for win-win solutions need not be abandoned. In the Pendle Hill case, the suggestion has been made by the Swarthmore Friends Meeting for Concerns that the study center provide professional training in conflict resolution to public school teachers and students, in exchange for tuition for its residents. Other nonprofits may similarly find ways to return to their communities services of tangible value, whether they be recreational, health related, or educational.

It is clear that tax-exempt third sector can no longer expect local governments to excuse it from taxability as a matter of entitlement. Such exemption will likely need, in the years ahead, increasingly to be demonstrated, earned, and continually justified.

## Boundary War 3: Sparring with Partners

The increasing fiscal crisis of government has brought a third consequence for third-sector organizations. They are increasingly called upon to provide services under contract to government, services that in an earlier era would have been provided by government itself.

Sometimes, as in Britain in the 1970s, these services have focused on providing low-wage jobs to individuals the market finds unemployable. More usually in the United States, the services contracted to the nonprofit organization have devolved from arenas of care, maintenance, and education of dependent individuals—be they young, delinquent, criminal, or mentally impaired.

The distinguished student of voluntarism Ralph Kramer has identified "vendorism" as the basic relationship between government and many nonprofit organizations in our time. In the vendor relationship, a governmental organization provides financial support to a nonprofit organization, which then provides the agreed-upon direct service to clients.

Vendorism is at the heart of a story I once recounted in my column in the *NonProfit Times* (February, 1993). Let me retell it here in full, because it suggests another aspect of the changing relationship between governmental and nonprofit organizations:

The story begins on a sunny fall afternoon, as two old friends greet each other after church. Both are successful and powerful individuals; one had risen to the position of city council chair before his party was removed from office; the second heads a major nonprofit organization. As they talk, it is apparent to the nonprofit exec that the politician has something he really wants to say: an election is approaching, and the support of every voter will be critical in permitting his party to return to power. There is a hard glint in the politician's eye as the message is delivered; this election is for keeps, and the support of the nonprofit community, and the clients they serve, may hold its outcome in the balance. The nonprofit leader will be expected to work hard for the party this fall, because "with the contracts we provide you, you need to remember that you work for us." (Van Til, 1993b)

We live in a time and place in which elected governmental office has become a job, one to which incumbents cling with an air of near desperation. In such a United States of Ambition, as Alan Ehrenhalt has dubbed it, it is all too easy to become ensnared in the political games of favor, patronage, and pseudo-friendship. One way of coping with these snares is to adopt, in theory and practice, the motto the nonprofit Housing Association of Delaware Valley borrowed from Friedrich Engels some years back—"No permanent enemies; no permanent friends; only permanent interests"—in their case, housing the poor. Perhaps such a motto could serve as a countervailing force to the prevailing political commitment to serve only the self-interest of the elected official.

## Conclusion: Resolving Boundary Conflicts

The three cases presented in this chapter—regulating nonprofit advocacy, taxing nonprofits, and using vendorism as a tool for political control—all suggest the persistence of conflict on the boundary between government and the third sector. The rapid rise in visibility of the third sector as both an advocate and a provider of service, particularly when contracted from government, accounts for the intensity of these often conflictual relationships.

Resolving these conflicts will not be easy, for they involve deeply held perquisites of power and authority in society. Nonetheless, there are lessons for organizational advancement to be learned from each of them.

Persuasive dialogue might be the only way to resolve the nonprofit advocacy question. It is recounted that Congressman Istook abandoned his efforts to restrict governmental payments to nonprofit organizations after he heard from third-sector leaders in his own district about the difficulties such legislation would bring to their groups and the communities they both represented. Since groups on the left and the right of the political spectrum engage in both advocacy and service, the argument can be made that the Istook sword cuts in both directions. However, the suspicion remains strong, particularly from the left, that the true desire of conservatives is to silence their progressive opponents. Since it is at least plausible to believe that the persons of wealth who predominantly support conservative efforts can fund their own advocacy, this somewhat conspiratorial belief is likely to persist in society's progressive corners.

The contracting issue seems best resolved by simple personal and organizational courage, unusual as its exercise often is within the daily run of organizational politics. The threat recounted in the story above was simply rebuffed by the third-sector leader to whom it was delivered. It turned out that the politician was unable or unwilling to deliver on the threat of retribution, and let the matter drop. Should such threats be advanced, however, it would appear that counter-thrusts involving the hint of public disclosure will often repulse the attack. This is not a time that tolerates open power-wielding against the interests of the needy, however unjust the overall distribution of income and wealth has become. The goodwill enjoyed by most non-profit organizations provides a substantial fund upon which to draw in times of political chicanery.

The taxation issue is the one of the three treated in this chapter that most directly invites policy innovation. Here we may have a chance to break through one of the dreary deadlocks that characterize relations between right and left in American society. Think of it this way:

- Maybe those conservatives who observe that no corporation, for-profit or nonprofit, should be taxed have a point. If all individual income, earned or unearned and from whatever source, could be taxed fully and fairly one time only, the corporate income tax could be repealed, and a significant difference between exempt and non-exempt organizations would be eliminated.

- Maybe those liberals have a point who observe that the time has come to join the rest of the industrialized world and impose a value-added tax, as has been suggested by President Clinton and a number of business executives.

- Maybe those progressives have a point who observe that high incomes, whether they issue from work or the ownership of equity, should be taxed at high rates if any semblance of economic justice is to prevail in our society. Before Ronald Reagan and his associates lowered the upper marginal tax rate from 71 percent to the low thirties, the United States had a semblance of a progressive tax system, and since then, a few modest efforts have been made to raise the rates paid by the wealthiest taxpayers.

The combination of repealing the corporation tax (which would remove 11 percent of the federal tax yield) and replacing it with revenues achieved from the imposition of a VAT and the reinstitution of a progressive income tax would have the effect of continuing the tax exemption of presently exempt nonprofit organizations. It would also eliminate a bone of contention between nonprofits and small businesses, and go some way toward deflating concerns that nonprofit organizations reduce governmental revenue. Further, it would smoke out the murky argument that some nonprofits provide services that governments would otherwise have to provide. And it would go a long way toward reducing the bloated after-tax salaries of some nonprofit, and many more for-profit, executives to a more defensible level.

As a piece of public policy innovation, this modest proposal might open a dialogue that could then address the adjustment of two remaining taxes: the property tax, upon which local governments heavily rely; and the charitable deduction, which rewards middle- and upper-income donors to selected charitable and educational nonprofits with a reduction in taxes approximately equal to one-third of their contribution. Reforms issuing from such a dialogue could go a long way to reducing the level of conflict between governmental and third-sector organizations. They might also serve as a useful reminder that the reason most third-sector organizations exist is not simply to be "non-profit," but rather to profit communities and society in ways that families, corporations, and even governments cannot.

# 4

# National Service in
# Theory and Practice

AmeriCorps, the program of national service established by President Clinton, has engendered a lively controversy on the boundary between government and the third sector. The very survival of the program is subject to recurrent challenges that center about the three issues discussed in Chapter 3: advocacy, taxation, and partnering dynamics. These issues are reviewed by means of an examination of the development of this program and its operation as a limited, but innovative, form of public-private partnership.

AmeriCorps is perceived variously in the context of three diverging perspectives of policy: the conservative vision of the primacy of the economy and pure voluntarism; the moderate vision of pragmatic partnership between sectors; and the progressive vision of a force capable of contributing to the establishment of liberty, equality, and fraternity in modern life. AmeriCorps is in many respects the most significant contemporary program on the boundary between government and the third sector, and the outcome of its political and organizational struggles will likely prove critical in shaping the future of these relations.

An informal definition suggests that *national service* involves governmental support of the performance of structured voluntary action by citizens, usually youths, toward the end of strengthening both values of citizenship and behaviors evincing caring and concern for others.

As a policy initiative, national service has been supported in principle by nearly every incoming American president in the 20th century. Few of these initiatives, however, have survived the press of other governmental priorities, and, in the last half-century, only the initiatives of Presidents Kennedy and Clinton have yielded legislation and programs. Kennedy's call to service gave rise to the Peace Corps and a variety of smaller domestic programs. Clinton's national service legislation resulted in AmeriCorps.

This chapter aims to explore how AmeriCorps, the contemporary program of national service, actually works—probing the experiences of those who serve in this program, the nonprofit organization managers under whose direction they work, and the opinions of the citizens who ultimately will decide the fate of this modest legislative initiative.[1]

## Building AmeriCorps

On the first day of March 1993, the 32nd anniversary of President John F. Kennedy's historic announcement of his Peace Corps plan to send American volunteers to work in the world's poor countries, President William Jefferson Clinton spoke at Rutgers University about implementing his campaign promise to develop a broad program of national service. The president stood before a full house of cheering students, faculty members, and community activists in the university's arena, and announced the initiation of a massive program of youth and student service. This program, the president explained, would achieve stirring national purposes:

> National service is nothing less than the American way to change America. It is rooted in the concept of community: the simple idea that every one of us, no matter how many privileges with which we were born, can still be enriched by the contributions of the least of us.

By September of his inaugural year, Clinton's national service initiative achieved congressional approval, and was promptly signed into law by the president. As Stephen Bates (1996: 27) recounts, this legislative triumph provided the Clinton administration its earliest clear-cut win:

> The new statute created a Corporation for National Service to administer a variety of service-learning programs connecting schools, universities, and community organizations (Learn and Serve America); to integrate a set of senior volunteer programs involving more than a half-million persons over 55 into a National Senior Service Corps; and to establish a new program of national service to be called AmeriCorps. The corporation directed $155.5 million in AmeriCorps

grants in the first year, principally divided among direct grants to service programs and grants to state commissions.

AmeriCorps itself was given the mission of engaging thousands of adult Americans (over 17 years of age) in a variety of community service activities, and provided living stipends and post-service educational awards in return for this service. AmeriCorps came to consist of three separate programs:

1. A variety of state and local programs called AmeriCorps*State and National. This is the largest of the three AmeriCorps programs, initially placing over 20,000 individuals annually in local service programs run by nonprofit organizations, local and state governments, higher education institutions, and a variety of partnerships among such organizations. By the year 2002, the program expects to enroll up to 100,000 persons annually. Members receive an annual stipend of $8,000, and an additional $4,725 is provided to cover future college tuition costs or reduce existing college loans.

2. A full-time residential program of service called AmeriCorps*National Civilian Conservation Corps, which focuses on environmental issues and disaster relief. This program draws on the traditions of the Civilian Conservation Corps of the 1930s, and enrolls just under 1,000 youths between the ages of 18 and 24 annually. These members receive a stipend of $4,000 and the educational award upon completion of a year's service.

3. A long-established anti-poverty program (VISTA—Volunteers in Service to America) now to be known as AmeriCorps*VISTA. These members number about 3,500 annually, are of a wide range of ages, and address a range of concerns of low-income communities, including education, health and nutrition, housing and homelessness, community and economic development, public safety, and the environment. The stipend for AmeriCorps*VISTA service amounts to $8,000 per year.

The legislative history of AmeriCorps is brimful of political bargaining and social debate. Steven Waldman's *The Bill: The Adventures of Clinton's National Service Bill Reveal What Is Corrupt, Comical, Cynical—and Noble—about Washington* charts the legislative history quite admirably. Standing behind these contemporary visions of national service lie a range of images that have appeared in the literature since the turn of the century. Principal among these are William James's "moral equivalent of war" (1910), Donald Eberly's "non-military service" (1988), Charles Moskos's "call to civic service" (1988), and William Buckley's "gratitude" (1990). These classic views, and others, are ably summarized in Stephen Bates's Cantigny Conference Report, *National Service: Getting Things Done?* (1996).

## AmeriCorps and the Moral Equivalent of War

Donald Eberly, a life-long advocate of national service, recalls the importance of William James's impact on national service in 20th-century America:

> [Societal] problems were less complex when William James proposed a form of youth service in 1906. In "The Moral Equivalent of War," James, while opposing militarism, said that young men are inherently energetic and have militant tendencies. He observed that these tendencies all too often find expression in war and street corner gang fights.

> As a constructive alternative, James recommended, instead of a military draft, "a conscription of the whole youthful population ... to coal and iron mines, to fishing fleets in December, to dish-washing, to clothes washing," and various other challenging, constructive, and energy-consuming jobs. "Such a conscription," James said, "would preserve in the midst of a pacific civilization the manly virtues which the military party is so afraid of seeing disappear in peace."

> James looked forward to the day when a force other than war could discipline a whole community. To date, there have been only isolated, short-term examples such as the San Francisco earthquake of 1906, which James witnessed first-hand a few weeks after giving his "moral equivalent" speech at Stanford University. Similar expressions of community spirit and service have been seen in the wake of major floods and hurricanes.

> The closest the U.S. has come to a "moral equivalent of war" on a sustained level has been the Civilian Conservation Corps with three million enrollees from 1933 to 1942, and the Peace Corps with 90,000 enrollees from 1961 to 1983. In talking with those who served in the CCC or the Peace Corps, one often gets the feeling that they as individuals absorbed James' objective. (Eberly, 1988: 188–89)

James's view of national service focused on three major values: selfless service, the obligation to participate in community activity, and the value of experiential education and training. These values have persisted in service concepts that have been developed throughout the 20th century. One of those programs was developed under the watch of Arkansas Governor Bill Clinton in the 1980s, and was known as the Delta Service Corps. This program, in its basic structure, was expanded to become the national program known as AmeriCorps.

## Building a Bipartisan Agenda

Bill Clinton was not the only recent presidential aspirant to hitch his star to the wagon of national service. His predecessor in the White House, George Bush, committed his support in 1990 to a program which would utilize volunteer programs to help inculcate the value of service. This program proved nearly invisible, but its purposes were high. Passed by the 103rd Congress on November 16, 1990, the National Service Trust Act took as its purposes to:

1. renew the ethic of civic responsibility in the United States;

2. ask citizens of the United States, regardless of age or income, to engage in full-time or part-time service to the Nation;

3. begin to call young people to serve in programs that will benefit the Nation and improve the life chances of the young through the acquisition of literacy and job skills;

4. enable young Americans to make a sustained commitment to service by removing barriers to service that have been created by high education costs, loan indebtedness, and the cost of housing;

5. build on the existing organizational framework of federal, state, and local programs and agencies to expand full-time and part-time service opportunities for all citizens, particularly youth and older Americans;

6. involve participants in activities that would not otherwise be performed by employed workers;

7. generate additional service hours each year to help meet human, educational, environmental, and public safety needs, particularly those needs relating to poverty.

A 1993 Cantigny Conference, convened by the Robert R. McCormick Tribune Foundation, focused its attention on national service. The conference aimed to cement a bipartisan approach, one that would smoothly link both civilian and military components of service. The conference summary observed that "President Clinton's national service program is intended to expand educational opportunity, reward individual responsibility, and build the American community by bringing citizens together to tackle common problems" (Ethiel, 1993). The report advised that a national service program "must address unmet educational, environmental, human or public safety needs" and "must improve the life of participants through citizenship, education, and training."

The Cantigny Conference, attended by policy pundits and Washington influentials, offered its assent to the values that Clinton was attaching to national service, and upheld the policy of national service as an avenue through which patriotism and service to the country might be renewed. The Robert R. McCormick Tribune Foundation's report concluded with the "hope that it will help our nation and its citizens find more and better ways to fulfill their responsibilities to each other."

With Bush and the conservative intelligentsia convened by McCormick on record that national service was an appropriate way to advance such values as service, community support, employment, and education/training (the William James values which presidential candidate Clinton had so adeptly articulated in his speeches and implemented in his Delta Service Corps), the way was opened for the new president to make both political and programmatic capital from his support of national service. His Republican opponents could oppose his initiative persuasively only by finding within it a programmatic flaw, a lesson that was painfully to be learned by Georgia Congressman Newt Gingrich, elected Speaker of the House in early 1995.

Buoyed by its electoral successes in both House and Senate, the new Republican majority moved quickly to implement its proposed "Contract with America," which outlined a set of free-market solutions for social problems and called for the establishment of a tight rein on public spending. AmeriCorps had no place on their agenda, for it was perceived to be a program more appropriately funded by private contributions than by public funds.

Among the most enthusiastic members of this new majority was the newly elected senator from Pennsylvania, Rick Santorum. Santorum, still in his 30s, had bested incumbent Democrat Harris Wofford for the seat Wofford had surprisingly won two years previously, in a campaign to succeed Republican John Heinz, who had died in an airplane crash. Wofford had bested Republican stalwart Richard Thornburgh in a 1992 special election, and quickly established himself as the leading senatorial voice for national service, a cause he had championed throughout a long and distinguished career, which included such service as the founding associate director of the Peace Corps and President Kennedy's adviser on relations to the civil rights movement.

The 1994 senatorial race between Wofford and Santorum was an unpleasant affair, filled with the mind-numbing sound bites that have become the staple of contemporary electoral discourse. Among the approaches Santorum found effective was the ridicule of national service. How better to unmask Wofford as a soft-headed intellectual unsuited to the new rigors of governmental service than to depict him as a supporter of as fuzzy a concept as national service? Santorum proffered images of long-haired youths of varying genders "sitting around the campfire singing 'Kumbaya.'" His message warned the voter not to support Wofford, who had after all spent several years of his life in as dubious a professional activity as the presidency of Bryn Mawr College. Wofford was soundly beaten in the election, and Santorum became Pennsylvania's junior senator.

The removal of Harris Wofford from the United States Senate provided, in one of the more remarkable ironies of recent American politics, crucial support for the establishment, and modest growth, of national service in the Clinton era. Clinton's legislative management of the national service initiative had run into an immediate roadblock with the 1994 election, as Speaker Gingrich indicated his desire to zero out congressional funding for the program. Led by Clinton crony Eli Segal, the newly established Corporation for National Service found itself isolated, with limited bipartisan support, as a principal target of the new Republican advocates of limited government.

Clinton responded to this massive Republican challenge with a master political stroke of his own by appointing the recently unseated Senator Wofford as Segal's replacement as the chief executive of the Corporation for National Service. Within a few short months, Wofford, drawing both upon his skills of persuasion and the personal ties established by his Senate service, quickly assembled a bipartisan legislative coalition strong enough to sustain a modest, but steadily increasing level of support for AmeriCorps throughout the Clinton years, and possibly beyond as well.

## Findings from the AmeriCorps Study

The Gallup Institute study of AmeriCorps I directed began with twenty questions. This brief summary presents the major findings of the study, which are presented elsewhere in greater detail (cf. Ethiel, ed., 1997).

AmeriCorps, we found in our study, is a program largely invisible to the American public, but one that rests on a broad, if shallow, base of public support. Part of the invisibility of the program reflects the reality of its process of initiation: AmeriCorps was founded without a single guiding vision. Rather, those who developed the program brought to it a number of varying images of what it should be about:

- Some saw the work of national service as the 1990s extension of the civil rights movement, in which young people of every race and class would work together to develop new institutions of justice and opportunity. In this camp were a few who saw this movement already betrayed by governmental bureaucracy and corporate power (cf. Horwitz, 1993: 43).

- Others rallied behind the flag of "experiential education," in which students would demonstrate that they learn best "by doing." "Service learning" had spread rapidly through the borders of the higher education curriculum, and many educators and committed students held to the view that the new federal program would greatly enhance this trend.

- Yet others, also behind a flag first raised by John Dewey, found sustenance in the educational vision of the "community school," in which universities and school systems join forces in opening schools to their surrounding communities, providing job training, continuing education, recreation, and a range of other collaborative social services.

- A fourth vision focused on voluntary action, framed in the context of democratic institutions and civic participation. This vision of national service focused on the need to bring students directly into the fray of civic life, addressing and advancing community needs by means of the same skills they would be required to use throughout their lives if they were to be active, rather than passive, players of their citizen roles.

Speaking to the Presidents' Summit on America's Future, the 1997 Philadelphia gathering co-sponsored by the Corporation for National Service, President Bill Clinton directed his appeal to the contributions of "citizen servants." This rather dubious term indicates the pitfalls inherent in articulating an overarching justification of national service. As many speakers both within and without the Summit's process indicated, the idea of national service is a complex one when considered in terms of political ideology. One person's "voluntary service" quickly becomes another's "servitude." The nation, even after the intense public relations effort that was the Summit, still stands uncertain of the roles and responsibilities its major institutions (family, corporate, governmental, and voluntary) each must play in the resolution of its manifold societal needs.

Results from the Gallup survey we conducted projected the image of AmeriCorps as largely unrecognized, but resting on a favorable base of public opinion. While only 24 percent of a 1995 national sample could identify AmeriCorps by name as the particular vehicle of contemporary national service, 77 percent reported that the program should be expanded or retained at its present level when given a description of AmeriCorps.

Underlying the various visions of national service are a number of core values that figure in most discussions. National service is said to provide an antidote to individualism in society, to encourage responsible activism, to fortify the moral currency of citizens, and to encourage the development of effective partnerships between governmental and voluntary organizations in society.

National service tends to be highly valued by those who see as appropriate a partnership between government, citizen, and voluntary organization in enhancing individual commitment to service and participation. For those suspicious of the role of government, however, national service takes on a more menacing appearance. From this perspective, it is seen as an arm of an intrusive and overarching state, seeking to extend governmental power in realms properly left to voluntary action. As such, then, national service tends to be viewed as an appropriate policy by liberals and a more suspicious one by conservatives.

As Stephen Bates notes in his Cantigny report, the operating values of national service tend toward, but do not achieve, a full consistency with each other. Summarizing the case President Clinton made for the program, Bates identifies five major goals: "getting socially useful work done, instilling an ethic of sacrifice, helping troubled youths turn their lives around, reducing the barriers between different races and classes, and reinvigorating an assortment of civic virtues" (1996: 33).

AmeriCorps participants interviewed in our study[2] concur with the applicability of these goals to their service. Both members and employers place "getting socially useful work done" and "instilling an ethic of service" as most highly characteristic of their view of AmeriCorps, with "reinvigorating civic virtue" and "reducing barriers" closely behind. Seen as least characteristic of AmeriCorps, but not without applicability, was "helping troubled youths turn their lives around." Thus the core operating value of AmeriCorps in the minds and hearts of its participants involves "community service," blending thereby themes of doing important work in a spirit of teamwork, diversity, and civic concern.

The operational goals of useful work and the ethic of service tend to be internalized by AmeriCorps participants. They speak of these goals as grounded in their everyday actions, imbedded into their lives, and spread throughout the communities in which they live and work. As one Colorado Springs member put it,

> I know with the program I did last year, they had us in all different areas of urban areas, and even if you didn't even change a lot around you, you made a lot of friends, especially with the senior population, the high school students, whatever area you were working with. You

were able to get those around you to get involved to help you with what you were doing, and when that happened it was big—as far as results.

AmeriCorps builds a broad range of social and economic diversity into its programs in manifold ways. While some programs are quite segregated in their membership (on grounds of class, age, race, and gender), others consist of remarkably well-integrated activities. The overall result is a program of some substantial diversity, both in terms of members and those served.

The impact of this diversity in action is often powerful within AmeriCorps, as the following comments of two members indicate. One recent college graduate recalled her first days in Chicago:

> For me race has been a huge issue in my placement. I am coming from the University of Colorado which is a predominantly Anglo school. I am working in a predominantly African-American community. I have dealt with a ton of racism. Police officers, public transportation. It has been a huge eye-opener and learning experience, in dealing with racism for the first time, and learning from a culture I am not used to. This has been a huge factor for me.

Another Chicago member described the route that brought him into the program, and the important protective role he came to play within it. Spencer, a resident of one of Chicago's poorest areas, had been homeless, but never gave up his interest in helping his community. A volunteer with a local church organization, he began to volunteer helping AmeriCorps members placed in his community. Before long, he signed on as an AmeriCorps participant.

> I think it's great that we can get out into the community and serve people in the community and the residents. We can go and talk and help 'em and educate the importance of lead poisoning. That's the field I work in and it's just wonderful to be there; this program does work and it helps people especially in the schools and the churches and things like that. I work for the Chicago Health Corps. It is good to have a team because we can learn each other's moves and how things are gonna go and who's gonna disagree and agree on a lot of things, because in the neighborhood we're in, there's more issues than just there for us. We have to go out into the field and we have to watch each other's back because its nothin' to play around with; your life is at stake. And in the community you go in you have to go in on a positive note. Where you have to go and do what you gotta do and leave.

The Gallup survey discovered that the American public overwhelmingly supports the core values of national service. Ninety-four percent of the sample positively evaluated "bringing young people of different backgrounds together" in national service, while 75 percent agreed that it was important for such a program to provide the opportunity of "performing worthwhile work that would not otherwise be done."

The initial image of AmeriCorps was of a program seeking to attract middle-class youth to service in lower-income communities. While the service beneficiaries largely remain as intended, those providing the service turn out to be considerably more diverse in their backgrounds. Some AmeriCorps members serve in their own communities, some in other communities. Some live at home and commute to their assignments; others establish a new home as they enter their service.

Participants in the focus groups in our study were aware that AmeriCorps attracts several distinct categories of Americans to its service. A principal category involves what one administrator called "the best and the brightest" young college students in or just after their college years. Then there are the "diamonds in the rough," young people who have grown up in the ghettos and poverty communities of the American urban wasteland, but who turn to AmeriCorps for the multiple purposes of finishing their GED, learning a skill, and giving back to their communities. A third category involves the "young at heart," persons of considerable skills and maturity who join AmeriCorps (usually its VISTA program) to provide their service.

The degree to which the AmeriCorps programs examined in Camden, Chicago, and Colorado Springs have been able to design programs to attract and sustain each of these categories of participants is quite remarkable. These programs allow the recruitment and maintenance of participation of persons of a wide variety of income categories, racial and ethnic backgrounds, genders, ages, and life experiences.

When thinking of the future mix of AmeriCorps participants and programs, one finding from the national survey seems particularly striking. In that survey, 35 percent of the respondents indicated a personal interest in themselves serving in a national service capacity. Included in this group were 60 percent of all black respondents, and 45 percent of all respondents between 18 and 24 years old. If a similar program were designed for older Americans, 50 percent of those between 55 and 64 expressed an interest in serving, along with 41 percent older than 65. Clearly there are resources of untapped interest waiting to be developed by AmeriCorps, and they reach far beyond the pool of job-seeking welfare recipients that are so much at the fore of contemporary policy interest.

AmeriCorps programs often succeed in providing participants with both the chance to serve and to advance their own socio-economic prospects for later employment. College students and graduates who are members report significant enhancement in job-related skills, and also receive a stipend which can be applied to further their formal academic education. High school drop-outs receive both formal job training and the educational stipend. Both groups engage in significant amounts of service learning activity.

Consider, for example, Malik, the AmeriCorps member in the YouthBuild program in New Jersey, who saw the program as his "second chance" in life. To Malik, AmeriCorps offers a seamless web that incorporates both skills and service learning.

> The services I'm doing. There's a lot of friends that want to enroll in the same school and do the same that I'm doing. They see that they can go somewhere, instead of always having someone on their back. They can take that extra step, change their life around. When they see me and Jerome [also at the focus group—JVT] working and going to school, they happy, they appreciate us. They back us 100%. Like "Stay in the program." It's a good program, stay in it. It's like when we get out of school, we talk to other people around the neighborhood and other neighborhoods. To try to join them the program. To let them know it's a really nice program—we let them know it's not all about the stipend. They try to help you out with your education. If you take up a trade, so you can have a good paying job for yourself and your family. So we try to have people in our community on the right track, let them know that there's nothin' out on the street for you. So enroll in school, do something positive with your life and make a big step to change. Let everybody in the community know you're giving back to 'em because AmeriCorps can give me a chance so I want to give something back to them. I'm going to help build up the community.

Malik describes the community response to his AmeriCorps team and their work:

> We help clean up the community, you can see the shock on people's faces. They think that, our community is a lot of African-Americans, we don't have a mixed group because of the population in Atlantic City. So, they have this shocked look on they face like, "I don't believe they here to help us, to help serve us." We just let them know that we not here just to do it because of school, we're here to help y'all because everybody need help too. So we've tried to give something back to them. I feel as though they feel appreciated for it because when we was on Texas Avenue cleaning up graffiti off a house and a store, and like two days later the block was totally different because there was no spray paint on the walls. A lot of people was looking out they windows, and standing on they porch looking like, "Well who are these people who helped clean up the community?" So, I guess, they probably got together and felt as though, "Well, if they can do this, so can we." So it's like, I see this coming together, little by little.

Malik is asked if AmeriCorps should be mandatory for all youth:

> I say for the parents in Atlantic City it should be mandatory. Because
> if you know that your son or daughter's not doing it then you should
> make it mandatory that they sign up in the program. You know, do
> something with they life instead of wasting it. Like the lady said
> down at the end, well, we've had to go feed the homeless or take care
> of the sick, no, it's more than just that, you know, it's help building
> up the community. I feel as though AmeriCorps shouldn't stop with
> their program because, for our program, see next month there's going
> to be two classes coming together. So continue the effort, you know,
> helpin' the youth that's out in the world who need help gettin' their
> first step in the door with these programs, you know, and lettin' them
> know that there's another way instead of going back the other way.
> So, I feel as though y'all should keep up the good job.

The themes that emerge in these statements by this black, poor,
ghetto-dwelling, dropout father of three would be remarkable if they
were uttered by any human being: the need for personal commitment
and economic advancement, the desire to give back in the form of service to the community from which one came, the willingness to involve
others in advancing socially valuable work, the moral suasion to others to keep the faith and to bring along the new generation. Is Malik
unique as a statesperson for the value of the AmeriCorps experience?
I turn to the Chicago transcript and start reviewing the comments of
Marcus, another YouthBuild AmeriCorps member:

> We feed the homeless and rehabilitate houses for them. It's really
> much help in the community of Gary, Indiana.

> There's about thirty of us. Two Mexicans, and the rest African-Ameri-
> can. And about five of us go to the school in the area and help out
> the young. We really get along with each other. There's really no in-
> terracial thing going on. Everybody is getting to know one another.
> Getting things done. If there's a problem we go to the counselor. We
> get education and studying, carpenter skills, wiring houses and such
> and building and community service. It's fun to me. I like it. We have
> a money problem though, we need more money. Yeah, in Gary Indi-
> ana, that's about it.

> I am very spiritually inclined. Psychology is what I want to take up
> and electrical engineering, probably a little carpentry work. I help
> everyone out spiritually. If you want to be a leader, you must first be
> a servant. . . .

The survey respondents would not be surprised by the impacts
AmeriCorps has made on Malik and Marcus. They strongly supported
the value of the work experience provided by national service. Ninety-
five percent of the sample indicated that this value was important, in-

cluding 98 percent of the black respondents and 97 percent of those of with lower incomes.

AmeriCorps participants bring a variety of personal and financial needs to their service: seeking experience, finding themselves, supporting themselves and their families. Providing a single stipending system to these various needs is already causing considerable strain in the lives of many participants, requiring some to seek public assistance, work two jobs, or borrow even further from parents or banks. As AmeriCorps becomes more diverse in its membership, these problems seem likely to increase.

Among the greatest strengths of the AmeriCorps programs represented in this study was their ability to create a sense of teaming and morale among their participants. Members reported a strong sense of commitment to AmeriCorps goals and process, and demonstrated an enthusiastic level of support for the program and its activities.

The constraints applied to AmeriCorps by the slim nature of its national legislative mandate create a set of difficult dilemmas for the field operation of the program. Participants are prohibited from engaging in a wide range of individual and group activities that are part of the conventional repertoire of the individual citizen. Members typically navigate through these waters by recognizing the constraints as a necessary, if dubious, characteristic of any governmentally supported program. Nonprofit employers of AmeriCorps participants respond with greater dismay to these constraints, in cases imposing an unwarranted remove from any activity that might be seen to involve advocacy or governmentally related action.

Positive outcomes for nonprofit organizations which serve as the employers of AmeriCorps participants tend to be of two sorts: 1) expansion of organizational capacities by assigning AmeriCorps members to relatively routine organizational tasks; and 2) expansion of organizational capacities by asking AmeriCorps members to develop new programs for the organization. Both tasks are appropriate to the program, and both are widely represented, in the view of both members and employers. Occasionally, members are assigned tasks of a "gofer" nature, compensating for absenteeism or other organizational neglect.

AmeriCorps members and their immediate supervisors report an impressive listing of skills developed from the service of members. Principal among the skills reported were: knowledge of how an organization works; understanding organizational culture and functioning; basic job skills; office and interpersonal communication; working with people; decision making; project management; mediation; time management; computer skills; teaching; listening; crisis intervention; public speaking; leadership; teaming.

AmeriCorps members serve to increase the involvement of the agency clients they work with in an indirect, and yet significant, fashion. Members report that they work directly with clients and listen to their statements of interest and need in an open and sensitive fashion. They then report back to their agency supervisors, sometimes in ways the employers find non-traditional, and in this fashion assist in providing a voice to those they seek to serve.

Stipending within AmeriCorps provides a modicum of flexibility, in that agencies are allowed to supplement the minimal stipend provided by the national program. Basically, however, the stipend takes the form of "one size fits all." And yet, AmeriCorps members are, as we have seen, a rather diverse group in terms of need and background.

The administration of AmeriCorps involves a certain level of bureaucratic structure and functioning, as is generally the case with federal governmental programs. Forms are often confusing and difficult to complete; payments often lag behind expectations of their delivery; regulations are sometimes interpreted differently by different administrative personnel. On the whole, however, the administration of the program is viewed from the local level as well intentioned and usually helpful when directly contacted.

## AmeriCorps, Voluntarism, and Democracy

In a limited way, it is possible to see AmeriCorps as enhancing the workings of American democracy. It addresses a widespread willingness among the population to engage in service to those in need; it builds a connection with communities into the lives of those who serve as its participants. But the conception of democracy involved is not a fully robust one, as the participation of AmeriCorps members is limited by a set of restrictions on the involvement of members with the processes of the communities they seek to serve. The citizen service thereby provided by the AmeriCorps program is somewhat more fearful and constrained than the democratic rights and responsibilities established by the Constitution might suggest.

The AmeriCorps case also illuminates the three boundary issues we began tracking in Chapter 3: advocacy, taxation, and political control:

### ADVOCACY

Advocacy is a central issue in AmeriCorps, as the grudging support given the program by many in Congress is conditioned on the setting of a strict boundary between service and advocacy. Service is permitted; advocacy is not. AmeriCorps members learn to approach this issue pragmatically, but their nonprofit employers live in constant concern that the line will be inappropriately crossed.

That a proper balance between service and advocacy has not yet been achieved within AmeriCorps is apparent from the conversations with the agency people who administer these programs. In the Chicago discussion, for instance, program directors spoke frankly about the difficulties and dilemmas the AmeriCorps prohibitions on advocacy created for their agencies' work with AmeriCorps members:

FEMALE: I think AmeriCorps could speak to many other problems if that limitation wasn't there. You have to be very careful in what you get AmeriCorps members involved in terms of activism. If we didn't have that prohibited, there could be other things we could do.

MALE: For me as a project director, I am scared to death of political anything—any discussion that involves politics. Anything—whether talking about alderman races or the mayor or Congress. They say we are supposed to encourage our members to register to vote and I don't even want to get into that, really, because that's close to a line of having a discussion and endorsing a candidate. It's such a big issue that they're always sending us memos on from Washington. I don't want to get involved in that because I don't want to jeopardize what we have going, which is a very good thing.

MALE: How do you differentiate between community service and what the leaders of the community do? It seems to me that you all need to work together in the community. But it's a nationally funded program and you can't take sides. But to try to split community service from democratic participation doesn't work.

MALE: The thing that ties our hands, and we try to juggle the best we can to get the learning experience in there, is that a couple of prohibitions really hurt us. Organizing is exactly one of them. We would love to spend our time teaching our participants to organize, and we do a little of it. Can they put it into action? is a totally other thing. I think this social change comment about AmeriCorps is totally false because you can't organize. Additionally, the AmeriCorps member can't fundraise to support the organizing project that you would love to see. So there are these things in place that keep you from moving.

MALE: What needs to be done is to be able to shake the cage and say, "Here's what's really going on in the community, I want to say something about it." I think AmeriCorps members have a talent in being able to relate to folks. But how far can we take it?

MALE: Education is our mission, and my members are educating each other. Our community is going through this welfare thing and so they're teaching each other about the new child care regs, the new food stamp regulations, the new cash benefit. In terms of influencing where that's going to go, I'm completely hands off. If they want to do that on their own time, that's up to them. But for our program, we say: "We are here to educate the children of this building," and that's it.

MALE: AmeriCorps members can't be excused from work to engage in politics. But on election day we close down. If they want to participate in a rally on their own time, that's OK as long as you don't have your AmeriCorps gear on. Be a citizen.

FEMALE: It's very clear you can't demonstrate. When the Democratic convention came, we got a lot of directives to be very clear as to how AmeriCorps was used. Members understand that, we are open as to prohibited activity. We spend time going over those activities.

MALE: Maybe it was a really intelligent person who thought of this, and thought let's do something about this innately American behavior to have someone else solve this problem. OK, I have a hole in front of my house— get a politician to do it. Making a separation makes it possible to do community building in the truest sense. Let's do something about this hole, not to demonstrate about it or write a letter about it, but just figure out what resource we can use in the community to solve this problem.

AmeriCorps members are also troubled by the advocacy restrictions placed upon them. Their response, however, tends to be more moderate and understanding than those of their supervisory elders. They seem to accept these restrictions as "something adults do," and work their way through their relations with the communities they serve in a pragmatic and productive way.

Consider these comments by Camden AmeriCorps members:

FEMALE: This has been the biggest and the hardest struggle for me as an AmeriCorps member, that you can't advocate at the legislative level.

FEMALE: Having been a member for the past three years, it seems that every year the rules get more strict about our political participation. The rules for this year are so strict that I'm not even sure if we can go to the Stand For Children which is a non-partisan activity, which is directly linked to our goal of stopping violence among children. AmeriCorps is an activity that makes a lot of the college students in our corps more aware politically of what's going on. When we can't even try to send a letter to our congressperson, and if they don't cut our budget, it's frustrating.

FEMALE: I agree with what's been said here. It is frustrating, and it almost feels like censorship. In order to be in this program you can't make any big waves, you have to be quiet. We can as private citizens, but not under AmeriCorps. I understand them not wanting us to lobby, but I feel as though, as a group, and especially when it's something that we participate in, we should be allowed to say, "Hey, this is what's going on here with this focus that we're dealing with, and this is what needs to happen."

A Chicago member echoed the same themes as the Camden participants:

> FEMALE: For me it raises a lot of questions. I work for "I Have a Dream." I believe that we have gotten to where we are because we have tried to stay middle of the road. We need AmeriCorps because we have been there. I find it weird that they don't suggest that we get more involved through alternative routes.

Even though the restrictions on advocacy seem weird to many participants, they tend to learn to work within them such that their effect is minimal on the basic relationship that counts for them: their relation to the individuals in the communities they serve. Some, like a Chicago member, come to see service itself as the subject of advocacy. He observed that "AmeriCorps definitely is an advocate for community service—serving the community and giving back to the community." A woman in the same group added, "I also take it as becoming a responsible working adult."

The AmeriCorps members learn to work around their restrictions, and they tend to be quite creative. As one Chicago woman member recalls:

> Last year we were trying to teach the kids voting responsibility. We had to phrase it in such a way that, well, we brought in an outside speaker so we the AmeriCorps members were not doing it. It was bipartisan. It is protection so that we do not influence the people we work with. Allow them their own right to free speech.

The survey completed by focus group members shows that the advocacy restrictions clearly concern employers more than members. Participants tended to rank their own ability to encourage activism, advance social change, and strengthen democracy considerably more highly than did their supervisors. But both members and employers are more likely to characterize AmeriCorps as a service program rather than an advocacy or change-oriented program. Clearly the legislative compromise engineered between the president and a handful of Republican moderates has heard the voice of those further right: no advocacy shall be sponsored by the federal government! But, equally clearly, the ingenuity of AmeriCorps participants has allowed them to find ways of encouraging activism and advancing social change that fit within the bounds of whatever administrative constraints Washington is able to devise and proclaim. Advocacy, it would seem, is a persistent part of the repertory of third-sector participants.

The provision of service is important, and often essential, to a thriving third sector. As Dorothy Height, the long-time president of the National Council of Negro Women, has often put it: "If a person is bleeding, they need a Band-Aid. But Band-Aids don't do much for cancer." What the American tradition of voluntary action provides its citizens is the chance both to dispense Band-Aids as needed and to stand tall in the call to action when required. It is this dual legacy of service and advocacy that governments confront when they seek to institutionalize national service programs. The issues raised in this process have troubled AmeriCorps as they earlier troubled community action programs in the War on Poverty. It is very difficult, if not impossible, to work with communities in need without entering, if only indirectly, the world of advocacy, protest, and direct action.

## TAXATION

AmeriCorps, as legislatively established and funded, is a program of the federal government. By the late 1990s, the cost of supporting an individual member for a year's service, when costs of the stipend, training, and administration are all included, came to about $15,000 (though this figure remains in some controversy between supporters and opponents of the program). With 40,000 participants expected by 1999, the total annual program cost came to about $60 million, or about 25 cents per citizen per year.

This cost seems eminently reasonable to Americans. Our Gallup survey in 1995 asked a national sample if they felt "the country is getting good value for the compensation" it pays for AmeriCorps: 76 percent agreed, and only 9 percent disagreed. When asked if the "money would be better spent on other programs," 16 percent agreed, and 71 percent disagreed.

On the whole, Americans see the benefits of AmeriCorps far outweighing its costs. Primary among the benefits are the following, with percentages of respondents agreeing:

94% Brings together young people from different backgrounds
94% Gives young people useful work experience
91% Raises self-esteem among the young people participating
83% Encourages healthy lifestyles among the participants
78% Helps reduce crime among young people
77% Encourages more people to do volunteer work generally
77% Helps reduce restlessness among young people
75% Participants perform worthwhile work that would not otherwise
    be done

Costs of the program are primarily considered in terms of undesirable values being inculcated, but are perceived by many fewer respondents:

29% Delays the start of the careers of the young people who participate
19% Sends the wrong message to young people—that they should be
    paid for volunteer work
19% Diverts some participants from further education

## PARTNERING DYNAMICS

The national sample questioned in the Gallup survey of AmeriCorps
was asked to assess a number of criticisms of AmeriCorps that had
been raised regarding problems of government-nonprofit partnerships. With the exception of only one item, most respondents did not
perceive these criticisms as serious.

The only item receiving agreement by as much as 50 percent of the
sample was hardly a criticism: "Adds more bureaucracy to the federal
or state government." Unless one takes an Aesopian view of government and expects it to provide services without expense, this is hardly
a major criticism. A similarly empirical statement, "Diverts national
resources from other worthwhile programs," received the agreement
of 27 percent of the respondents.

The most substantial criticism pertaining to the impact of Ameri-
Corps on nonprofit organizations, "Makes it more difficult for private
organizations to find volunteers," found only 23 percent of the respondents in agreement.

Survey respondents were not convinced, however, that the federal
government should be the lead agency in assuring national service.
When asked which one of the following "is best able to organize and
manage AmeriCorps," the respondents' choices were:

50% Non-governmental organizations
18% Federal government
13% State government
11% Local government

The national survey reveals several important findings pertaining
to this difficult issue. First, African-American respondents demonstrate a far greater trust in the federal government to operate the program than do whites. Indeed, whites overwhelmingly support the
management of AmeriCorps by a non-governmental organization
(53%) as against the federal government (15%). African-Americans, on
the other hand, favor the administration of the program by the federal
government (38%) as opposed to a nonprofit (33%).[3]

Interviews with nonprofit managers and governmental administrators of the program suggest that the partnering relationship, while
not always easy or smooth, usually proves workable.

Choosing which agencies will become suitable receptors for national service participation is an important decision. In the public-voluntary partnership of AmeriCorps, this choice is made in a joint fashion between national and state governing agencies. Federal Policy shapes and constrains the fields of placement, which were initially limited to education, recreation, law enforcement, and elder care.

The Corporation for National Service sets the policies that place AmeriCorps participants in programs throughout the land. Strong political forces may compel them to choose among only those agencies whose purposes are so bland and generally acceptable that they arouse little political opposition. Considering the power that "veto groups" exercise in American democracy, it would seem unlikely that service participants will ever have the chance to work for such agencies as Greenpeace, Focus on the Family, or the National Abortion Rights League.

The issue of the selection of agencies is one that was addressed only indirectly in the present study. But the range of agencies who provided members and employers to our focus groups suggests a wider range of agencies and programs than might have been expected in the context of AmeriCorps's political controversy. Some agencies that provided us respondents were primarily oriented toward advocacy, though they made certain to assure that the AmeriCorps components of their programs conformed to the advocacy proscriptions. Others focused on citizen education, and yet others provided core services in the basic fields of education, recreation, law enforcement, and public health.

A major issue facing AmeriCorps policy during the period of study (early 1997) involved the selection of agencies and programs that fit administration initiatives of welfare reform. As one Chicago employer described the situation:

> We went to D.C. for a new program directors' conference, and it seems to be the trend in AmeriCorps to use it as a "welfare to work" program. So I don't see it just as a program of college grads providing service. I see it as a program to get some folks child care and some money for school and skill development—a program that brings people together for a lot of reasons. Some people who care about service and have had some advantages in life, some getting into program for other reasons.

A state director noted that the introduction of a program that focused on bringing in welfare recipients met with considerable debate within the state commission, and was ultimately approved only with great caution. AmeriCorps would innovate, he asserted, but it would also seek to stay faithful to the spirit on which it was founded.

When the 1999 Reauthorization proposal was sent to Congress, mention was sparse on the impact of welfare reform. But principal among the goals were two pertaining to partnering dynamics: "Giving more authority over national service programs to the states" and "Strengthening partnerships with traditional volunteer organizations." Devolution is clearly an important dynamic in the continuing evolution of the AmeriCorps program.

## Conclusion

A critical first-hand report by Cunningham (1993) found that the first wave of what became AmeriCorps' 1993 Summer of Service participants seemed to be unswervingly directed toward themselves. Many of their objections begin with boilerplate therapy lingo: "'I feel uncomfortable when you say . . .'" (Cunningham, 1993: 7). Her article concludes with a bitter satire of bored and rowdy youth delighting when their clients did not show, leaving behind a messy picnic ground as they left in their vans. "All that remained of the day . . . witnessed that America Had Been Served."

Critics of national service, like Cunningham, might detect a twinge of egotism in the testimony of the AmeriCorps members interviewed for the present study, but this principal investigator did not. Rather, I recall as characteristic of the participants I talked with the comments of a former teenage single mother now serving as an AmeriCorps participant in a program directed at current teens:

> I work with teen moms, and what we do is, every night before we get in our group all the girls get in a circle. We have to be in a circle before we have a presentation or before we even start having a discussion we all have to be in a group, so we have to look at each other and, you know, you're more comfortable, like if someone's sitting behind you really can't see, you know, what she's feeling or what she's saying. So we always get in a circle, and the girls like it, they talk more when they're in a circle looking at each other.

The image of the circle is a powerful one in AmeriCorps. It was used by then U.S. Senate candidate Rick Santorum (R-PA) as a criticism of then Senator Harris Wofford in their bitter 1994 campaign. Santorum, it will be recalled, warned that public funds should not be used to support young people sitting around campfires singing "Kumbaya." A few years later, the defeated and yet unbowed Wofford, now the director of the Corporation for National Service, told of visiting an AmeriCorps group high in the California Sierras, where they had been clearing trails. They planned a campfire to regale Wofford, but needed to send a delegate down from the high country to the nearest library to find both the words and the tune of "Kumbaya."

By the middle of the 1990s, national service found itself in the uncomfortable position of having become an issue of considerable political controversy. On the one hand, President Clinton clung tenaciously to its support, calling it one of the most important pieces of legislation passed during his administration. In opposition to this view, the Speaker of the House, Congressman Newt Gingrich of Georgia, identified national service as a prime example of the kind of wasteful government spending the new Republican majority had been brought to power to eliminate.

This debate is an ongoing one, addressed annually in congressional struggles over budgetary appropriations and legislation. However, the issues raised by the president and the Speaker will continue to face American society whatever the fate of the current national service initiative: Does the federal government have a role to play in supporting service? Or should service emerge only if initiated and entirely supported by voluntary organizations? Should the federal government play a direct role in helping equip youth to serve others? Or should such service be left to state and local governments to provide in a redesigned welfare state that sees a greatly lessened role for the federal government.

To the participants in the AmeriCorps program who joined the focus groups of the Gallup study, the value of their mission seemed clear. They were distressed, however, that so few people took the time to learn about that mission and the work it provided in the communities they served. They complained that the media consistently failed to report the work they accomplished, even when painstakingly invited to visible community events. They feared that the impact of their contribution was vanishing into the miasma of a nation fixated on the lives of the rich and famous and the violence of the slums and ghettos of America's cities.

The invisibility of so much of AmeriCorps's work was dramatically underwritten by the interviews we conducted with a purposive sample of community leaders in each of the three cities. Time and time again, major leaders of educational, business, governmental, and civic organizations admitted that, while they knew in general about the national struggles over AmeriCorps, they could not identify a single AmeriCorps program in their own community. In Chicago only one of the sixteen leaders interviewed had a strong knowledge of local AmeriCorps programs. In Colorado Springs, that same situation was replicated, one in seventeen. In Camden, five of sixteen leaders showed an informed knowledge of the workings of at least one AmeriCorps program in their community.

Time and time again, the local leaders rehearsed the same position. It sounds like a valuable program, but it hasn't come across my screen here in Colorado Springs, here in Chicago, here in Camden. When the interviewer filled in a few of the blanks about the workings of AmeriCorps and asked the leaders if the program sounded like one that would assist their community, the responses were overwhelmingly positive. Even in conservative Colorado Springs, that bastion of limited government, only one of the seventeen leaders interviewed held to the view that the fact that AmeriCorps members were stipended meant that community agencies should not find considerable advantage in bringing them to service.

AmeriCorps has a difficult road ahead, if it is to survive the Clinton years and enter the 21st century. It must learn to continue to serve effectively, even if that means participating in an occasional act of surreptitious advocacy. It must continue to receive legislative funding, even if that means convincing reluctant congresspersons to bring their thinking into line with the overwhelming majority of their constituents. And it must remain vigilant and sensitive to the dynamics of partnering in an age of rapid devolution. Not an easy task—but neither an impossible one. No small piece of the survival of American democracy will rest in the outcome.

# 5

# The Emerging Field of Nonprofit Policy Study

Contemporary liberals and moderates speak of the importance of "public-private partnerships," in which government and third-sector organizations work together to achieve public ends. Today's neo-conservatives, on the contrary, hold to the primacy of the two "private" sectors—business and voluntary—and call for the minimization of government—save for the enforcement of various "moral values." These differences in viewpoint give rise to the basis for clear distinctions in what we may call "nonprofit policy"—or the proper orientation of third-sector organizations toward directing the focus of its efforts.

Differences in orientation toward nonprofit policy often center on issues of "philanthropic sufficiency or insufficiency" and the proper role of volunteers. The 1997 Presidents' Summit on America's Future brought these issues closer to the fore of American public life, and this milestone event receives particular attention in this chapter.

## The Presidents' Summit

As was seen in the previous chapter, the new Republican majority in Congress moved quickly upon its election in 1994 to implement its proposed "Contract with America." This document outlined a set of free-market solutions for social problems and called for the establishment of a tight rein on public spending.

The predominantly Republican-led initiative that became known as the Presidents' Summit on America's Future proved to be a highly significant event in the development of third-sector policy. The Summit, viewed as a visible convening of all the living U.S. presidents and their spouses in support of principles of voluntary action, was the brainchild of the late George Romney, a former governor of Michigan, unsuccessful candidate for the Republican presidential nomination, and founder and long-time board chair of the National Center for Voluntary Action—currently known as the Points of Light Foundation. Romney persuaded Robert Goodwin (CEO of the Points of Light Foundation) and Wofford to join him in advancing this vision, and died within days of that meeting. Subsequently, Goodwin won the commitment of his Points of Light Foundation board chair (former President George Bush), and Wofford secured the support of his boss (President Clinton) to move to advance the Summit.

The design of the Summit was placed under the leadership of Gregg Petersmeyer, who was Bush's director of the Points of Light initiative during his administration. Petersmeyer, a thoughtful practitioner, had spent "decompression and reflection" time at the Indiana University Center on Philanthropy after Bush's electoral loss to Clinton. His views tended toward valuing direct individual volunteering, and he had been known to express skepticism about the motives and contributions of nonprofit professionals and the formal nonprofit organizations they administer.

Petersmeyer set about approaching the five principals (in addition to Clinton and Bush—Ford, Reagan, and Carter) carefully, recognizing that each required the same delicacy of approach as would surround inviting the head of a sovereign nation. Jimmy Carter, distressed by Clinton's refusal to invite him to the 1996 Democratic national convention, initially indicated a willingness only to participate through an off-site television linkage. Bush, still smarting from his 1992 electoral loss to Clinton, indicated that he would not share a stage with anyone who spoke positively about the contributions of AmeriCorps, which he viewed as a misguided initiative by an opposition politician. Last-minute understandings were achieved even as Bush and Clinton made their way to the late 1996 press conference announcing the forthcoming event.

Form necessarily preceded content in the planning. The initial planning committee was heavily weighted toward publicists, who liked the idea of holding the event on Presidents' Day. Reason prevailed, though, when one thought of likely Philadelphia weather in February, as well as the need for program content. The substance of the event gradually took the form of amassing "commitments" from businesses and other organizations. These commitments were aimed to extend to the year 2000 in five areas: mentoring, safe places to learn and grow, health, marketable skills through education, and community service.

Considerable focus and weight was given the effort when the

highly popular, and oft-considered candidate for the Republican presidential nomination, General Colin Powell (ret.), signed on as general chairman of the effort. The Democratic Secretary of Housing and Urban Development, Henry Cisneros, was named as associate chairman, besting retiring Senator Bill Bradley (D-NJ) for this position. Senator Bradley was thought to be too strong an eventual presidential contender to Vice-President Al Gore to be selected for so visible a position.

Powell quickly asserted his vision of the Summit: it should address as its key concern the fate of at-risk youth. His vision came to predominate, moving to the margins of the event George Bush's preferred image of volunteering and Bill Clinton's desire for a focus on citizen service. The press, however, delighted in the plurality of foci, alternating between references to the event as the "Volunteerism Summit," the "Service Summit," and the "Youth Summit."

Attendance at the April event was by invitation, with some 2,400 delegates representing 143 cities and other areas and all 50 states. The city delegates were named by local panels including an official from AmeriCorps or a related program. A relatively small number of national association leaders were invited, and a last-minute invitation brought several hundred AmeriCorps participants to the event.

The Presidents' Summit on America's Future played itself out with as much variety as the forces that stood behind its planning. Powell's "Youth Summit" vision predominated, tightly packaged and delivered during what turned out to be a rather successful three-day "infomercial." The five themes of the Summit were constantly put in play: Mentor! Protect! Nurture! Teach! Serve!

Community delegations varied widely in their perceptions of the process provided for them, which focused heavily on the use of nominal group techniques, staffed by an army of organizational trainers and consultants. Delegates from teams who had prepared for the Summit tended to be impatient with the corporate training styles of their at times hyper-enthusiastic trainers. As one delegate put it, not wishing to be identified for quotation: "In our group, there's a hard edge of realism. Many of our group have had senior leadership positions in voluntary nonprofit organizations, and they're asking how is this effort going to be any different or any more successful."

The Philadelphia team, one of those which had prepared well for the Summit, thrived under the leadership of Mayor Ed Rendell, the Summit's local host. Rendell worked long and hard with his strong and increasingly cohesive team, which moved to commit to reaching 30,000 youths on all five of the Summit's goals. "This means," noted team member Ira Harkavy, the director of the University of Pennsylvania's community partnership program, "that we will be looking for places in the neighborhoods of the city to provide all five of the Summit's goals, be they schools, community centers, or higher education institutions."

Oneonta (NY) delegate Cathy Martinez worried about the way in which Summit commitments would reach her town. "We will obviously be looking for our local folks to make their commitments, but in an area that's economically depressed, with a high level of unemployment and lots of problems already, lack of resources is a big problem. For example, how do we tap into the commitment Lenscrafters made when we don't even have a Lenscrafters store in our community?"[1]

The follow-up vehicle to the Summit, "America's Promise: The Alliance for Youth," was introduced to the delegates only at the final session of the conference. It identified itself as a "fluid alliance" aimed to "propel the mission and goals of the Summit forward." Alliance staff present at the Summit noted that the program was still in invention, and cancelled a press conference to announce its structure, leaving the only mention of its presence to General Powell's concluding conference statement.

How to evaluate the Summit and its subsequent Promise? I ventured my evaluation in the pages of the *NonProfit Times*. Should it be:

A (for active and accurate)? Not yet, for far too many problems of youth do not fit in the five goal format. As pollster George Gallup observed, among those problems are the alcoholism of many parents and children, the role of responsible fatherhood, and the contributions of religious organizations. Other themes ignored: service-learning by universities, civil education in the schools, a defined role for nonprofits, the uses (and limits) of corporate volunteerism, and ways of dealing with what Jeremy Rifkin calls "the end of work."

B (for bright and building)? Maybe, for the TV was crisp and effective. But not enough evidence has yet been given as to the Summit's ability to work with its primary clients, youth (who were largely ignored and isolated at the conference) or to engage its primary providers, nonprofit organizations, to warrant this grade.

C (for caring and compassionate)? Well, this was Theme number 1, but will the endless stream of speakers who stayed so directly on message actually do anything but breathe a sigh of relief when they return to the post-Summit daily grind? Infomercials, after all, have a way of going in one ear and quickly passing out the other.

D (for daring but disappointing)? This was the grade assigned by Jeremy Rifkin, an early Summit organizer, who worried that bringing the presidents together had entered the miasma of political posturing, particularly as the Powell image mounted to dominate the event. Rifkin also noted the near total absence of any critical deliberation on themes like the role of the third sector in effecting change at Summit sessions.

F (for friendly but fascistic)? This theme was raised outside the hall from critics on both the right and left. Conservative pundit Robert Novak raised the theme on TV's "Crossfire," and the manifesto presented by the protesting National People's Campaign recalled the work of the late Bertram Gross, who saw the nonprofit sector as easily manipulable by corporate and governmental forces dedicated to keeping people poor but pacified.

My grade: Incomplete. With hard work and effective networking, maybe as much as a C+ or even B– by the year 2000. But don't forget that an F is also possible. There's a lot of work left to do, folks, and not all of it can be done by the volunteers.

The Summit's follow-up organization, America's Promise, had begun by the end of 1997 to conduct some follow-up activity in a number of the Summit cities, and youth-serving organizations reported a perceptible upturn in the number of persons calling them to volunteer. A national survey disclosed that 10 percent of the adult population had been moved by the Summit to increase their volunteering activities, a not inconsiderable accomplishment for a media campaign in an information-saturated society.

By late 1998, the only one of the five summit goals clearly being advanced was the fifth: to involve at-risk youths themselves in active service. Leadership in this effort was provided by the Corporation for National Service. Once more, Corporation CEO Wofford had shown his ability to work in a bipartisan environment to advance the goals of citizen and youth service. Moreover, his enthusiastic service in all phases of the Summit's process assured a productive working relationship with General Powell, who remained, despite all statements to the contrary, a formidable candidate for an eventual presidential draft, if not in 2000, then in some subsequent election. It is difficult to imagine that a Powell presidency would disband AmeriCorps, a small program which had secured, against all odds, a political beachhead against the opposition brought to it by Gingrich, Santorum, and many other Republican conservatives.

President Clinton, his political senses highly tuned, had mastered the politics of voluntarism through his participation in the Presidents' Summit, and had seemingly secured a place for his major domestic initiative, AmeriCorps, such that it would persevere into the administrative watch of either Powell or Gore.

## The Problem of Philanthropic (In)Sufficiency

The Presidents' Summit was not simply a political challenge or a public relations exercise. It was also a serious effort to set policy for the third sector. Those who stood behind its organizing process believed that voluntary action could impact in a decisive manner the quality of life of America's most troubled youth, the two million youngsters whose lives were at risk to forces of poverty, racism, and neglect.

Among the Summit's supporters were some, like person of wealth Ariana Huffington, who held to the conception of voluntarism that sees government as the bumbling enemy, while private enterprise is viewed as the source of truth, justice, and the American way. Also on the Summit's organizing committee were progressives like Jeremy Rifkin, individuals who saw Huffington and her ilk as ideological dinosaurs preserved in a set of pre-Depression era myths of Lady Bountiful and the benevolence of the corporate rich.

It is perhaps not surprising that persons of wealth tend to take on the rather provincial views that often characterize their lives of comfort and the protection it offers from the rigors of ordinary life. Teresa Odendahl, in her classic study *Charity Begins at Home*, documents clearly the ways in which the ideologies of the rich lead them to seek to control the thoughts and deeds of recipients of their largesse.

From this perspective often emerges the theory of "philanthropic sufficiency," in which it is imagined that the combined forces of philanthropy, voluntarism, and nonprofit organization will suffice to meet the pressing social needs of our times. Critics of this view offer two major arguments in reply: 1) they claim that the theory of philanthropic sufficiency ignores the fact that the vast majority of third-sector services are provided to members of the middle and upper classes, and not those most sorely in economic need; and 2) they note that philanthropic contributions remain only a small percentage of total societal expenditures addressed toward the meeting of social needs.

Research by Johns Hopkins policy specialist Lester Salamon indicates that the governments of our land—federal, state, and local—spent in 1989 nearly $1 trillion on social welfare activities of all sorts (1992: 33). When pensions and public education expenses are not included, the federal government's spending share amounted to some $382 billion, while total nonprofits spending amounted to just under $300 billion.

While this massive governmental spending was undertaken, the annual contribution of individuals and businesses amounted to some $15 billions of dollars to social services, while churches provided another $4.5 billion (including pro-rated volunteer time) to their provision. An additional $12 billion was directed to nonprofit organizations by governmental sources, to provide social services on contract. The instruments of the welfare state, therefore, outspent the philanthropic sources in assisting the poor and needy by a ratio of nearly 6 to 1. At the same time, the institutions of the third sector were directing over

$90 billion to programs in such fields as the support of religious con-gregations, "private" education, nonprofit health care, arts and cul-ture, social causes, and other purposes largely directed to the interest of middle- and upper-income persons. In other words, nearly nine of every ten dollars contributed philanthropically were not aimed di-rectly toward the requirements of the poor and needy.

Thus, while it is true that some voluntary organizations do pro-vide services to the poor and needy, the U.S. government has, over the past half-century, assumed major responsibility for such service through the instrumentalities of the welfare state, both directly and through the subvention of voluntary organizations.

Defenders of this position need not argue that the welfare state holds some clear moral superiority to the third sector. As Peter Drucker, himself no friend of big government, puts it: "Some of the toughest problems we face are those created by the successes of the past—the success of the welfare state, for example." The welfare state has be-come, like so much of philanthropy, itself the captive of middle- and upper-class desires. Upper-middle-class citizens who enjoy the re-wards of the homeowner's tax deduction, maximum income tax rates that barely top 30 percent, and the forgiveness of capital gains taxes on the sale of homes know all too well who benefits the most from governmental programs. As Turner and Starnes (1976) have observed, the "wealthfare state" that undergirds so much of the flourishing eco-nomic life of well-off Americans far exceeds in financial scope and governmental scale the (increasingly weakened) welfare state that seeks to provide a safety net for those in economic and personal dis-tress.

## Launching Third-Sector Policy Studies

As the third sector has grown in most modern societies, so has the for-mal study of this emerging field. As David Horton Smith, founder of this field of study, has indicated, its study begins with categorization of organizations and the study of individual voluntary activity. As the field of study matures, its significance in terms of direct societal im-pact becomes a topic of increasing concern. Research begins to move beyond the "bean counting" phase, and toward a fuller assessment of the significance of voluntary action and nonprofit organization in so-ciety.

The study of the third sector has blossomed with the expansion of third-sector organizations in society. The distinguished historian of nonprofit organizations Peter Dobkin Hall (1992: 62) has noted that in 1940 it was possible to identify no more than 12,500 charitable tax-exempt organizations. By 1989 the number had reached one million, and current estimates put the number closer to 1.5 million.

What sense can be made of this astounding growth? Surely it is not possible to argue that the general welfare has increased during this period by anything like the more than 100-fold increase in nonprofit organizations during the past 60 years. Indeed, it has recently been observed that

> After decades of narrowing the gap between rich and poor—brought about by policy and economic growth—the last two decades have seen rising inequality in income and a growing concentration of wealth, with 1 percent of the U.S. population currently owning 35 percent of the wealth. . . . This inequality is exacerbated by the changing access to technology and education, revealing the specter of a permanent underclass in the United States. This not only bodes ill for social peace, but it also means the loss of potential talent and innovation for society and economic growth. Addressing the needs of the poor has acquired new urgency, especially in light of the termination of welfare entitlements. . . . [W]ithin the nonprofit sector itself, there is a growing disparity between those institutions capable of mounting major drives for endowments and those grass-roots organizations struggling to achieve their missions.

This gloomy vision of the rich getting richer while a "permanent underclass" develops, boding "ill for social peace," has not been penned by an angry and isolated academic neo-Marxist. Rather, it is the collective work of over 90 corporate and foundation leaders, meeting in April 1998 in the sumptuous surroundings of Los Angeles's Getty Center (American Assembly, 1998: 9).

It is remarkable that these elite observers see as the cause of the contemporary crisis in inequality the combined workings of governmental policy and economic growth. Apparently they do not believe that a "rising tide raises all boats," but neither do they see that the burgeoning third sector has been able to make any perceptible impact on the level of social distress.

Those who gathered in the Getty Center represented the moderate liberal leadership of the third sector. Their views can certainly be distinguished from those of the field's neo-conservatives, whose views have been most influentially promulgated by Milwaukee's Bradley Foundation, which recently financed a "'National Commission' on Philanthropy and Civic Renewal," chaired by long-time presidential hopeful Lamar Alexander.

The central message of this commission combines traditional Republican skepticism about government and foundations with a faith in the power of community-based organization that would warm the heart of a 1960s radical. Its major points can be boiled down to four contentions:

1. More giving needs to be effectively directed to the benefit of those most in need.

2. Many of the best charities are local and independent of government.

3. Donors are well advised to become "civic entrepreneurs," strategically involved in the organizations they support.

4. Organized philanthropies often focus too heavily on research and theory, failing to provide simple and direct service solutions to pressing problems.

Of these four points, it can be sensibly observed that the first two make a lot of sense, but are hardly original, while the third and fourth imaginatively repackage the traditional right-wing distrust of big, "liberal" foundations and progressive community demands for social change.

A genuinely progressive theory of the third sector, while occasionally essayed, has yet to be fully developed, and I will discuss this possibility later, in Chapter 13. The basic elements of such a theory, however, will be found in the quest for a civil economy (one which provides not just growth but also fairness), in the search for an active democracy (one in which effective citizen voice is exercised and heard), and in the development of a robust and vital third sector in which both service and advocacy are evident and valued contributions. We stand, indeed, on the cusp of some very exciting days in the development of third-sector policy.

## Four Parties, Four Sectors

It is important to recognize that there is no agreement as to the proper direction social policy and social change should take among the leaders of the third sector. This arena is riven by the same set of ideological preferences and conflicts that characterize governmental and economic life. And there is no reason to expect that things should be different. The third sector is very much a creature of the society in which it has formed.

American life contains within its institutions a variety of views as to how society should be structured. These divisions appear most clearly during the election campaigns for the presidency, as the 1996 election indicated. In his acceptance speech for the Republican presidential nomination that year, candidate Bob Dole railed against the followers of his opponent, Democrat Bill Clinton, who claimed that economic issues should take precedence in the campaign. Clinton's people claimed that "It's the economy, stupid." But Dole dissented: "All things do not flow from wealth or poverty. . . . All things flow from doing what is right."

In spite of this recognition, the lengthiest comments in Dole's speech dealt with nakedly self-interested reasons to support his candidacy: "It means you will have a President who will reduce taxes across the board for every taxpayer. It will include a $500 per child tax credit for low and middle income families. Taxes for a family of four making $35,000 would be reduced by more than half—56 percent to be exact. . . . It means you will have a President who will end the I.R.S. as we know it. In other words, it's the economy, stupid!"

Dole's ability to sustain contradictions (opponents would call it "talking out of both sides of his mouth") was certainly rivaled by Clinton, who demonstrated he was a liberal only some of the time by his willingness to sign a "welfare reform" bill that, in the words of fellow Democrat Patrick Moynihan, punishes children in the feeble hope of reforming their parents. But Dole represented in his comments two very different views of the world that many Republicans seek simultaneously to include within their party dogma.

One way of understanding these differences is provided by a collection of essays edited by Don E. Eberly, *Building a Community of Citizens* (1994). Eberly, a policy specialist of impeccable Republican background, included in this collection a remarkable essay by A. Lawrence Chickering, titled "Citizenship: Transcending Left and Right." In this essay, Chickering argues that both the American left ("liberals") and right ("conservatives") are themselves divided into two quite distinct groups, depending on their valuing of freedom or order.

Chickering writes: "Conservatism is therefore divided into libertarian (freedom conservative) and traditionalist (order conservative) parts; and liberalism includes freedom liberals (anarchists, the counterculture, most civil libertarians) and order liberals (socialists, welfare state liberals)."

This very useful schema allows us to understand why the two major parties go through such contortions in their efforts to include so much diversity under their various tents—the Republicans including the more libertarian Colin Powell along with the moralistic Pat Buchanan, the Democrats tolerating their free-wheeling president even when he rails against the evils of crime or absent parenting. If a major party contented itself with ideological consistency, it would lose the next election to the party that successfully erected a tent big enough to house the followers of more than one ideological camp.

This conceptualization also assists in understanding that within the third sector, a similar division of ideological persuasion may be found. Freedom conservatives inhabit think tanks like the Cato Institute while Order conservatives predominate in fundamentalist churches and think tanks like the American Enterprise Institute.

On the progressive side of things, Freedom liberals predominate in the American Civil Liberties Union and Americans United for the Separation of Church and State, while Order liberals prevail at the Brookings Institution, the Foundation on Economic Trends, and the National Center on Economic Alternatives.

As with their political cousins, the ideologists of the third sector play their favorites among institutional sectors. Freedom conservatives place their faith in the primacy provided by the unregulated markets of laissez-faire capitalism, and minimize the role of government and those third-sector organizations that seek to expand government's role. Order conservatives similarly prefer market solutions to those of the state, but place their greatest emphasis on the importance of stable family life. Markets should not be allowed to provide pornography or hallucinogens, they assert, and neither should the state easily allow divorce or welfare. Like their libertarian cousins, Order conservatives value charity, but are suspicious of third-sector organizations that seek to act as social movements.

Freedom liberals, on the other hand, worry about the ways in which markets follow the rule of gold, and tend to find in a strong and active government, backed by an activist third sector, the surest path to individual growth and development. Their cousins on the left, Order liberals, are more inclined to support the development of formal governmental programs to organize and distribute the blessings of economic life.

The remedies for society's ills that pour forth from these sources of policy thought are lengthy: Family! Church! Lower taxes! Community participation! Rights and responsibilities! An end to failed programs of big government! Increased health care benefits!

But do these answers, fitted with each other, amount to a solution of our national ills? What is not being addressed? It is a recurrent observation of mine that no set of answers will solve society's needs unless it shows how each of the elements of our multi-sector society can work together to provide real solutions. Dole, for instance, saw clearly what might emerge from a cultural restoration of family and religious values, but seemed unaware of the ways in which community life sustains these values, as well as the ways in which a workplace plagued by underpaid, over-ruled, and insecure employees functions in direct opposition to the creation of a truly "civil" society. Others in his party, such as those who rallied around the legislative initiatives of Congressman Ernest Istook, missed the ways in which citizen action restrains the power of money to subvert the democratic preferences of ordinary citizens.

Clinton, on the other hand, appeared to perceive the need for all four sectors to work, but typically failed to connect each of his piece-meal observations into a whole vision of needed social change. While his wife, Hillary Rodham Clinton, understood by her book title that *It Takes a Village to Raise a Child*, President Clinton continued to address the concerns of an enormous number of organized interests, trying to please them one by one.

Speaking with the columnist's voice, the present author has fre-quently hectored his readers with the view that all four sectors need care and attention if society is to function smoothly and fairly:

> Solutions will come when it becomes widely recognized that both tra-dition and change are important, that both freedom and order must be secured. This will only happen when the contributions of each major sector of society are recognized: when cultural values sustain family, religious, and community life; when third sector organiza-tions organize both collective action and service freely and effec-tively; when business organizations discover and serve the humanity of their employees as well as their consumers; and when government assures a level field of opportunity and a fairness of result in policy, economic reward, and individual expression. (Van Til, 1996)

# Part Three

---

*On the Boundary between
Business and the Third Sector*

# 6

# Making Money, Wielding Power, and Other Temptations of Nonprofit Life

Third-sector organizations are often instructed to become more business-like. Grants are provided to them to improve their business practices; trade newspapers and magazines offer them advice on fund-raising and computer use; universities develop degree programs to certify their skills in management; and giving is often conditioned on their demonstration of business-like practices.

The boundary between business and the third sector is a complex one: it not only is marked by efforts to emulate business practice, but it also involves the transfer of funds and power from corporate profit and control to nonprofit organization and action. Corporate employees directly provide voluntary service and individual contributions to third-sector organizations; corporations themselves assign workers to third-sector activity and provide funding to the sector; and corporate profits are sometimes committed to the formation of foundations, which then distribute the fruits of such donations to appropriately certified charitable and educational organizations.

While these boundary issues have been sorted through in recent years, a number of prominent nonprofit organization leaders have found themselves enmeshed in a set of remarkable scandals. The ranks of the nonprofit sector's "hall of shame" have grown to include a prominent set of child-molesters, womanizers, embezzlers, charlatans, and other self-seekers. The use of nonprofit organizations for "fun and profit," the motives Edward Banfield once attributed to urban rioters, may of course be duplicated in the plunder of the first sector by robber barons and the deflection to private advantage of the second sector by corrupt politicians. But these experiences do lead to the conclusion that there is often nothing particularly special about a nonprofit organization or leader.

The next three chapters explore the largely uncharted boundary between business and the third sector. This chapter presents an introduction to boundary issues viewed as unfair competition with for-profit concerns, and the general temptation faced by many nonprofit leaders to emulate an often inappropriate set of business ideals and practices.

## The Persisting Problem of Nonprofit Competition with Small Business

On July 31, 1998, readers of *The Philadelphia Inquirer* learned, in a front-page story, that one David J. Cohan has owned and operated a fitness center in suburban Philadelphia since 1986. The "Sports Club," as Cohan's establishment is known, makes state-of-the-art machines and weight equipment available for the use of its 3,000 client-members.

In 1998, the *Inquirer* story continued, the neighboring Ridley Area YMCA began to expand its five-year-old nonprofit facility, adding a fitness center and day-care rooms. Businessman Cohan, in response to this competitive challenge, filed a complaint with the Pennsylvania Department of State, charging that, under the state's newly adopted "Purely Public Charity Act," a nonprofit organization may not use its tax-exempt status to compete unfairly with small businesses. An arbitrator, readers were informed, will soon hear Cohan's complaint.

Five years previously, readers of the same newspaper were overwhelmed by the presentation of a week-long investigatory report on the nonprofit sector titled "Warehouses of Wealth: The Tax-Free Economy." The seven-part series was authored by Gilbert M. Gaul and Neill M. Borowski, and included an exhaustive 18-month study of 6,000 tax returns of nonprofit organizations. The series was later published in book form under the title *Free Ride* (1993).

The *Inquirer,* a distinguished newspaper long in Pulitzer Prizes for similar series, provided its readers with the revelation that the National Football League, whose president receives an annual salary of over $1.5 million, is a nonprofit organization. So is the Motion Picture Academy of Arts and Sciences, which annually spends many millions of dollars to bring the world the thrill of the Oscars presentations.

The series' lead announced: "They're called nonprofit businesses, but that doesn't mean they can't make money. They do—billions of dollars. At the same time, their tax exemptions cost government more than $36 billion a year." A table details these costs: $18 billion for chari-table deductions from individual income tax returns; $16 billion for tax obligations that would have been collected from hospitals, univer-sities, foundations had they not been nonprofit; and $2.5 billion in tax-exempt bonds and postage discounts.

The series proceeded with daily chapters that focused on the fol-lowing:

- Hospitals: "In return for free care for the poor, hospitals didn't have to pay taxes. Now there's less charity care. But hospitals are still ex-empt."

- Colleges and universities: "While colleges stockpile millions every year from investments and research, tuition climbs out of the reach of more and more Americans."

- The IRS: "The IRS doesn't have the staff or money to adequately police nonprofit businesses. An audit of them all would take years. So they operate unfettered."

- Executive salaries: "Wanted: Top Executive to run a nonprofit or-ganization. Salary: $350,000 to $400,000 a year, plus bonus. Perks: Luxury car, country-club membership, interest-free house loan. Do-mestic help provided."

- Cheap money: "Tax-exempt bonds have fueled a construction boom. Taxpayers underwrite the loans. The purpose was to meet society's needs. Some are stretching the definition of those needs."

- Foundations: "Foundations became tax-exempt because of the grants they give. Now they earn far more than they give away."

Each article was chock-full of facts. For example, the chapter on executive compensation was replete with tables detailing the salaries of hundreds of foundation heads, trade association leaders, college and university presidents, hospital executives, and heads of charitable and cultural organizations. Gaul and Borowski noted: "Americans were shocked by the $463,000 salary of the former United Way presi-dent [William Aramony]. His pay was not unusual." University presi-dents like Temple's Peter Liacouris and Columbia's Michael Sovern, it was noted, bring in annual salaries in excess of $400,000 annually.

Gaul and Borowski set the context for a growing suspicion of non-profit organizations in American society, a suspicion that many of them simply serve as tax-exempt businesses. Faced with such chal-lenges as that of Sports Club owner Cohan, nonprofit leaders face four possible responses: denial, defense, offense, and concern.

1. DENIAL: Let it all blow over. Even if all tax exemption was re-moved, tax collections would only increase by 3 percent. Govern-ment has better things to do than worry about our salaries and how we spend our money.

2. DEFENSE: Why shouldn't there be equity between the salaries of nonprofit and for-profit executives? Among health care executives, the *Inquirer* couldn't find a hospital administrator making more than a million, while Thomas F. Frist of the for-profit Hospital Cor-poration of America did himself proud with a 1992 compensation package of $127 million. We've got a long way to go, baby!

3. OFFENSE: All for one and one for all. What's important is that we use the muscle of our 1.5 million organizations to articulate the val-ues that remain the core of our sector: caring for others; building community; enhancing the quality of life. So the NFL is a non-profit. Let's use that opportunity to make sure that it and its for-profit members (the football teams themselves) contribute their share of public service TV spots linked to the United Way, and con-tinue to make those visits to local hospitals. As for the Sports Club, what's this "club" word doing in its name anyway? Maybe it's the business that's unfairly competing with the nonprofit organization in this case: we're the realm of clubs, associations, and other mem-bership-type organizations.

4. CONCERN: Following Groucho Marx, do all nonprofit organiza-tions really want to be a member of a club that almost anyone, in-cluding themselves, are allowed to join? Do they really want to be in bed, albeit legally, with the National Hockey League, the MITRE corporation, and a wide range of wealthy health care providers? Or is it time to rethink the concept of the nonprofit sector, dividing it particularly into those which are self-serving and those which serve a broader public interest?

The issue here is one of determining how to set the boundary be-tween nonprofit and for-profit organizations. Nonprofits enjoy several advantages over businesses: 1) they hold a presumption of serving a valued societal purpose; 2) they are generally tax-exempt; and 3) they sometimes provide their supporters with the chance to deduct a por-tion of the contributions made to them from the giver's taxable income.

It is a small wonder that persons seeking to advance their own eco-nomic advantage would search out the possibilities involved in the nonprofit form. If they succeed, of course, they will be able to engage in fund-raising as a tax-exempt entity—thereby committing some of the most infuriating behaviors wrought by third-sector organizations.

# Would You Get That Phone!
## The Problem of Nonprofit Organization Fund-Raising

According to the 1993 annual report of the Attorney General of Massachusetts on Charitable Fundraising, The Association for Retarded Citizens of the U.S., a nonprofit organization, retained Heritage Publishing, a for-profit firm, to assist them in a fund-raising campaign. Over $382,000 was raised in the name of the association, which eventually received 29 percent of the collected donations ($110,000). In the same year (1992) and the same state (Massachusetts), the New Bedford Police Association retained the fund-raising firm Eastern Advertising for campaign assistance. It raised $62,255, of which 29 percent ($18,180) made its way to the association.

These two campaigns are notable for only one fact: each provided a rate of return to its sponsoring organization at the average level received from a fund-raising campaign conducted by external consultants in Massachusetts. That average return, from the 158 identified in the report, saw 29 percent of the moneys raised by fund-raising firms actually delivered to the association in whose name the funds were solicited. Moreover, in nearly one-third of the campaigns (49), the average return of the campaign was 15 percent or less of the collected funds to the sponsoring organization.

The problem of fund-raising costs of this sort twists observers of the nonprofit sector into a variety of intellectual contortions. Where should the line be drawn regarding excessive fund-raising costs? How seriously do donors take questions of fund-raising costs? Should fund-raising abuses by nonprofits be regulated? If so, by whom? And where do we draw the line between what is business and what is not-for-profit in these cases?

At about the same time the Massachusetts findings came to light, the major trade newspaper in the nonprofit sector reported the following (*NonProfit Times*, November 1993):

- A front-page graphic indicating that 70 percent of the public in the prime giving ages over 47 report that information about fund-raising and overhead costs is "very important" in their decision to donate.

- An article reporting a "general sentiment" of focus group respondents interviewed by Independent Sector, who agree that "if 75 percent of their money wasn't going to services, then something was wrong."

- A listing of fund-raising and administrative costs of the largest 100 nonprofit organizations, which indicated that two-thirds of them met the above-mentioned "75% for program" test.

- A lead story that reports that AIDS organizations typically raise half their income from special events, each of which may return as little as half their cost to the organization.

- Another front-page story that reports the widening use of fraud and deception statutes by state attorneys general in regulating charities that refuse to inform donors of their fund-raising costs.

- An editorial that warns of the futility of relying on government "bureaucrats" to regulate excessive fund-raising costs: "Those who work below the level of honesty and disclosure in the name of charity will find ways around bureaucratic ineptitude."

One set of bureaucrats, those who issued the attorney general's report in Massachusetts, did not seem insensitive to the role of the nonprofit sector. Among their observations are the following:

- "We all have a stake in ensuring the successful future of charitable organizations."

- "Charitable giving, especially by individuals, is often the only support charitable organizations receive."

- "In tough economic times, when government cannot meet the needs of all who require its assistance, charitable organizations depend heavily on individual donors."

The Massachusetts report did not seek to set a line of "earnings share" beyond which a nonprofit can be deemed guilty of inadequate attention to program responsibility. Their report does note, however, as do leading scholars of fund-raising like Indiana University's Richard Steinberg and Northwestern's Wesley Lindahl, that nonprofits use fund-raising campaigns for many legitimate purposes beyond the simple raising of funds. Among these associated purposes that may be involved in a campaign are the gaining of name recognition, educating the public about causes and services, and increasing bases of members and volunteers. As nonprofit management specialist David Mason has observed, separating out these costs for accounting purposes is as difficult as dividing the benefits in fire fighting between the water used to douse the flames and the gasoline that propels the truck to the scene of the fire. Clearly we need to do better in estimating these costs in our research and accounting, difficult as that task may be.

The Massachusetts report also observed, clearly and correctly, that professional fund-raising firms are employed by only a handful of nonprofit organizations. Massachusetts has over 28,000 registered public charities; only 158 fund-raising campaigns were conducted by professional solicitors in 1992. Nevertheless, the Massachusetts report found that the hiring of a professional fund-raising firm yielded only 29 percent of the take for the nonprofit. Two bucks and change for the for-profit fund-raiser; one for the nonprofit—quite a difference from the "75% for program" rule desired by the Independent Sector's focus groups.

As before, the usual four choices are presented to nonprofit leaders in evaluating this situation: Denial, Defense, Offense, and Concern.

1. Denial says: What's the big problem? A few fund-raising firms find that it's a hard go to get people to give. And so it is for many nonprofit causes, especially when they are new and little understood.

2. Defense says: Who says? A bunch of government bureaucrats trying to make a name for themselves. When did they do an honest day's work for their pay?

3. Offense counsels: The only way nonprofits are going to take their rightful place is by limiting the reach of government. Courts have ruled that fund-raising costs aren't a valid indicator of fraud. Let's recognize that fund-raising costs will vary, and not adopt solutions that are worse than the problem.

4. Meanwhile, Concern cautions: Look, folks, there is some bad action out there, and it doesn't take a lot of rotten apples to sour the cider. But it is also important to communicate the fact that a good campaign can provide a nonprofit with much more than funds—especially if we clearly present the program goals we aim to advance in such a campaign.

Once again, I think Concern is warranted here. Concern counsels that it is important to confront instances like the following culled from the Massachusetts reports:

- the firm whose cost overruns led them to bill the World Wildlife Fund for over $6,000 after keeping all of the $59,000 raised in their name in a fund-raising campaign;

- another fund-raising firm which conducted nine campaigns for such nonprofits as the American Association of the Deaf-Blind and the Multiple Sclerosis Association of America, raised over $6 million for these causes, and kept over $4.7 million of those funds for their own expenses;

- a third firm which was retained by 13 different youth-serving organizations and consistently returned 13 percent of the funds collected by their efforts, including $1,079 of the $8,632 collected for the Braintree Babe Ruth League and $431,637 of the $3,453,096 received for the Massachusetts Special Olympics.

The costs involved in nonprofit organization fund-raising are not confined to the retainer fees of for-profit consultants. There's also the problem of how much blood a particular turnip can produce. For the nonprofit whose cause is obscure, whose name is little known, or whose case is particularly difficult to sell, it simply may not be possible to raise the money required to support its service. Surely there comes a point when we have to ask if a cause is worth pursuing by conventions of funded nonprofit action. Once fund-raising and administrative costs, accurately assessed, move significantly beyond the 25 percent standard, the question may need to be faced directly: Can this need be better met by government (whose fund-raising costs, by means of taxation, are low and under long control), by business (whose record, granted, in throwing bad money after good in the creation of advertised wants is often more atrocious than that of even the most disreputable of nonprofits), by a wholly volunteered response, or even by a system of tax-based nonprofit sector revenue sharing?

Each case will need to be judged on its own merits, to be sure. But it may well be that the relief of AIDS sufferers should be assumed as a public responsibility, in light of the obvious difficulty this cause has in attracting voluntary support. A similar argument can be made for the care of the homeless, whose cause has also been subject to considerable philanthropic fatigue in recent years. And throw in the various police and fire retirement associations, which regularly allow the fund-raisers to keep seven of every ten dollars raised by their campaigns. In each of these cases, a well-conceived public program might well yield a more effective and equally satisfactory program to those provided by most nonprofits. At some point, it simply becomes indefensible to maintain an organization whose fund-raising costs approach the costs of its programs.

Nonprofits cannot do everything, and part of the art of managing nonprofits is to know when it is time to move back to advocacy and give up trying to provide services that simply cannot be supported by individual giving. An even bigger part is to reject the lures offered by dubious fund-raising firms. Any nonprofit organization that uses such a firm deserves to lose more than the revenues it will never see.

Leaders of nonprofit organizations need to remember that it is in their direct interest to drive ineffective and unethical fund-raisers out of the nonprofit sector. Ill-considered campaigns divert moneys donors might otherwise have given to reputable nonprofits using effective means of raising funds. This "crowding out" of good money by bad fund-raising not only tarnishes the image of the third sector, but it directly reduces its resource base.

## How to Succeed at Nonprofit Mismanagement without Even Trying

If it isn't bad enough to be called by for-profit fund-raisers just when dinner is being served, have you heard the one about the nonprofit organization director who started treating his organization like a personal oil well? Power corrupts, we have been told, and the power of a nonprofit manager who combines his own force into an iron triangle with that of a complaisant board and a fearful staff has few limits. A remarkable book by John Glaser, formerly a key associate of United Way of America's shamed executive, William Aramony, shows how easy it was for a nonprofit manager to forge that iron triangle into a force that provides one with all the wealth, sex, and power that anyone could wish for. (Of course, the down side is that you might get caught, as did Aramony, be tried and convicted, and spend most of the rest of your life in prison.)

Glaser's book is about United Way's head, heart, soul, and various other bodily parts at United Way of America in the Aramony years. Glaser gives us a peek behind the veil of nonprofit piety, beginning with his own initial employment interview with Aramony. Glaser was a community organizer and activist, and Aramony is quoted as saying to him: "Your resume is full of shit, Glaser, but I like your eyeballs" (Glaser, 1994: p. xxiii). Later on, Glaser recounts, a similar test was applied to the women who worked for Aramony: "[I]t often appeared that raises and perquisites were increased in direct proportion to their attractiveness."

With their pleasing eyeballs and feminine charms, his staff accepted their rewards in higher-than-competitive salary, and swallowed the abuse that Aramony dished up on the slightest pretense. The madhouse that was the elegant United Way headquarters in Alexandria is described in a vivid dissection of Aramony's leadership style. The workplace was a roller coaster that shifted rapidly through the ranges of manic and depressive moods of the leader. Aramony would scream, "Fire his ass" about an employee, and then agonize when he learned that his order had actually been implemented. "Only when Aramony was out of town could the staff begin to do productive work" (Glaser, 1994: 74–75).

"Aramony required planning for everyone but himself." "[H]e felt he 'owned' people because of the high salaries he paid them" (Glaser,

1994: 81, 91). Glaser (1994: 104–106) presents a powerful recounting of the staff roles made available in Aramony's fiefdom:

- the Chief Financial Officer, a friend or long-term associate who "rarely, if ever" questioned Aramony's expenditures;

- the Office Wife, the administrative assistant who traveled with the boss, occupied a room connecting to his, and was available for personal service 24 hours per day;

- the Bagman, who handled Aramony's private financial affairs and discharged unwanted employees (a role Glaser apparently played for several years);

- the Court Jester, a male who bonded with the chief and joined him in his favorite pastimes of dining, gambling, and playing the horses; and

- the Golden Boy/Girl, the new member of the team who was counted on to resolve any organizational problem, but then quickly fell from favor.

Board roles played during this organizational interlude were no more flattering. While in daily life playing the game of corporate or nonprofit management with apparent success, board members clearly were invited to check their good judgment at the door when entering United Way meetings. Aramony staged his board meetings with meticulous care, making members as comfortable as he could, and accepting in return their consideration of him as not only "the expert," but also one who embodied "all of the noble virtues of those who spend their lives serving others." Among the board members of United Way of America and its infamous spinoffs were such notables as then Girl Scouts of the U.S.A. executive Frances Hesselbein, identified by Glaser as a "close Aramony colleague" (Glaser, 1994: 167).

Readers of Glaser's volume will wonder why he allowed prominent nonprofit attorney Bruce Hopkins to write both an Introduction and an Afterword to his volume. These chapters do offer some comic relief on the matter, especially when Hopkins (p. xix) observes: "Readers will find this statement hard to believe, but I will repeat it: Bill Aramony did not break a single federal law."

In a splendid concluding chapter on "lessons learned," however, Glaser (1994: 235–48) redeems himself by offering the following 13 pieces of advice, presented verbatim below:

1. A charity is a charity. It is part of the voluntary sector, not the business sector, and must abide by the constraints imposed by the history, ethics, and public perceptions of the sector.

2. Charitable activities must be defensible in the court of public opinion.

3. Charities must represent constituents.

4. Character is more important than administrative ability.

5. Boards must really evaluate staff.

6. Boards must know their legal responsibilities.

7. Boards should have conflict of interest statements.

8. Boards should have viable internal standing committees.

9. Boards should have a risk management plan.

10. Boards should set acceptable salaries and ranges.

11. Boards should enforce equal application of policy.

12. Boards should set terms of office.

13. Boards should bring in outside evaluators.

Glaser suggests that the basic lesson in the United Way fiasco involves the development and sustenance of countervailing points of power and influence within the nonprofit organization. The painful case that he recounts reminds us that there is no special virtue that inheres in Section 501(c). As the distinguished scholar of nonprofit action, Ralph Kramer (1998), has demonstrated in summarizing a quarter-century of comparative research on nonprofit organizations: the legal "ownership" of an organization—whether it is governmental, nonprofit, or for-profit—may be far less important than the quality of services provided by the organization. Form may mean much less than function in assessing the nonprofit world.

The price of effective organization is continuing vigilance, for nonprofit organizations can be useful vehicles in society. When led by someone of dubious will and character, however, they are among the easiest of organizations to corrupt, as John Bennett showed when he brought his seemingly good intentions to the fore with his "Foundation for New Era Philanthropy."

## How to Succeed in Nonprofit Entrepreneurship without Even Trying

Become more entrepreneurial, nonprofit execs are often urged by trainers, authors, and other pundits in the field. Find a service niche, your own place in the nonprofit market, and make it pay for your organization! Don't be so nice about it. Learn to be more aggressive!

When the scandal at the Foundation for New Era Philanthropy hit the press in 1995, it was clear that Jack Bennett, New Era's founder, was as consummate a nonprofit entrepreneur as the field has ever known. He played every emotional chord perfectly to convince his donors of his personal commitment to the variety of causes, largely religious, to which his foundation was apparently dedicated.

Donors and donees alike were shocked by the revelations, as well they might be, having handed over sums up to the $11 million given by one hapless Rockefeller, and down to the $300 provided by a group of school kids in West Philadelphia, purportedly for the purpose of learning about philanthropy. (What a foundation!: everyone a donor, no one a beneficiary—save for the nonprofit exec himself, of course, and a few family and friends.)

One disillusioned New Era–ite confessed to his own dismay at judging character when he reflected on Bennett's frequent participation in Philadelphia-area prayer breakfasts. Bennett, this acquaintance noted, "prayed so well." Another New Era broker, a minister, solicited donations from putative "donees" and then had the audacity to invite a further donation in the form of a "thank offering" to his own nonprofit front organization.

How were Bennett and his New Era partners consummate nonprofit entrepreneurs? Let us count the ways. First, they knew how to talk the talk: their work at the foundation was "pro bono"; they acted as true volunteers; their work aimed only at the purposes of doing God's will on earth. And, second, they could walk the walk: they knew how to set up for-profits to self-deal with; they fabulously enriched themselves by contracting with their own firms for services; they knew how to take their pieces of the action.

The word "entrepreneur" is best translated from the French as "the middle-man who takes"—"entre" meaning "between"; "preneur" meaning "taker." Bennett put himself between the donor and the donee, and how he did take!

The concept of entrepreneurship was introduced into the social sciences by the Austrian political economist Joseph Schumpeter, and has been lionized since in business schools as the answer to a variety of ills: first the rigidity and bureaucratization of traditional corporate structures, and more recently the failure of the economy to provide jobs for business school graduates. The rise of nonprofit management as an arena for education and training has moved the concept into our field, for similar reasons.

But entrepreneurship without ethics can be a dangerous force. Without a grounding in the traditions, values, and ethics of voluntary action, without a rooting in organizations accustomed to abiding by both the letter and the spirit of the law, the entrepreneur is nothing but another middle person out to grab and take, a broker in it for self-interest, a corrupter of the nonprofit dream.[1]

## And Now, Social Entrepreneurship!

The latest concept to appear on the boundary between business and the third sector is that of "social entrepreneurship." For a considerable tuition, it is possible to become trained in its arts at Britain's School for Social Entrepreneurs, a brainchild of sociologist Michael Young (now Lord Young of Dartington). The octogenarian Young, who placed the concept of "meritocracy" into good currency some years back, has developed a curriculum built around the Open University's course Managing Voluntary and Nonprofit Enterprises. Students enrolled in the program are required to work on an ongoing project for a range of voluntary organizations.

On this side of the Atlantic, a Center for Social Entrepreneurs has been developed. The center's director, Jerr Boschee, defines social entrepreneurs as "nonprofit executives who pay increasing attention to market forces without losing sight of their underlying missions." Balancing these forces, Boschee observes, is at the "heart and soul of a movement that is rapidly accelerating throughout the sector" (Boschee, n.d.).

Boschee observes that many people approach the concept of "social entrepreneurship" warily, articulating such concerns as:

- "This smells like making money off the backs of the poor!"

- "What happens to quality when we start emphasizing the bottom line?"

- "This sounds as if we're setting up a two-tiered system—are we going to ignore the people who can't afford to pay?"

- "Will we lose our hearts when we find our wallets?"

- "How can we protect our nonprofit status?"

- "How can we manage such rapid growth?"

Despite the odds, however, Boschee continues, "more and more nonprofits are becoming social entrepreneurs, either by adopting earned income strategies (designed primarily to cover more of an organization's costs, not necessarily to turn a profit) or by creating social purpose business ventures (whose primary purpose is to make a profit)."

## The Increasingly Blurred Boundary
## between Business and Nonprofit

When the distinction between what is business and what is nonprofit becomes blurred, the distinction between the businessperson and the nonprofit worker also begins to disappear. Rudolph Bauer (1998: 4), in his seminal work, notes that this blurring occurs particularly among third-sector organizations when they directly confront the market forces involved in fund-raising, relating to individual donors, seeking commercial sponsorship, and competing for foundation grants.

The blurring of the business-nonprofit boundary has profound implications for the advocacy-service dimension, implications for financial support, and partnership complexifications. *Advocacy* becomes particularly problematic in this condition, because the financial resources standing behind many social change interests pale in comparison to the *resources* that are daily mobilized in support of the status quo. As the third sector becomes increasingly populated by nonprofit-making *firms*, the focus of their efforts increasingly becomes services that can be supported by fees and donations. And as tax-generated revenues are increasingly displaced by self-generated resources, the tilt of beneficiaries of nonprofit service inclines ever more strongly in the direction of those capable of paying for the service provided to them. In such a scenario, the third sector increasingly comes to resemble the world of business: them that has gets; the rich get richer and the poor poorer; and needs that can only be met by *partnerships* between public and private support and public-serving organizational capacities become displaced by the simple ability to pay.

Lester Salamon (1997: 47) describes this situation as a four-part crisis: "This challenge is part fiscal, part economic, part political, and part philosophical and moral. Nonprofit organizations are being forced or enticed into modes of behavior that diverge increasingly sharply from public expectations and norms, and too little is being done to bring either the reality back into alignment with expectations, or expectations into better alignment with reality. The upshot is a dangerous crisis of confidence and legitimacy for one of the oldest, most venerated, and most critical components of our national heritage."

The crisis Salamon describes will either be met directly, with a rediscovery of the necessity to address the needs of what one advocacy organization calls "the disenfranchised" in American life, or it will be met by the commodification of the nonprofit sector and the rise of a "business and charity" approach. If the third sector is to reinvent itself in this time of crisis, it presents a potential payoff of substantial dimensions: we might discover through such a process of reinvention that the reason the third sector exists is not to be "nonprofit," but rather to profit our communities and society in ways that families, governments, and corporations—each acting alone—cannot. The third sector might, in other words, discover a soul that has been lost by many contemporary nonprofits, blinded as they are by their quest to be both "business-like" and "tax-free."

# 7

# The Art and Business of Nonprofit Organization Management

As the number of tax-exempt nonprofit organizations continues to expand meteorically (100-fold over the past 50 years), the task of making them achieve the ends they have set for themselves has emerged as an important administrative profession. This chapter reviews a number of challenges faced by today's nonprofit manager, and offers advice in ways of dealing with these perplexing issues. We begin by looking at several important nonprofit organizations, and try to figure out why some are administered better than others.

## Making a Nonprofit Organization Work Well

Deborah Gardner, in an important case study, illuminates the processes of nonprofit governance, leadership, and management. It is a study of the founding process of the Nathan Cummings Foundation, and is titled *A Family Foundation: Looking to the Future, Honoring the Past.*

In this monograph, Gardner describes, step by step, the transformation of one man's vision into an effective and humanely administered nonprofit organization. The visionary, a grocer named Nathan Cummings who came eventually to direct the Sara Lee Corporation, established the foundation in 1949. The enterprise moved into high gear when Cummings died in 1985, leaving it assets worth $200 million.

Nathan Cummings hoped his foundation would allow his grandchildren to join in common cause, and "accustom them to the understanding that we must contribute to worthy causes, thus sharing our good fortune with those less fortunate than we are" (p. 10). His children and grandchildren pitched in enthusiastically to this task, and participated actively as volunteers in building what has become one of our country's most active and enlightened philanthropies.

Gardner's study of the foundation rehearses familiar lessons of organizational development, lessons not always learned or followed by leaders of many nonprofit organizations. She shows how the Nathan Cummings foundation struggled in its process of growth, and ultimately built into its very structure five enduring truths of successful nonprofit management:

1. The organization embodies, and does not outgrow, its founding spirit of voluntary concern. In the Nathan Cummings case, family members committed to serve the board without compensation, and that tradition continues to this day as non-family members play increasingly central board roles.

2. Board members are selected with an eye toward the future as well as a respect for the past. Gardner shows how non-family members were carefully selected, with the assistance of a search firm. At the same time, younger family members were groomed for eventual board service by being selected as "board associates."

3. The Board enables itself to struggle with the definition of its role, its workload, and its relationship to the executive director. In the Cummings case, the board worked hard to shape its own agenda, eventually adopting the practice of a regular retreat session to work through tension and workload issues.

4. The inevitability of board-staff tensions is recognized, confronted, and resolved—at least for the time being. The relationship between an active and vital CEO, like Cummings's Charlie Halpern, and a powerful and committed board, like the one built at Cummings, was never all sweetness and light. Gardner quotes Halpern, a prominent public service lawyer: "The proper line between management and board had to emerge from a process, not start as a given. I started with it as a given" (p. 40). As the organization matured, direct lines of communications were developed and encouraged between board members and mid-level staff, and considerable progress was achieved in developing a sense of "harmonious partnership" among all members of the organization.

5. While the internal organization of a nonprofit is a crucial requisite for its success, its ultimate test lies in the generation of an effective external program to advance its mission and goals. At the Nathan Cummings Foundation, evaluation became a central activity of the

foundation's annual retreat, or "decision-making forum." Gardner writes that "The end result was an entirely new way of evaluating grant programs, proposals and projects, dubbed 'Objectives, Strategies, Outcomes,' or OSOs for short."

These five simple, but also powerful, tests—voluntary concern, quality of board, executive leadership, partnership with staff, and external productivity—can be applied to any nonprofit organization. Consider, for further examples, three major Washington-based groups: CIVICUS (the world alliance for citizen participation); America's Promise (the follow-up vehicle to the Presidents' Summit on America's Future); and NCRP, the National Committee for Responsive Philanthropy, a leading advocacy organization in the field.

CIVICUS, founded in 1994, was governed in 1998 by a board of directors chaired by the distinguished Indian community developer Rajesh Tandon. The board was composed of citizens of nineteen different nations, working in tandem with Executive Director Miklos Marschall, the former deputy mayor of Budapest. Its founding board process was a lively one, as members assembled twice yearly from various corners of the earth. In 1997 a board retreat was held, facilitated by an outside expert.

A recurring concern at these meetings has been a choice between organizational models: on the one hand the traditional North American nonprofit model of a strong director as primary among board equals, on the other the traditional European model of a strong board chair guiding the efforts of a staff cum secretariat. Marschall, who himself came to see the values of the strong executive model, reports that dialogue on this issue remains lively, and that a "hybrid" model has emerged, in which conflicts are frequent, but typically resolved by "tolerance and patience" (interview with the author).

CIVICUS quite clearly passes the five tests derived from the Cummings experience: its board members volunteer to gather from the corners of the globe; they have been carefully selected to balance a wide range of diversity concerns; they struggle actively with their role and their relation to the director; they directly face, and seek to resolve, the inevitable board-staff tensions that characterize the modern nonprofit; and, together, board and staff have succeeded in creating an organization that has been extraordinarily productive.

Few organizations so young can point to the range of achievements CIVICUS has amassed in four short years: two highly successful world assemblies, a small bookshelf of useful publications, policy positions hammered out by widely varying, and influential, constituent participants. Its current agenda involves a major role in the United Nations' emerging "Millennial Forum," and the creation of a process to strengthen ties between corporations and civil society organizations throughout the world. As board chair Tandon puts it, these efforts are being designed to create a future in which nonprofit organizations will fill "front-row seats" in all aspects of the global development process.

America's Promise, the second nonprofit I hold to the Cummings tests, has chosen a very different organizational approach than CIVICUS. As was noted in Chapter 5, an important part of the difference reflects AP's founding conception as being a temporary organization, intended to complete its work by the year 2000.

Organized during and immediately after the Presidents' Summit on America's Future of April 1997 as its follow-up vehicle, AP's first year has been organizationally turbulent. Within its first year of existence, AP was already under its third executive director; the organization has also experienced a fair amount of turnover among its board of directors, as well.

Applying the Cummings tests, one sees that AP is taking a few tentative steps (Test One) toward incorporating the voluntary spirit it so vigorously advocates into its own organizational life, particularly if the provision of roles for interns and board spouses are counted as volunteering. Its board, however (Test Two), appears to have been selected on the most traditional of grounds from the ranks of corporate and political America. That AP has not chosen to include young persons on its board, including reclaimed youths at risk, seems to counter its elevated rhetoric regarding youth service and empowerment.

As this organization ages, it has yet to demonstrate a maturation of its board (Test Three). America's Promise has yet to harness a board fully committed to providing the accustomed work, wealth, and wisdom. Three figures continue to dominate its process: Board Chairman Colin Powell, philanthropist Ray Chambers, and Senior Vice-President Gregg Petersmeyer. The result?: an organization that strongly favors the traditional European model (and probably, a wag might observe, its Prussian variation).

Compare (Test Four) the CIVICUS board and staff resolving their conflicts through tolerance and patience with the observation of a Presidents' Summit volunteer, there at the founding. She recalls seeing AP's first director completely distraught, having received the order from General Powell to completely reassemble several hundred copies of a press packet because one telephone number listed therein was off by a single digit.

Operating in a mode of continuous short-term, or even crisis, planning, America's Promise is certainly beginning to make its mark within circles of corporate and community life in many American cities (Test Five). Its real impact, however, remains to be assessed—the direct impact it will ultimately be found to have had on the quality and quantity of attentive response to the needs of millions of American youth at risk in hundreds of cities and towns.

The third organization to be held to the Gardner test, the National Committee for Responsive Philanthropy (NCRP), was founded in 1976 out of the Donee Group of the Filer Commission, a major review of philanthropy's structure and process. As the Donee Group, an informal component of the Commission's process, those who would come to call themselves the NCRP represented a set of organizations whose interests, they feared, would continue to be ignored by major philanthropic institutions. These interests and organizations represented an array of individuals and groups disadvantaged by structures of privilege and power in American society, a coalition NCRP would come to identify as "disenfranchised" from participation in the recognition and rewards of philanthropic giving.

By 1978 NCRP the group had taken its organizational form, and filed an amicus brief in a lawsuit challenging the fairness of the Combined Federal Campaign (the CFC), a struggle it would persist in for two decades. In the following year, the NCRP held its first national conference, on the topic of alternatives to the United Way, another interest it continues to hold until the present day.

As the NCRP developed in its work, a range of issues was addressed, foremost among which were the accountability of philanthropy, the accessibility and monopoly of United Way, the openness of the Combined Federal Campaign, the impact of community foundations, corporate giving to racial/ethnic populations, and the emerging role of conservative philanthropy and public policy. By 1998, NCRP, led throughout its entire organizational life by Robert Bothwell, had become widely recognized throughout the philanthropic world as an important advocate for social justice and fairness in philanthropic practice.

Applying Gardner's tests to NCRP, we see that NCRP has sought to build a strong board into its structure (Test One), and to develop a lean staff of persons well acquainted with philanthropic practice into its structure.

Its board (Test Two) has been carefully selected to represent the diversity of its principal constituencies: activist organizations and particularly those representing groups disenfranchised from conventional philanthropic process—women, people of color, poor persons, and the like.

As this organization aged, it gradually came to the recognition that its leadership was beginning to "age in place" (Test Three). After 22 years of executive service, Robert Bothwell, long perceived as the very spirit and voice of the organization, announced his resignation to assume a three-year research position with the group. The replacement process promised to present severe challenges to the organization, accustomed as it had become to Bothwell's steady and devoted leadership.

The NCRP board committed itself to a determined process of governance, decision making, and conflict resolution (Test Four). Board meetings were regularly held, and occasionally took the form of retreat-type reflection.

As a national advocacy organization, whose recommendations are based on solid research, NCRP clearly made its mark in circles of third-sector policy and practice. Like the Nathan Cummings Foundation and CIVICUS, it found that a partnership between an able and determined executive and a willing and independent board provided the best path to achieving its organizational goals.

## Leadership Style and Its Meaning for Financial Development

Nonprofit organizations are like businesses, and like governmental agencies, and like families on one critical resource issue: it is difficult for them to survive if they don't bring in as much income as they spend. Those who lead nonprofit organizations must be every bit as cognizant of this bottom line factor as a businessperson, a bureau director, or a parent. As this awareness has grown among nonprofit organization leaders, new ways of approaching the generation of resources have been developed. In this regard, Colin Powell's entry to the third sector has proven both illuminating and perhaps prophetic.

A common factor between the three organizations just considered involves their leadership by men of considerable intelligence, determination, and interpersonal skills. The leadership style of General Powell, more characteristic of the military than the philanthropic world, contrasts importantly with those of Marschall, Bothwell, and Halpern with their backgrounds in public life, both governmental and voluntary.

As former Senator Harris Wofford (CEO of the Corporation for National Service) tells it, Powell takes relish in applying his "sweat test" to those he believes have the resources to increase their philanthropic giving. Wofford recounts the tale of a panel presentation shared by Powell and the CEO of a major corporation. The CEO, turning expansive during the discussion, offered a contribution to Powell's America's Promise organization that was quite substantial. Powell, not missing a beat, asked if he could find it possible to increase that commitment ten-fold. Noting the sweat appearing on the brow of the CEO, as he reflected upon the possibility and then concurred with it, gave Powell the sense that he had set his "ask" at the proper level.

Twentieth-century Americans have become accustomed to two kinds of giving: mandatory and voluntary. The quintessential mandatory gift is the one we provide the IRS at tax time. This contribution supports many valuable, and some dubious, services. It has become fashionable in many circles to view the payment of taxes not as a public responsibility, but rather as succumbing to a kind of unwarranted theft of what is rightly ours. Nonetheless, we pay our taxes because that is the law, and the law's command is evaded only with considerable risk to our resources and our personal freedom.

Voluntary giving is what we have learned to provide when we believe we are behaving as benefactors. We expect the solicitor of our gift to be deferential and polite. After all, it is our resources which are being requested, and we are in full control of their disposition. Philanthropy involves tender-minded benefaction: give, but only if you choose.

The coming of the "farewell state" (see Chapter 1, above) dramatically changes these cultural forms of giving. The farewell state shows us the backside of the disappearing "welfare state"—it wishes those in need well as it waves its ungiving hand: Farewell! In the farewell state government can no longer be counted on as the ultimate benefactor to those in need. But need remains, and is intensified as income, wealth, and work become more unequally distributed. Into this equation enters the new benefaction: tough minded rather than tender; no longer just a voluntary act, but tinged with a social obligation to contribute.

For General Powell, benefaction becomes a stern personal responsibility, an opportunity to give which requires a considerable donation, because negative consequences in the form of public humiliation await those who fail to give. Thus, the CEO to whom the "sweat test" is administered must either give what he has foreplanned to contribute, thereby publicly refusing the fund-raiser's request, or spontaneously commit to a contribution far in excess of what he thought either possible or reasonable.

Such publicly pressured giving is almost as mandatory as the giving involved in taxation, and is far more visible. To the publicly pressured donor, whether an individual or a corporation, giving loses much of the control involved in its more traditional conceptions.[1] As one business student asked me after the Summit, in discussing the "sweat test": "Where does giving end and extortion begin?"

It may be helpful, in understanding the new benefaction, to focus on the issue of control. In the case of the taxation example, it is clear that the governmental agent is in control: taxes are owed because of law, and that is that. In the case of voluntary giving in its 20th-century American form, control has been seen to rest with the giver, whose wealth and income are viewed as private possessions to which others will have to defer as the disposition is made. The Powell model reverts to older traditions of religion-based philanthropy, where obligation predominates over voluntarism.[2] In some of these traditions, public recognition rewards the donor in much the same way that the Powell model lauds the highly public contributions of corporations rendered in the form of "commitments" by their chief executives.

Publicly pressured giving blurs the line between the coercive nature of taxation and the voluntary nature of traditional philanthropy. As General Powell enacts it, some causes are so important that the reluctant donor must be publicly motivated, up to the point of being publicly shamed, to give far more generously than would have otherwise been contributed. The consequences of not giving, or not giving sufficiently, involve the risk of public recognition of an unwillingness to contribute as fully as the fund-raiser has determined should be done.

In each case—taxation and publicly pressured giving—a conception of a need for community justice stands behind the request to give. In traditional democratic theory, taxation allows the community, through the vehicle of self-government, to redistribute resources authoritatively from a central source. You or I might want to assist the poor and needy, the theory goes, but we cannot do so effectively acting as individuals. Only the commitment of the entire community, working through a democratic government, will provide a thorough and far redistribution of power, wealth, and other resources.

Similarly, publicly pressured giving bases the firmness of its demand on perceived community need. Governmental power, this theory asserts, has become far too weak and far too compromised to be effective in dealing with human need. What is needed is a massive infusion of resources that appear to be given freely by concerned and effective individuals and organizations (read: corporations). Behind this facade of voluntarism, however, often lurks the same spirit of "give or else" that has reduced the image of taxation as an appropriate means of modern giving.

A tough-minded approach to giving may not be all that new, if one considers the recent reflection of Quaker scholar and administrator Thomas Jeavons, writing as general secretary of the Philadelphia Yearly Meeting. "Questions about money," Jeavons writes, "really become questions about commitment and loyalty." Updating the biblical citation "Where your treasure is, there will your heart be also," Jeavons paraphrases: "You want to know what someone really cares

about? Look at how they spend their money . . . or . . . their time" (Jeavons, 1998: 2).

Of course, some would argue that traditional Christianity, with
its focus on blurring the distinction between self-love and the love of
others, has confused things immeasurably. Piety itself does not feed
the hungry, whatever the source or motive of the giving. And pious
responses, General Powell asserts, will simply not suffice. Nor will the
passing of the hot potato from government to church to corporation
to individual giver. These are tough questions, indeed. Ones surely
worth some sweating over.

## Nonprofit Management Education at a Crossroads

Every ten years, the educational elite who direct America's emerging
centers of nonprofit management education also gather in California.
First in 1986, and then again in 1996, these leaders met to share papers
and perspectives on their work.

The first thing to understand is that the field of nonprofit management education is growing. Naomi Wish and Roseanne Mirabella reported that their research has identified 102 colleges and universities
offering graduate courses in nonprofit management and 46 providing
undergraduate courses in this field.

The field is not only growing; it is changing as well. In 1986 the
call was for the blooming of many flowers. In the conference volume,
*Educating Managers of Nonprofit Organizations,* conference organizers
Michael O'Neill and Dennis Young observed that a separate field of
study, along the lines of business or public administration, might
emerge, but so also might tracks within other established fields of professional study.

From the 1986 conference came a recognition that a "three circle"
curriculum might meet the needs of the field. Circle 1 would contain
basic courses in generic management, which could be shared with programs in business and public management; Circle 2 would present
courses on the history, traditions, and structures of the nonprofit sector; and Circle 3 would inculcate specific skills pertinent to the many
specializations within the field: arts, social service, advocacy, and the
like. Research that Gabor Hegyesi (Hungary's leading educator in the
field of nonprofit education) and I have been conducting for the International Society for Third Sector Research confirms the attractiveness
of this model to nonprofit management educators on an international
scale.

But professional education involves more than a choice of curriculum. As Professor Stuart Nagel of the University of Illinois has noted
for the field of policy studies, choices need to be made regarding level
of degree (certificate, B.A., M.A., Ph.D.) and emphasis on substance or

methodology, discipline or interdiscipline, teaching vs. research, level of organization (international, national, regional, or local), and ideology (liberal vs. conservative).

These choices, for universities, will ultimately be made by deans and faculty members who control those curricula, and the 1996 conference was presented with one particularly challenging major presentation urging a rethinking of curricular approaches in the field. In this talk, Johns Hopkins University's Lester Salamon, a major figure in the field, suggested that the idea of a separate curriculum for nonprofit management may be a force whose time has passed.

What we have learned about the three sectors (government, business, and nonprofit), Salamon suggested, was that their basic relationship is one of interdependence, not independence. Career paths often cross the boundaries of the sectors as individuals move from business to government to nonprofits, and then return. Patterns of grant making and contracts move money freely from private wages to taxes to contracts with nonprofits (what Salamon calls "third-party government"), or from corporate profits to charitable contributions, or from wages to charitable donations to tax deductions.

What is true of the broader society should be true for university programs in the field, Salamon continued. Separate programs in nonprofit management do not reflect the interdependent realities of institutional life, and should reform themselves as multi-sectoral in their curriculum and thrust. Pointing with pride to his own university's graduate program in "professional citizenship," Salamon urged the educators to make the interdependence of the three sectors the central focus of their instructional programs.

One of the most remarkable papers presented to the conference was the one prepared by Professor Maria Josefa Canino and Eugenia R. Echols of the Public Administration department at Rutgers University, Newark. Professor Canino, a long-time leader in Latino affairs in New Jersey, and Ms. Echols, a graduate student whose energetic presentation won long applause from the attendees of her session, addressed the challenge facing their department as it contemplates developing a new graduate program in the nonprofit field.

They knew that this program should address the needs of Latino organizations in their state, but instead of hanging a shingle and offering a program to whoever might attend, they did something else, something as refreshing as their presentation: they went into the field and asked the nonprofit managers of Latino organizations what they wanted and needed from the university.

The responses of the managers were intriguing, to say the least. First of all, the managers themselves hardly needed another degree. One-fourth of them already had earned a B.A.; more than half had earned a master's; and 20 percent were holders of a doctoral degree.

And, secondly, what they wanted from the university was technical assistance and training rather than another degree program. When asked how Rutgers-Newark might contribute to the organizational survival and development of their community-based organization, their responses were first for the assignment of graduate interns to their program (67%) and the development of short-term customized training programs (67%), second for the provision of technical assistance (53%), and only third for the presentation of summer training institutes (47%) or a master's program (47%).

The broad-based efforts of a consortium of educators and service providers in St. Louis also illustrates the wisdom of asking before one offers a degree. The directors of the nonprofit programs at four regional universities in the St. Louis area have joined with a group of support providers (private and agency-based consultants and trainers), foundation leaders, and nonprofit executives to develop the Nonprofit Services Consortium to provide training and technical assistance. This center offers a full range of services to the nonprofit community, including courses and degrees through its four cooperating universities, certification programs, continuing education modules, technical assistance training, and consultation to individual organizations.

As the field of nonprofit education continues to develop, it faces a continuing series of challenges. The largest denizens of the nonprofit world have already secured their educational beachheads in schools of education, public health, social work, and religion. Nonprofit management is thus left to forage off the sector's bottom for its students and legitimacy. If it becomes a track in a business or public administration program, it risks being marginalized by the central focus of its host school; if it sets up its own degree (most common is the MNO—Master of Nonprofit Organization), it runs the risk of providing a degree that will be seen as less "valuable" than the lordly MBA (Master of Business Administration). And, in any case, there remains the question of fitting the degree to the particular sections of the nonprofit world to which the students' interests are focused. Already, an emphasis on management over board concerns, and a drift of attention away from community-based organization and toward the better-financed interests of larger nonprofit organizations, may be discerned in these new curricula.[3]

## From Collaboration to Merger to Acquisition

As business-like organizations, nonprofits have been increasingly forced to contemplate issues of collaboration, merger, and acquisition. Social work educator Stephen Wernet and his colleague and wife, nursing educator Sandra Jones, have studied the processes by which nonprofit organizations explore closer relations with each other. First, they find, the talk is of collaboration. Then the idea of merger may be presented. And, finally, in some cases issues of takeover and acquisition are moved to the fore.

Wernet and Jones examined in detail relations between two agencies in an unnamed town. One was a well-established provider of social services, which they called the Family Service Organization (FSO). The other, the Substance Abuse Treatment Organization (SATO), was newer and less well known, but growing rapidly.

FSO had its good reputation and an energetic board, but it faced a turbulent fiscal environment. It was highly dependent upon external funding, and these sources (both third-party funding and United Way) were proving increasingly unreliable.

SATO, on the other hand, had expanded its services steadily since its founding in the early 1970s, and had become a multi-million-dollar organization. It ran like a well-oiled corporation, and competed effectively in the provision of treatment, prevention, and educational programs in an expanding target area.

As professional colleagues, the directors of the two agencies had often worked jointly in community partnerships and strategic, though limited, collaboration. It was the executive of the FSO who first proposed to explore a merger, in part from his own wish to relieve himself from the burdens of management. It was his professional goal to focus much more directly on clinical responsibilities for the remainder of his career.

The boards of the two organizations quickly came to see a strategic fit between their organizations, and a merger committee was established. As Wernet and Jones tell it, "For the larger firm, the merger provided a means of fulfilling one aspect of its strategic plan by adding an outpatient family treatment service. For the smaller firm, the merger provided a means to procure new and more stable revenue source as well as to expand its base of operations" (Wernet and Jones, 1992: 374).

Organizationally, however, the fit was more precarious. The FSO took a traditional orientation, aiming to serve a clearly defined target population within a prescribed area. SATO, on the other hand, took an entrepreneurial and corporate approach, extending itself in both services provided and area served. Nevertheless, a merger plan was approved by both organizations.

The plan provided for the SATO director to become the CEO of the new organization, in which the FSO director would head an independent division (in effect, the former FSO). Only grudgingly did the FSO members of the merger committee agree to accept a lesser number of seats on the board of the new organization, by a ratio reflecting the financial strengths brought by each to the merger. Only gradually did they come to recognize that what began as a merger was rapidly turning into an acquisition.

Summarizing their research, Wernet and Jones explain that collaboration involves a continuum. In its extreme forms—merger and acquisition—it involves the creation of a new organization, and the full mingling of formerly independent organizational resources. In more limited versions, organizations retain their autonomy but may contribute resources to the "joint venture." Steps along the way may be identified as cooperation, collaboration, merger, and acquisition.

At every step along the way, collaboration provides a challenge to the nonprofit organization. Research shows that successful collaborations involve a multi-step process:

1. Collaboration begins with a vision of how the world might be a better place if two or more organizations were to work together, a vision usually developed by a single visionary leader.

2. The vision is tested by "mental experiment" to assure that it respects the domain and autonomy of the potential collaborators.

3. The idea is then shared with the potential collaborating organizations, who are invited to join in the process of exploration of what might be created jointly.

4. A collaborative team is appointed to define more clearly the limits and extent of the joint venture.

5. The process is invigorated by the development of complementary roles and the development of a productive joint process.

6. Each partner regularly reviews the progress of the collaboration to assure that its purposes are being met, and that its own organizational integrity is being respected.

It is the possibility, always present in this game, that collaboration may lead down a slippery slope to ultimate takeover and acquisition that gives rise to the greatest fear of entering into the collaboration process. The fear of loss of control and organizational identity strikes terror into the hearts of many nonprofit managers, and, it must be noted, it is never wholly clear at the outset where a collaborative exploration will lead.

Among the unpredictabilities of the process are the following:

• The Executive may (secretly, or known only to a few trusted board members and colleagues) wish to be relieved of the burdens of management, and welcome the ultimate acquisition of the organization by another, more enterprising and energetic, leadership team.

- Staffers assigned to the collaborative team may take on the role of "boundary spanners," developing new loyalties to the mission of the collaborative enterprise that may raise questions about their previous commitments to the organizations that employ them.

- Either (or any) of the collaborating partners may discover, as the process develops, that changing environmental or internal forces have brought the potential of merger and acquisition to the fore.

In light of these unpredictable factors, it may be best to view merger and acquisition as one of a set of potential outcomes of collaboration that may, from time to time, be in the best interest of even the organization that loses its former organizational identity and autonomy. After all, it is not as though the loss of a single free-standing nonprofit will necessarily diminish the sector; nor is it likely that the loss of one formerly autonomous organization will be missed. What is most important is to learn that processes of birth, courtship, marriage, and death have become inescapable realities of the contemporary nonprofit world.

## Everyone a Businessperson, Some in Nonprofits

Chapter 6 concluded with a discussion of "social entrepreneurship" as a source of contemporary buzz in the nonprofit sector. This chapter has reviewed some of what it takes to manage a nonprofit organization creatively and thoughtfully. In each case, the argument of the chapters has pointed toward the importance of balancing vision and reality, mission and the bottom line. Both leadership and management would seem required of the nonprofit executive, and the danger may be that the latter skill, in a time of financial uncertainty, will be given primary attention.

Consider the hiring process for an endowed professorship at an urban campus of a leading Midwestern university. The job definition involved both professorial and management responsibilities, the latter entailing the oversight of several public-related centers and institutes.

One might first observe that this is not, strictly speaking, a nonprofit sector position. The university, after all, is a public institution. A quick examination of budget, however, indicates the limits of that conception. As with the quintessential nonprofit organization, public university funding comes from three major sources, and often in fairly equal amounts. Yes, the university is chartered by the state, but only one-third of its funding typically issues from state sources. Tuition and fees, and outside funding sources, both governmental and philanthropic, provide for the other two-thirds of State U's support. More accurately, the state university has become a "public-related" institution, whose management tasks have also come to closely resemble those of the quintessential nonprofit organization.

Candidates for the endowed position were granted an initial screening interview, and were provided three questions to ponder before this conversation. Remember, the position is that of an endowed professorship. These, however, were the areas of focus for the interview:

1. the candidate's vision of community collaboration

2. the candidate's ideas for substantially increasing grant and contract activity

3. the candidate's ideas for mobilizing faculty for increased multi-disciplinary research

Question 1 pertains to leadership capacity, calling for the articulation of a quest for shared vision, mission, and partnership. Question 2 pertains to resource mobilization, calling for the willingness to translate vision into the often slow and unpredictable quest for external funding. And question 3 pertains to the management savvy required to bring a set of relatively independent contractors together in a variety of organization-serving matrices.

Skills in leadership, resource mobilization, and management have become essential for the contemporary professional—whether she or he is employed by a nonprofit corporation, a university, a church, a governmental agency, or a business organization. Differences in tradition and mission remain, of course, among these organizations, but they do not allow escape from the basic triad of skills. We live in an organizational society, and, increasingly, if we are to advance or even persist, we will be required to show our skills in collaborative leadership, business-like resource development, and effective organizational management. In a very real sense, we have all become, at least in part, businesspersons. It is just that many of us pursue our business in the organizational milieu of the third sector.

# 8

# When the Business
# of Nonprofits Is
# Increasingly Business

Calvin Coolidge, Ronald Reagan's favorite predecessor in the White House, was said to observe that the "business of America is business." As we have seen in the previous chapter, nonprofit organizations, particularly over the past two decades, have been hectored to become increasingly businesslike. For-profit subsidiaries are created, and unrelated income increasingly comes to be earned. Increasingly one confronts the worry: Has the nonprofit sector become the home to too many organizations which act essentially as tax-exempt businesses?

This chapter focuses on the role of nonprofit organization in the arenas of health care and education. For these enormously important social institutions, what difference does it make if one is for-profit or nonprofit?

## Enter the For-Profit: The Case of Hospital Buyouts

American health care is increasingly coming under the control of formally for-profit organizations, and this tendency is particularly pronounced among hospitals. Between 1980 and 1989, Lester Salamon (1997: 30–31) notes, the number of for-profit hospitals increased by 28 percent, while the overall number of hospitals continues to decline. In 1994 alone, 31 nonprofit hospitals were bought by commercial firms, and this number increased to 59 in 1995, with several hundred additional take-overs still in discussion. As of 1996, 15 percent of the nation's community hospitals were under the control of investor-owned for-profit corporations.

Economics journalist Robert Kuttner explains that this process is part of a national movement to privatize nearly everything that can conceivably be bought or sold. Kuttner devotes a long chapter of his study of the privatization process, *Everything for Sale*, to questions of "Markets and Medicine."

Kuttner (1997: 126) notes that "investor-owned" hospital chains are "growing explosively," usually the result of "merger-and-acquisition binges orchestrated by entrepreneurs. Historically, the for-profit hospitals were locally owned; now they are held by absentee companies." According to Kuttner (p. 126), the typical acquisition pattern is this:

A chain like Columbia/HCA [founded in 1988 and now the owner of 346 hospitals], armed with investor capital and its capacity to borrow in financial markets, comes into a community that has excess hospital beds, and makes a struggling nonprofit hospital an offer it can't refuse. The chain also promises town officials that a tax-exempt institution will be converted to one that generates tax revenues. It often buys off key trustees and other key hospital officials. Once a hospital is "in play," the sale becomes almost a foregone conclusion; the only questions are who will buy it, on what terms, and who will benefit. After a hospital has been acquired, Spartan cost economies are instituted—layoffs, increased hours and reduced pay for remaining medical personnel, closing or trimming of facilities deemed unnecessary.

To Kuttner, the important point in this process is the way it allows for the market to make decisions that enrich a few and beggar the broader community of providers and consumers of health care. What the community loses in this process is an "asset value [that] represents many decades of benefactors' making donations"—including "charitable contributions, local government subsidies in the form of foregone property taxes, and slightly below-market fees accepted by doctors for the good of the community. . . . Under the well-established common-law doctrine, a charitable corporation that has raised funds for one set of purposes is not free to convert its assets to new purposes, nor are executives of charities free to convert assets to personal benefit. But that is precisely what occurs when a for-profit buys out a nonprofit."

Kuttner argues that the process by which a community-based nonprofit hospital becomes transformed into a chain-bought for-profit entity negates the fundamental legal criterion for a nonprofit organization: the non-distribution constraint. This constraint assures that, if the nonprofit closes its doors, its assets cannot be transformed into personal gain, but rather shall be distributed to other nonprofit organizations. Kuttner notes that some hospital conversions have sought to conform to law by "transferring assets to a nominally nonprofit foundation that is closely controlled by the parent for-profit corporation," and that these conversions are currently under investigation in several states.

Vigorously dissenting from Kuttner is "conversion foundation" director Roger Hughes, who has directed Phoenix's St. Luke's Charitable Health Trust for the past three years. Hughes explains that his foundation emerged from the sale of the nonprofit St. Luke's Health System to for-profit OrdNa (now owned by the Tenet Healthcare Corp.) for about $120 million in 1995:

> After paying off a $60 million debt, a charitable trust was formed with the remaining $60 million and about $13 million from St. Luke's nonprofit hospital foundation, its fundraising arm. Three years later, that $73 million is $110 million, and about $8 million has been returned to the community through a comprehensive grant program.
>
> The philosophy and purpose behind this conversion were straightforward: If a nonprofit hospital system with a long history of serving the community is to be allowed to sell its assets to a private owner so that it can more effectively compete in a crowded marketplace, then public ownership of those assets, vested through years of tax-exempt operation for the "greater public good," must be perpetuated through the proceeds of that Sale in such a manner that the public good is neither diminished nor compromised, but ideally is enhanced.
>
> Over the past two years, we have given approximately 30% of our grants for direct medical services/charity care, another 30% for projects focused on strengthening and expanding a healthcare infrastructure for impoverished populations, about 20% for professional health education programs, and another 20% for public education and advocacy around specific public health issues. (Comment to ARNOVA-L, e-mail list of the Association for Research on Nonprofit Organizations and Voluntary Action, 1998)

Hughes observes that "In the opinion of many in this community, the conversion has been a win-win situation for everybody. The Charitable Trust is able to do far more with its 'charitable' dollars than a stand-alone nonprofit hospital focused strictly on medical services and indigent care." He notes that the important question—Which is better: charity or strategic philanthropy?—is raised by the buyout situation. Are "tax-exempt dollars better 'invested' in direct medical services or in finding ways to improve both the systems and public policies that govern the provision of those services?"

The debate over the ease with which the hospital buyers are able to lay aside the fundamental legal basis of the nonprofit organization, the non-distribution constraint, is a vitally important one. On the one hand, Kuttner's argument suggests that everything is for sale, and that the only portions of the third sector that are defended from privatization are those services that no entrepreneur can imagine a way to profit from. As Lester Salamon (1997: 31) has observed, it may not be far-fetched to argue, as did an author recently in the *New England Journal of Medicine*, that "nonprofit health plans are a product of the past."

Despite the obvious risks of privatization, other nonprofit and hospital experts find little cause to worry about its impact on the welfare of the communities involved. Mark Pauly of the University of Pennsylvania has been quoted (*Philadelphia Inquirer*, July 26, 1998, D1) to the effect that "It's really hard to find a dime's worth of difference between how nonprofits and for-profits behave." And renowned Princeton health expert Uwe Reinhardt adds, in the same article, "The nonprofits are just as much at each other's throats" as for-profits would be. "I really don't think for-profit makes that much difference."

The second-largest for-profit hospital chain in the country, Tenet Healthcare Corp., owns 123 hospitals in 18 states. In the fiscal year that ended June 30, Tenet secured for itself profits of $540 million on revenues of $9.9 billion. Tenet approaches the purchase of a nonprofit hospital with all the sweetness of Lady Bountiful herself, offering a "Compact with Communities," a manifesto that employs the traditional verbiage of voluntarism and eschews any shred of possible capitalist greed:

- Tenet recognizes its vital responsibilities as a member of the community: as a provider of healthcare, an owner of hospitals, in partnership with other providers and as a part of the spectrum of healthcare delivery.

- Tenet will operate with the highest standards of business and professional conduct, and it empowers its employees with the strongest ethics and compliance programs in the healthcare industry.

- Tenet pledges to honor without interruption, the charity care policies of the hospitals it acquires or with which it affiliates.

- Tenet believes in local governance of its hospitals by local physicians and community members. It expects governing boards at its hospitals to ensure that services are tailored to meet specific needs of the communities they serve.

- Tenet recognizes that it can best serve its shareholders only if it best serves its patients' interests first. It has not paid dividends, choosing instead to reinvest net profits into its hospitals and services so that both the company and the community enjoy the long-term benefit of having the best possible healthcare.

- Tenet pledges to work cooperatively with other healthcare providers in every community in which it operates to help meet the needs of vulnerable populations through the support, creation, and maintenance of concrete programs.

- Tenet honors the commitments it makes in each community it serves, and it welcomes full disclosure and monitoring of its fulfillment of these commitments by an attorney general or appropriate authority.

- Tenet vows to provide leadership within the business community in advocating for responses to the healthcare needs of vulnerable populations.

Kuttner (1997: 131) puts an interesting spin on the point that for-profits seek to sound like traditional voluntaries, suggesting that at the same time, the nonprofits tend to act much more like predatory capitalists:[1]

> [I]n this entrepreneurial environment, non-profit institutions find themselves behaving more and more like for-profits—"avoiding the burden of caring for expensive and hardship cases, limiting costly research and teaching, advertising for market share, conceiving of the healing enterprise as cost centers versus profit centers, and entering into dubious joint ventures that contradict the spirit of their original mission. To exquisitely complete the circle, the defensive imitation of for-profits by nonprofits then allows the big chains to argue that non-profits are really not so different at all. Why, Columbia/HCA repeatedly asks in its public-relations materials, should nonprofits get special treatment?

In the case of the 1998 buyout of Philadelphia's Allegheny hospital system by Tenet, Kuttner's point was driven home with a vengeance. As the nonprofit hospital chain sank into bankruptcy, it raided its endowment funds for inappropriate expenses, made preferential payments on loans to its executives, hid its predicament from its employees, and, in general, acted as deceitfully and desperately as the local oriental rug store throwing its annual "going out of business" sale. In Phoenix, conversion foundation executive Hughes observes that "While Tenet–St. Luke's continues to operate as a hospital system, they face considerable market pressure from the consolidation of several nonprofit chains which are able to give the for-profits a real run for the money—and not to put too fine a point on it, that's the goal. 'No margin, no mission,' as the Good Fathers say" (comment to ARNOVA-L).

What do these issues mean for the nonprofit sector? In dollar terms, health care amounts to 56 percent of its expenditures (Salamon,

1992: 24). And hospitals amount to 40 percent of all health care expenditures (ibid.: 59). As hospitals increase their rush from the nonprofit sector, they abandon both their considerable presence as nonprofits and thereby threaten the structural underpinning of their traditions of voluntary service to their communities.

Gone when that check from the for-profit is cashed is an important legal base for a long-developed tradition of community support for a vital human service, and an important structural support for the conception that medical care is about caring for people in need. Nor have the boards of the new "conversion foundations" yet demonstrated their independence from the corporate control of both the new and old hospital owners and managers.

## Is Higher Education Far Behind?

As we have seen in considering the rise of for-profit mentalities and instrumentalities in the area of hospital care, the future may contain both a loss of mission and a loss of scale for nonprofit entities. The same questions arise for the sector's second largest constituency, education (which amounts to 26 percent of the sector's expenditures). Here, too, for-profits have entered the arena, both through the Whittle Group's ventures in secondary education and the collegiate developments by the for-profit University of Phoenix and numerous corporate training facilities. And here, too, the steady escalation of fees (which educational institutions have generally called tuitions) threatens the loss of whatever uniquely nonprofit qualities these institutions may have possessed.

An expensive liberal arts college presently bills its students over $30,000 a year for its services. One such institution, Swarthmore College, explains that the true cost of one year of its services amounts to almost $50,000. (For the derivation of that figure, see Swarthmore graduate Peter Passell's article in the *New York Times* of July 29, 1994, "One College's Price Tag: Why So Low, and So High?") Swarthmore prides itself on being need-blind in its admissions process. It strives to meet the full need of those students it accepts, as calculated by its own financial aid formula. What this means is that a low-income family (at $20–$30 thousand) will be asked to pay less than 15 percent of its income to the college, while families at the $50–90 thousand range can expect to pay up to 18 percent of income for their college costs. Over $100,000, the family contribution rises to 25 percent, but it begins to fall after $140 thousand, and continues to do so through the highest income levels. No one is charged more than the sticker price of $29,800 (as of academic year 1997–98), and so the upper-income family with an income of $300,000 or above will pay less than 10 percent of its income for college, a smaller percentage than that charged the family with a $5,000 income.

The net effect of this pricing scheme is that the upper-income family not only pays a smaller percentage of its income for college than the poorest family, but it also enjoys the benefits of a "hidden scholarship" of almost $20,000 received by each attending student. This hidden scholarship exists because the sticker price is lower than the estimated cost of the college's service. This gift to rich and poor alike is funded by the college's endowment and is a result of philanthropic contributions like the recent unrestricted gift of $30 million from alumnus Eugene Lang, a gift sufficient to fund a year of hidden scholarships.

It has become fashionable for nonprofit college economists to bewail the abandonment of the private college by so-called affluent bargain hunters, individuals who act on the recognition that quality public university services can be purchased for one-third the price of upscale nonprofit service by persons of middle income and above. Such reformers worry that well-off students will "crowd out" the "natural constituency" of the state schools: able students of incomes too modest to afford the nonprofits.

State colleges and universities, at the same time, have raised their own tuitions rapidly, knowing that they will remain bargains for most of their students, and hoping that those federal funds remaining available will allow for a continuing presence of low-income students among their ranks. These universities are vigorously introducing a variety of "honors programs" and "merit scholarships," aiming directly to attract able students away from their nonprofit competitors. It is their hope to forestall their own crisis of underfunding, which also takes a direct toll on low and moderate income students and their families, by becoming better situated politically to buttress their dwindling claim to general public funding.

The net effect is a crisis in higher education finance that extends far beyond the already complex problem of nonprofit pricing. As policy analyst Lester Salamon notes in his recent Cummings Foundation study of the nonprofit sector, *Holding the Center* (1997), economic struggles to attract and retain clients and customers are raging in the health care and social service arenas, as well as in education. And nonprofits are losing many of these struggles: Salamon shows that for-profits accounted for 70 percent or more of the growth in employment in such service industries as day care and home health care between 1977 and 1992.[2]

The downside of any reform in the current chaos of higher education funding involves the price sensitivity of the rich. What if Penn or Brown continued to charge only $30,000 a year while Harvard and Swarthmore kicked their tag up toward the $50,000 level? Would the best and the brightest be drained toward the cheaper places? Probably not, or at least no more than the Universities of Virginia and Wisconsin now drain the Ivy League. As long as parents continue to believe that their children are significantly advantaged by the content and contacts available from associating with offspring of the elite during the formative college years, students are likely to continue to struggle for positions in those, largely nonprofit, colleges identified as "elite" and "competitive."

Second, concern would exist that such a stiff price might discourage wealthy parents, or alums whose parents paid the premium price, from giving as generously in their later gifts to the college. Is, in other words, the likelihood of a major gift enhanced when the givers have the sense that they have already gotten a bargain? (This theme echoes in the recent philanthropy of James Michener and Eugene Lang—but both were poor boys when they attended Swarthmore, and now they recall the generosity of those who made it possible for them to go there.) One might anticipate some slippage in parental giving, but a substantial decline in giving from loyal, and rich, alums would appear unlikely.

Extending the sliding scale would allow elite colleges to provide more generous financial aid to their middle- and lower-income clients. And it would enable second-tier colleges to follow suit, charging their widely varying fees to students unable to gain admission to the elite level.

## Health and Higher Education as Markets

As the preceding discussion indicates, higher education, like hospital service, has taken on many market trappings. Colleges and universities offer their products for sale with the same vigor and even shamelessness as any for-profit organization. On the day this sentence is composed, to take an example, the *New York Times* reports on the slick television advertisements currently being run by such publicly supported universities as Auburn, Minnesota, and Penn State.[3] Does anyone expect the nonprofit "private" colleges to be far behind? Swarthmore, to take an example, published considerable puffery about its one-year rank as "Number 1" by a national news magazine that many of its faculty members privately dismiss as a reputable source of news pertaining either to the United States or the world.

As health care and higher education increasingly take on the form and function of business enterprises, one may wonder what difference this transition actually will involve for those who seek to teach and learn within such institutions. As with the hospital transformation from public and nonprofit to for-profit, will the impact be noticeable in any important way? Or, rather, will the proof continue to be found in the pudding provided by each institution—public, for-profit, or nonprofit—as Ralph Kramer has searchingly asked?

For the moment, there is little question that a valued commodity at many elite colleges is the enrollment of individuals of minority racial background, particularly African-American, and especially if such an individual has emerged from a childhood of urban poverty. Journalist Ron Suskind's account of the pathway Cedric Jennings takes from the Washington ghetto to the halls of Brown University describes this valuation. Mr. Jennings, an eminently deserving and ambitious young man, is granted early admission to Brown even though his SAT scores amount to 960, a full 400 points below the average of his entering class.[4]

Such remarkable mobility may be provided more easily by a nonprofit than a public college, but that does not dissuade public institutions from similarly seeking to provide educational advantages to those of deprived backgrounds. Surely the fact that charitable donations undergird the financial offers of the nonprofit allows them to skim the cream of minority applicants, but the lower tuitions of the public institutions give some continuing advantage as well. It is doubtful that for-profit institutions will give more than lip service to the racial/ethnic backgrounds of the students they will seek to serve.

It would seem plausible that differences will narrow between public, nonprofit, and for-profit institutions as the market principle takes hold within their various structures of administration and service delivery. The creation of departments and research centers as "profit centers" is well established within universities of all auspices, and the dependence of even the most highly endowed institutions on tuitions and fees is evident. To be sure, the appointment conditions of boards of directors vary somewhat, and it will be more difficult for profit-seeking institutions to launder contributions into charitable foundations that will undergird their support. But just as differences between public and private colleges have declined in recent years, the blurring of the boundaries will surely continue apace.

## The Discovery of Society's Third Space

As health care and education increasingly become market driven, a corresponding loss can be expected in traditions of philanthropic support, nonprofit governance, service to those underserved by market and state, and asset protection under terms of the non-distribution constraint. Increasingly, observers of the nonprofit sector are beginning to confront the implications of the shifting boundaries between the sectors.

Elizabeth Boris, director of the Urban Institute's Center on Nonprofits and Philanthropy, is one who approaches the subject with some delicacy. "Businesses and government entities often provide services similar to those of nonprofits," Boris observes. "As a result, there may be few obvious differences among nonprofit, for-profit, and government services such as substance abuse programs, child care centers, and hospitals. Although there is growing concern over the potential impact on communities of the conversion of hospitals from nonprofit to for-profit status, there is little documentation of the consequences" (Boris, 1998: 2–3).

Boris, a long-time worker in what Peter Dobkin Hall calls the nonprofit "industry," finds some "positive effects" in the "overlap" between the sectors: "For instance, nonprofits may create for-profit subsidiaries that allow them to make a profit in one program that can be used to subsidize services in another. Nonprofits also use services provided by businesses when it is cost-effective to do so. Many colleges now provide commercial food services for students, for example."

Boris concludes her discussion of boundary relations with an observation that was frequently made about voluntary action before there was as much concern with the workings of a nonprofit "sector" as there is at present: "These changing boundaries can lead to innovation and new opportunities for problem-solving. Sometimes, for instance, the nonprofit sector may pave the way for government and business to meet a social service need that they may not have known existed." The example she uses is the area of AIDS prevention and treatment.

Boris's argument is important in that she recognizes the limited differences that often characterize the services of public, nonprofit, and business enterprises. But it may well be that it is the quality of the service, and not the formal structure of the provider, that is most important. This is the point social welfare scholar Ralph Kramer makes in his Aspen Institute working paper "Nonprofit Organizations in the 21st Century: Will Sector Matter?"

Kramer's most significant research throughout a long and distinguished career detailed the ways in which governments relate to nonprofit organizations, particularly in the contracting of service.[5] In his Aspen Institute paper, Kramer (1998: 1) identifies two contrasting perspectives that have emerged on the nonprofit sector during its rapid growth over the past quarter-century:

[T]he dominant one emphasizes the rapid institutionalization of a third sector partner with government in the provision of human services, culture and the arts, and as a mainstay and advocate in the civil society. The other view is skeptical of the sector as a model based on corporate form, and instead, finds blurring of the boundaries and convergence between government, the market economy, and non-profits in a post-industrial society.

Kramer reviews a number of theories drawn from the fields of political and social economy, organizational ecology, neo-institutionalism, and mixed systems. He concludes that "how a service is delivered may be more significant than its auspices; consequently an emphasis on the importance of organizational ownership or corporate form in service delivery can divert attention from social policy goals and values such as access, effectiveness, and quality."

The concept of a statistically large nonprofit, third, or independent sector has been attractive during the process of its "invention." But there has always been a bit of the Wizard of Oz in this construct, as the principal "biggies" in that sector—hospitals, insurance associations, colleges, and religious institutions—do not acknowledge that they are part of a distinctive third sector. These institutions retain their own professional networks, educational niches, and particular institutional identities.

This left the inventors of the nonprofit sector with a dilemma: Should they continue to proclaim the reality of this reluctant center? Or should they return to the traditional conception of a smaller, but more focused, "voluntary sector," consisting largely of smaller social service organizations, community organizations, and social action groups?

These areas of concern fit best with the principles of voluntarism and philanthropy, and offer most clearly what neither state nor market can provide. They are also the activities that the philosopher Franklin Gamwell (1984) sought to identify when he pursued the "teleologically prior" segments of the third sector: the corners of society in which the soul of the sector could be found. These are vital and distinctive institutions in society, which can be seen as situated in social territory that lies in spaces in between what is strictly "business," "government," and "family."

Social theorist and activist Harry Boyte (Evans and Boyte, 1992: 17–18) has referred to this territory as host to society's "free spaces"—"the environments in which people are able to learn a new self-respect, a deeper and more assertive group identity, public skills, and values of cooperation and civic virtue. Put simply, free spaces are settings between private lives and large-scale institutions where ordinary citizens can act with dignity, independence, and vision. These are, in the main, voluntary forms of association with a relatively open and participatory character—many religious organizations, clubs, self-help and mutual aid societies, reform groups, neighborhood, civic and ethnic groups, and a host of other associations grounded in the fabric of community life."

Boyte tends to see free spaces as primarily, though not exclusively, consisting of smaller and more informal organizations located in what I have been calling the third sector. But there is more than a bit of blurriness in the boundaries between these organizations and the activity that occurs in what I have called the informal sector—the locus not only of families and kinship systems but also of many informally organized gatherings of persons within neighborhoods and communities. Also small and intermediate between family and large institutions are the variety of reform and civic groups and networks that address their concerns toward governmental, and, sometimes as well, corporate structures. The kind of space we are now exploring increasingly takes the form of a wide range of places particularly noted for their position "between" other sectors, rather than their identity as a sector unto itself.[6]

Building on the depiction of social space presented by Victor Pestoff (see above, ch. 2), the German scholar Adalbert Evers envisions the third sector as occupying a particularly important public space within contemporary society. He begins by seeing this space located within a triangle of basic institutions: market, state, and informal. Thus, third-sector organizations are seen to play a variety of economic, social, and political "intermediating" roles with each of the other forms of organization.

Evers's (1995: 160–61) vision of the third sector is strongly spatial. He emphasizes that the third sector involves a wide range of action and organizations—many of them "hybrids, intermeshing different resources and connecting different areas" that involve "synergetic mixes of resources and rationales." The boundaries between the third sector and the other major institutions are not at all distinct. Rather, the third sector is a space "which opens up when conceiving the state, market, and informal sector as cornerstones of a triangular tension field."

Viewed as located between and within the institutional structures provided by business, government, nonprofit organizations, and families/kin groups/communities, the spaces envisioned by Boyte and Evers may prove crucial for the sustenance of a healthy modern society. Rather than a product of a large and heavily bureaucratized third sector, this societal arena may be better seen as a "third space" in modern society. Not the space where business and economic gain are the order of the day or the bureaucratic space where the workings of governmental authority and organization prevail; and certainly not the family space of society, within which most individuals live out their most important human relations. A third space—a place between the mega-organizations of society and the tiny islands of our family lives. A place to link, to network, to communicate, and to live out the fact that modern life involves connecting individuals to larger systems that affect their daily lives.

Among the varieties of the third space: It was in the third space of the basement of Ebenezer Baptist Church that Martin Luther King Jr. rallied what became the core of a great movement following the arrest of Rosa Parks. It was in the third space of the Magic Lantern Theater that an ex-convict named Vaclav Havel met with his peers to design a peaceful revolution that led him within several months to the Presidential Castle. In the third space of an organization called PEN, fellow writers stood bravely to share the hit placed by an Iranian ruler on Salman Rushdie. And first in the third space fronting Upper Darby (Pennsylvania's) 69th Street Terminal, and later in the kitchen of a government-built homeless shelter, citizens of Delaware County nightly, over the past decade, have provided over 30,000 meals a year, cooked in their own kitchens, to their hungry and homeless neighbors.

The concept of the "third space" suggests that the third sector may not primarily be about organizational structures—nonprofits instead of corporations or governments. Rather, the special contribution of this realm of human activity may rest in a particular combination of spirit and organization.

And it may be that spirit comes first. If a human action is infused with a voluntary spirit, it may take place within any type of organization—be it nonprofit, business, governmental, or family. Such "voluntary action" may characterize the businessperson who chooses to be a volunteer in a community organization or a whistleblower reporting corrupt or illegal behaviors of his boss; such "voluntary action" may characterize the elected official who dedicates herself to the building of a new social contract between citizen and state; such "voluntary action" may even characterize the decision of a mother or father, tempted to leave her or his family in a time of stress, to remain with spouse and children as both a source of support and a role model for the future.

Voluntarism, consisting as it does both of individual and organizational actions, is a force that has been seen as being capable of revitalizing a society. The third space may be where we find it; indeed it may be precisely where we happen to be at any given time.

We will surely need to find ways to deal with a health care industry controlled by for-profit organizations, and an education industry controlled by for-profit modalities and mentalities. And the way may be: Join with us in the third space to explore your aims and programs! Hear what it is that your clients and customers and citizens and neighbors need and expect from you.

What remains when one subtracts the large and essentially nonvoluntary nonprofit bureaucracies from the third sector is still a vast and significant realm: the realm of individual acts in any walk of life or institution, and the special value of religion, arts, social service, and civic organization. Roger Lohmann has called this area "the commons." The rest of this book will focus on this ground and its significance for the human experience—society's third space.

# Part Four

---

*On the Boundary between
Culture and the Third Space*

# 9

# Civil Education: Moving to Define an Ambiguous Tradition

Americans are sometimes said to be the most giving people on earth, both in terms of time and money. But traditions of participation, voluntarism, and philanthropy are under siege in an age of personal and cultural privatism. In a variety of confusing ways, the third sector figures in the "culture wars" of our times. This chapter gives primary focus to the critical role schools may play in the development of patterns of socially active behavior, while ensuing chapters in this section look at the role of religion and community development.

## Educating for a Civil Society

No societal institution faces a larger, or sterner, set of masters than the school. Whether it is a neighborhood elementary school, a district high school, or a state university—educational institutions daily face the often conflicting expectations of students, teachers, parents, tax- and tuition-payers, and just plain concerned citizens.

Schools are expected to make students literate, to equip them for a changing world of work, and to instill in them a set of values on which their elders fail to agree. And they are expected to provide these outcomes equitably, without regard to differences in class, gender, ethnicity, religion, or race. To paraphrase the old Gilbert and Sullivan line, the educator's lot is often not "a happy one."

In recent years, rediscovering a tradition first established by John Dewey and his followers, educational institutions have begun to take on the task of educating for democracy and civil society. At the collegiate level, this has meant the development of course and program work in such fields as "service learning" and "experiential education." At the secondary level, this has meant infusing the curriculum with opportunities to engage in a variety of community service projects and activities.

The educational initiatives involved in the service learning movement are intended, their proponents assert, to be an important part of a transforming society toward greater democracy, justice, and economic opportunity. These efforts are seen to provide a realistic starting point for students to see the world as it is, and to begin to explore the many other steps needed to address the many challenges the future will present.

Proponents of service learning see the school as able to infuse many skills and career learnings into the processes of what the Partnering Initiative on Education and Civil Society calls "civil education." The school, a basic institution for the transmission of a society's culture to the rising generation, is assigned the critical responsibility of playing a primary role in assuring democratic character in society.

## Re-engaging Young People

A comprehensive white paper published by the Association for Supervision and Curriculum Development (ASCD), a principal organization in the Partnering Initiative on Education and Civil Society, presents the case for "civil education" with both clarity and intelligence. The paper begins by noting the widely observed decline in democratic participation in the United States. The research of Robert Putnam is cited to demonstrate the decline of many forms of public participation, "from attending public meetings to working for a political party" (Robelen, 1998: 2). National tests also show declining levels of student understanding of how governmental institutions work. Keeping current with political affairs is a value now held by only 27 percent of college freshmen, compared with a high of 58 percent on this measure in 1966.

The ASCD paper notes that schools are not the only societal institutions responsible for building democracy, but a powerful quotation from John Dewey is presented to buttress the argument that schools have an important role to play:

> We have forgotten that [democracy] has to be enacted anew in every generation, in every year, in every day, in the living relations of person to person, in all social forms and institutions. Forgetting this . . . we have been negligent in creating a school that should be the constant nurse of democracy.[1]

The ASCD paper identifies a range of "competencies for democratic life" that are necessary for active citizenship. Among these traits are listed "respect, empathy, honesty, integrity, tolerance, trust, belief in justice, responsibility for self and others, cooperation, and patriotism" (p. 2). These competencies, required for effective democratic participation, are complemented by a set of skills in group participation that underlie the approach commonly known as "character education." ASCD deputy executive director Diane Berreth[2] observes that character education extends beyond the curriculum: "It's not just addressed in the classroom, but on the playground, on the bus, in athletic programs, in discipline programs." The ASCD paper observes that character education "can include teaching conflict resolution, practicing cooperative learning, teaching values through the curriculum, and creating a democratic classroom" (p. 3).

Building service into the curriculum is a challenge that can be met in many different ways. Increasingly, it is also a challenge schools are seeking directly to meet. Of a national sample of 8,000 students interviewed in April 1997 by the National Center for Education Statistics, over half reported that they had participated in community service during the past year. And of those who reported having served, half reported that their service had been integrated into the curriculum (Robelen, 1998: 4).

The ASCD paper finds a variety of state-level policies have been adopted in the area of service learning, character education, and citizenship education: "Maryland requires community service to graduate, 10 states allow school districts to award credit for student community service activities, and a handful of others encourage such service. Many states also have either enacted or are considering legislation that mandates or encourages character and citizen education" (p. 6).

This trend is growing. In June 1998 Philadelphia's school board voted to require all 213,000 of its public school students to do community-service work. In Philadelphia, beginning in 2002, students will not be able to graduate from the fourth, eighth, or twelfth grade without having completed a community-service project. In Chicago, high school sophomores are required to serve for 40 hours, and if they fail to meet that requirement they are not allowed to graduate. In Louisville, high school students are required to perform 30 hours of service as a condition of graduation.

The ASCD report reviews the positions of critics of service learning from both right and left. On the right, Chester Finn and Gregg Vanourek see such programs as distracting from essential school programs: "Our schools, which have been botching their core mission of transmitting basic skills and essential knowledge, are now diverting time, energy, and money to non-academic matters."[3] On the left, Rutgers University political theorist Benjamin Barber, an advocate of mandatory citizenship education on the college level, opines that such programs are only justified when they use a "language of citizenship" rather than a "language of charity."[4]

From the pragmatic center, Gordon Raley, executive of the National Assembly of National Voluntary Health & Social Welfare Organizations, worries that, "When these things are not planned out well, we may dissuade young people from volunteering as much as we encourage them." Raley adds: "Maybe we should rethink making it mandatory. Given everything we know about teenagers, we should probably forbid them to volunteer and they would be out there in droves" (quoted in Dundjerski and Gray, 1998: 32).

Both democracy and community should be built into whatever service-learning curricula are developed, the ASCD report urges, following the lead of the University of Pennsylvania's Center for Community Partnerships under the leadership of Ira Harkavy. The Center worked closely with the Philadelphia school district to develop a set of "community schools" in Penn's neighboring West Philadelphia area. Harkavy, who began this effort in the late 1980s in colleagueship with two fellow historians, Lee Benson and Sheldon Hackney (who also happened to be president of the university), now lists over seventy academically based community service courses in the various departments and colleges at Penn, many offered by its most prestigious and best-known faculty.[5] Penn's list of separate university projects serving its surrounding community numbers in the hundreds.[6]

## Developing Civil Education

Several national efforts are underway to clarify and advance the goals of civil education. The National Commission on Civic Renewal, a bipartisan group chaired by former Senator Sam Nunn (D-GA) and former education secretary William Bennett, reported in 1998 four recommendations in this area to schools:[7]

- Schools should reorganize their internal life to reinforce basic civic virtues such as personal and social responsibility, by giving students far more responsibility for maintaining cleanliness and discipline in classrooms and on school grounds.

- Every school should offer serious, age-appropriate instruction in civic knowledge and skills, focused on founding documents—the Declaration of Independence, the Federalist Papers, the Constitution, and other significant writings from the rich quarry of our political and social history.

- Whenever possible, civic education should include the regular reading and discussion of newspapers, because the habit of newspaper reading has been shown to enhance civic information and participation throughout adult life.

- Every state should require all students to demonstrate mastery of basic civic information and concepts as a condition of high school graduation.

One hears echoes of parental voices in these injunctions—"Clean up your room; read your newspaper"—and also notes that the Commission failed to come to an "agreement on mandatory community service for high school students." The Commission does, however, report being "impressed with the ways in which well-designed community work carefully linked to classroom reflection can enhance the civic education of students" and with "the positive civic consequences of programs that bring students into direct contact with government at every level," and urge "more schools to forge ties with them." The Commission calls for the establishment of a Civic Education Project to advance its recommendations.

Two years previous to the Commission's report, a group of 60 educational and community-based organizations formed a coalition which goes unmentioned by the National Commission on Civic Renewal. This coalition, the Partnering Initiative on Education and Civil Society, was organized by policy analyst Jeremy Rifkin and Corporation for National Service deputy director Susan Stroud. It seeks to define the basis for civil education in contemporary life. The Partnering Initiative's "Declaration on Education and Civil Society" begins with the following Preamble:

> The shift from the Industrial Age to the Information Age is transforming our civilization. Vast economic, social, and political changes are already underway. As we enter the Information Age, we face the very real challenge of redirecting the course of American education so that young people will be ready to wrestle with the demands of the new global economy, the new realities facing government, and the new challenges of a multicultural world. We need to bear in mind that the strength of the market and the effectiveness of our democratic form of government have always depended, in the final analysis, on the principles of democracy and community that have served as the cornerstones of our civil society for more than 200 years. The civil society is the wellspring of our spirit as a people. Preparing the next generation for a lifelong commitment to civil society is one of the most important challenges facing educators and communities. Our schools, colleges, universities, and community organizations can play a key role in fostering America's civic values by helping to weave

a seamless web between schools and communities. (Partnering Initiative on Education and Civil Society, 1998: 1)

The Partnering Initiative's "Call to Action" is both more far-reaching than that of the National Commission, and also much more detailed. This set of recommendations also focuses on the third sector as the locus of civil education, rather than government, as with the Commission:

- Expand opportunities for young people and adults to become more involved in meaningful service with neighborhood and community organizations by making service learning an integral part of the educational experience.

- Encourage students to explore the twin issues of character development and responsible participation in the civil society by integrating service learning, character education, and citizenship education opportunities into the classroom.

- Weave the historical legacy and values of the civil society into a broad range of curriculums and community programs.

- Extend the values of democracy and community to the classroom by engaging students in the design of their own learning experiences.

- Elicit more direct involvement between community organizations, civic associations, businesses, local schools, colleges, and universities.

- Ensure that faculty, students, staff, families, and community organizations have a genuine voice in school, college, and university-level policy making.

- Make every effort to ensure that the human, financial, and community resources needed to accomplish these goals are made available.

The Partnering Initiative presents an agenda that is community-focused, applicable from kindergarten through college, student-empowering, and resource-aware. The National Commission, on the other hand, advocates a program that is more heavily government-focused, pre-collegiate, adult-centered, and resource-unaware. Which of these two visions will dominate in the years ahead will depend on the quality of public dialogue these two entities, and their various supporters in the world of philanthropy and public affairs, will be able to generate. But the differences in their approaches are substantial, and the outcome of their contest will be important for the future of civil education.

## Shaping Civil Education Programs

As teachers, school administrators and leaders, parents, and students confront the future of civil education, the issues that divide the Commission and the Partnering Initiative will have to be resolved, along with others that arise almost daily in such programs. Civil education has swept into the arena of educational reform as a social movement capable of transforming both school and society. Such hopes have been dashed before in the annals of both education and social policy.

The sense that schools and colleges should make a central place in their curricula for service learning arrived late in the 1980s after several "me-decades" in which student interest rarely extended beyond fantasies of personal wealth and success. Like so many "megatrends," this one emerged almost simultaneously in a number of states. In 1985, a group of 12 university presidents founded Campus Compact, an organization that now boasts 225 member colleges and universities. A second federated organization, the Campus Outreach Opportunity League (COOL), drew campus leaders from 206 different colleges and universities to its 1989 conference.

The sense that something was amiss in education, and that service learning might address that problem, permeated the celebrated 1988 commencement address by Rutgers University president Edward J. Bloustein:

> [T]he naked pursuit of individual interest and material gain is a hopelessly inadequate source of personal satisfaction. It is also a thorough distortion of the ideal of civic virtue in the democratic state. Moreover, it is a dangerously obtuse response to the global condition in which we find ourselves. . . .
>
> Giving is no less part of the good life than receiving. . . . Higher education already makes important contributions to teaching the virtues of sharing and caring, but I propose that we do more. I propose that we look at community service as a necessary component of the learning experiences which constitute a liberal education. . . . I urge that we consider . . . making service to others a requirement of the undergraduate liberal arts degree.

Bloustein went on to explain that such a requirement might be undertaken "unwillingly" by some portion of the student body, but that it should be seen as a way of meeting a curricular requirement for "social and cultural literacy." He concluded his address with a passionate call for service learning:

> We must rediscover, as a nation and within this university, the satisfactions of caring for others as we would have them care for us; we

must rediscover and teach civic responsibility as a liberalizing art. I believe that, in finding ways to modulate our individualism with altruism, we will thereby foster greater individual gratification, and bring ourselves into greater harmony with an increasingly heterogeneous and tumultuous world.[8]

An illustration of how programs of civil education have grown may be found on the urban Camden campus of Rutgers. In 1988 students in my Urban Studies course, "Communications in Urban Society," learned by seeking to communicate with troubled urban high school students in the neighboring Juvenile Resource Center, as they served as "mentors" to these youths. Within a decade, that program in Camden, now known as Camden ACE (Associates in Citizen Education), was placing several hundred students per year in field placements as part of course work in such varied departments as English, History, Political Science, and Psychology. Typically, students receive training in communications and intergroup skills during the first three weeks of the term, and then provide five or more hours of service in a community organization setting for the remaining eleven weeks of the term. Regular class sessions are held to provide for lectures, discussion, and reflection on the meaning of the service. A final paper builds on a journal that details the students' experiences throughout the term, and relates that experience to course readings and other collegiate learnings.

Building voluntary service into the core of the college curriculum was no easy matter, at Rutgers or anywhere else. Many faculty, students, and administrators remain convinced that the only good learning comes from the classroom, and that community service is only a "frill." Moreover, the personal schedules of many contemporary students overflow with commitments—other courses, part- or even full-time employment, and a dizzying range of family obligations.

Camden ACE was established by the Rutgers Camden Faculty Senate in 1989, predating the university's Civic Education and Community Leadership program. The Senate unanimously affirmed the university's obligation to provide courses involving experiential community education available to students, while assuring that such participation would remain a voluntary choice for each student.

Camden ACE provided students the opportunity to serve the urban community surrounding the campus while earning academic credit. Courses offered in a number of departments connect community placements to academic problems; reflection is provided in regular class meetings; and ample time is provided to assure effective placement activities. Working with community partners, Camden ACE allows experienced students to participate in the leadership and management of the program as well as to assist in applying their education to the resolution of pressing social problems.

Camden ACE developed an infrastructure that served both the students on campus who perform community service and its community partners. Students were selected as "Leadership Fellows" and played leading roles on campus in program planning and development. Simultaneously, the Rutgers-Camden Department of Urban Studies and Community Development developed the Rutgers Urban Literacy Partnership. Beginning in 1991, approximately 60 Rutgers students yearly enrolled in courses in which they teach less-than-literate Camden residents how to read, and work as mentors to juveniles in alternative high schools.

Camden ACE, like hundreds of similar programs on other campuses of American colleges and universities, faces a number of dilemmas it has yet to fully resolve. Among these challenges are:

- What role can be found for advocacy activities in such programs, or is their community work to be limited to service functions alone? In a public school or university, the First Amendment proscribes classroom activities that directly advance religious institutions, as well as campaigning for political candidates. But experience shows that direct service is often the preferred activity of students as well as the sort of work most conventionally developed for them by organizations.

- How should the pursuit of productive service be weighed against the political pressures that weigh on schools and colleges? The sensitivity of administrators to the potential of political pressure can be extreme. Some years back a Rutgers dean vetoed a proposal I had brought her to house a "homelessness advocate" on campus, on grounds that the university might suffer political embarrassment from the leadership of the same suburban communities from which a majority of the campus's students were drawn.

- Should the program of student service be voluntary or mandatory for students? Rutgers colleague Benjamin Barber, the distinguished political theorist, has been a strong advocate for a degree requirement of participation in a citizenship and service-learning placement. I have held to the position that such participation should be voluntary, arguing both on philosophical and pragmatic grounds.

Philosophically, I have argued that not only is it an oxymoron to develop service programs along principles of "mandatory voluntarism," but that it is important to recognize that democracy itself offers its citizens the right not to participate. Barber, to the contrary, observes that educators appropriately take on an adult role in establishing curricular requirements, and that requiring students to be literate in civic education is quite similar to requiring them to be accomplished in English or Math. (When I begin to find attractions in that argument, my administrative prudence takes over, and I begin to contemplate the difficulties involved in providing civic education, and the associated field placements, for every last business and medical technology student on campus.)

## Conclusion: Learning about Citizenship by Learning to Be a Citizen

Former President George Bush once spoke of public service as a valuable way to commit young people to a "civic contract." The citizen education responsibilities of schools and colleges involve, in considerable part, socializing young people into their adult roles as active citizens and participants in society. Contemporary efforts to achieve this goal are central to the building of a new civic and social contract.

Schools in the United States, as we have seen in this chapter, are increasingly moving to include lessons on the ways of civil society into their curricula. Through such involvement, and the reflection on its meaning that follows in the classroom, students may learn to navigate the many social interactions required of an effective citizen, worker, and person in our multi-faceted world.

A recent symposium illustrates the magnitude of the educational challenges that face society in the years ahead.[9] Contributors to the symposium included a teacher, two economists, and a noted policy analyst. The teacher, Stan Karp, noted the terrible toll inequities of class and race exact on his students. The economists, Richard J. Murnane and Frank Levy, observed that college graduates have sustained their role in the economy better than high school graduates over the past decades, and that employers will continue to be selective in hiring for the best-paying positions in the years to come. And the policy analyst, Jeremy Rifkin, stated that the microchip is steadily disemploying people world-wide, creating possibilities for either increasing misery or increasing leisure.

How are students, educators, and citizens to confront this triple challenge of poverty, educational inequality, and technological dislocation? The policy analyst urges that we recognize the increased role of third-sector organizations in a world in which both government and business downsize to the point that voluntary community activity becomes a survival skill rather than a trendy frill. The economists urge that basic skills be inculcated in every high school graduate, confounding the lot of the employer by presenting a larger number of qualified job-seekers for every position made available. And the teacher cautions that schools must be joined by other institutions if necessary changes in politics, economics, and culture are to be achieved.

If the American future requires an active and effective citizen force to defend the rights of all to productive work and decent income, it would seem imperative that citizens learn from school and community how to mobilize the uniquely powerful resources of the third sector. In that way the teacher's interest in equality would be addressed, the economist's skillful students would be enabled to find good jobs, and the policy analyst's faith in the power of citizen action in the third sector would be redeemed.

The contemporary movement toward citizenship and service education puts democracy to the trying test of everyday individual choice and action. The next two chapters of this book examine this process in a variety of civil society's contexts: faith-based organizations, colleges, and residential communities.

# 10

# On the Contemporary Hope
# for Faith and Charity

The rediscovery of the urban church has given rise to a hopeful literature that banks on the commitment of urban ministers and their
remaining congregations to meet the social needs of children and
communities at risk. National commissions have touted such efforts as
uniquely meritorious of philanthropic support, and studies have
emerged identifying the power of faith-based local voluntarism (cf.
Cnaan, 1999). This chapter examines the place of faith-based communities in meeting contemporary social needs.

## The Entry of Faith-Based Nonprofits

Let me begin with a parable, as befits our subject: I was meeting with
a group of colleagues on a panel that had been asked to identify individuals with the greatest power and influence in the nonprofit sector.
All was relatively low-key until I suggested a prominent man of the
cloth, whose face and voice are familiar to most Americans. It might
have been Jesse Jackson or even Minister Farrakhan. "But he's not a
nonprofit manager," I was told. "He's a minister."

I'll let you in on a little-known fact, dear reader. Ministers *are* nonprofit managers, churches *are* nonprofit organizations, and what we
better soon learn to call "faith-based organizations" *are* rapidly being
positioned as heavyweights in America's civil society.

Quaker administrator and scholar Thomas H. Jeavons, in his
study of Christian service organizations (1994), notes that such or-

ganizations are both infused with the values of their respective religious traditions, and partake of the myriad challenges that confront the
development and management of other voluntary organizations. Jeavons identifies ten principal foci that require the consideration of those
who lead and manage such organizations: vocation, witness as well as
service, means as well as ends, servanthood, stewardship, engagement
in ministry, caring, creating and sustaining a Christian organization,
integrity, and leadership.

These foci may be reduced, Jeavons (1994: 223) concludes, to two
basic requirements:

> First, being mindful of Jesus' call to feed the hungry, to aid those in
> need, and to care for the sick, and of His call to be good stewards of
> the resources with which they are entrusted, these organizations
> have to provide needed practical services in accordance with their
> missions and vocations as effectively and efficiently as possible. Sec-
> ond, mindful of another call that echoes through the New Testament,
> the call to share the good news of God's love for the world, these or-
> ganizations need to operate in ways that make the provision of the
> services they offer a living testimony to that love.

To Jeavons, religious organizations "can and should be viewed as
integral parts of the American tradition of philanthropy and voluntary association" (p. 39), and indeed comprise the initial "social space"
from which other forms of voluntary and nonprofit organization later
emerged and flourished (p. 37). "The essence of this argument is that
religious groups—often 'sects and advocates of marginalized faiths'
rebelling against established and state religions—established the right
of voluntary association for themselves, and that right came to be
transferred to other charitable and values-expressive organizations"
(Jeavons, 1994: 37).

Statistics also indicate the centrality of religious organization
among nonprofit organizations: more than half of the charitable giving of Americans goes to support religious organizations. But churches
have been widely ignored by students of American voluntarism, sometimes viewed as present in "the nonprofit sector" only because of some
unexamined coincidence between the First Amendment and the Internal Revenue Service.

Three recent reports on the state of America's third sector counter
that conventional assumption. The American Assembly, the Council
on Civil Society, and the National Commission on Civic Renewal each
observe that the role of faith-based organizations is growing in American life.

The American Assembly report, developed by a group of third-sector leaders who met at Los Angeles's Getty Center in 1998, puts it this way: "The faith-based institutions in the nonprofit sector should be more broadly recognized as key actors in the philanthropic endeavor, particularly in their roles of engaging individuals in giving and volunteering and in creating community at the local level" (American Assembly, 1998: 23).

The National Commission on Civic Renewal, a group co-chaired by former Senator Sam Nunn (D-GA) and former education secretary William Bennett, quoted George Washington's Farewell Address: "Of all the dispositions and habits which lead to political prosperity, religion and morality are essential supports. . . . And let us with caution indulge the supposition that morality can be maintained without religion."[1]

But it is the Council on Civil Society that most fully supports an extended role for faith-based organizations.[2] A creature of the Institute for American Values, the Council was composed of 24 national leaders, including a number of prominent public intellectuals. The Council's central interest lies in the elaboration of what it calls "transmittable moral truth." Such truth is said by the Council "to exist" and to be "accessible to people of reason and good will" (Council on Civil Society, 1998: 12–13).

The Council on Civil Society gives hints as to where moral truth is to be found, but it does not fully elaborate on its contents. We are told that moral truth does not involve "expressive individualism," and that it does involve an understanding of "humans as intrinsically social beings" who live in communities and "only through such connectedness . . . approach authentic self-realization" (pp. 13–16). Further, moral truth may appropriately be interjected into a "moral economy"—as markets can appropriately be restrained in their production of morally dubious products of consumption and processes of wants-creation.

The briefest expression of moral truth, we are told, is "inscribed on our coins: 'In God We Trust.'" And "the renewal of a common moral life . . . will not take place unless faith communities and religious institutions play a leading role, since vigorous communities of faith are vital to the discernment and transmission of moral truth" (pp. 12, 21).

Don E. Eberly, a member of the Council, elaborates upon this "leading role" religion is seen to play in conceptions of "civil republicanism." He stakes out Alexis de Tocqueville as his intellectual predecessor in identifying religion as "the first political institution" (1998: 192). This position emerges because religion and freedom march "hand in hand," religion shaping and "nourishing the habits of restraint, industry and tranquillity that were thought necessary to maintain republican institutions. In other words, religion was a welcome source of influence in the shaping of civil society and the broader culture" (Eberly, 1998: 193).

Eberly's recommendation is two-fold: first, to provide for "wider freedoms of expression and participation for religious citizens," and second, to acknowledge "that religious belief has played a constructive and pivotal role in shaping our culture and union, and that it still exists as a socially renewing power in spite of attempts to partition it off from society and politics. The first recommendation gives rise to thorny issues of separation of church from state; the second, more important to Eberly, "concerns whether to welcome a far broader role for religion in the noncoercive realm of civil society, premised upon an acknowledgement of pluralism" (1998: 193).

The Council on Civil Society devotes five of its 41 recommendations to religion, another indication of the priority it gives to "faith-based institutions." Churches should, the Council advises: 1) recognize their crucial role in society; 2) strengthen families; 3) call on business to restrain materialism; 4) work actively in anti-poverty programs; and 5) compete equally with other nonprofits for governmental contracts.

That faith-based nonprofit organizations have truly arrived was signaled by *Newsweek* in its June 1, 1998, cover story, "God vs. Gangs." "What's the Hottest Idea in Crime Fighting?" asked the cover. The answer: "The Power of Religion." Cover-person Reverend Eugene Rivers is depicted dispensing his toughlove to gang drug-dealers from his base as director of the Ella J. Baker House in Dorchester, Massachusetts. Rivers aims his ministry at the reduction of violent crime in our nation's most dismal ghettos, and he seems to be succeeding. Police, teachers, social workers—all play roles in this redirection of religion to replace the tutelage and concern of absent fathers and disaffected neighborhoods. This part of the nonprofit sector never sleeps; it stays with its charges "24, 7, and 365."

Political scientist John DiIulio has become the principal source of research and public intellectual support for the role of faith-based organizations in returning order to the lives of poor inner-city children. DiIulio puts his conclusions directly:

> Based on four years of research and direct observation, I believe a necessary condition [for improving the prospects of poor inner-city children] is the support of churches, synagogues, mosques, and other faith-based grassroots organizations that perform youth and community outreach in the inner city.
>
> Supporting inner-city churches means helping sustain, at the street level, clergy and volunteers whose faith in children is manifest not

just in compassionate words but in daily works. It means identifying and "lifting up" the unsung people of urban faith communities who monitor, mentor, and minister to the basic needs of the poorest of the urban poor. It means assisting those who reach out every day—in acts of faith, hope, and charity—to innocent toddlers, illiterate adolescents, pregnant teenagers, and young males on probation. . . . It means standing with people motivated by religious sentiment, who invoke spiritual language but work mainly on behalf of children who are not "churched." These religious witnesses do not make profession of faith, conversion, or church membership a condition for entering their buildings and receiving their services—or for receiving their sometimes tough but unconditional love. (1998: 7)

DiIulio recognizes that "religious institutions alone cannot cure America's social and civic ills," but affirms "growing empirical evidence" that faith-based initiatives can "transform lives, revitalize neighborhoods, reduce poverty, prevent violence, improve education, and yield other morally desirable social consequences" (1998: 7). Particularly effective in achieving these desired outcomes are smaller urban ministries, or "blessing stations" that address the needs for "spirituality plus" by means of a proximate and available presence in the inner city. Both liberals and conservatives, the *Newsweek* article observed, "are beginning to form an unlikely alliance founded on the idea that the only way to rescue kids from the seductions of the drugs and gang cultures is with the only institution with the spiritual message and the physical presence" to reclaim poor inner-city children: "the church."

Adds DiIulio: "Say amen" (1998: 7).

## Assessing the Faith-Based Movement as Policy and Practice

Academic critics of Eberly and DiIulio have become increasingly respectful over the years. Formerly, they would preface their observations by noting the conservative proclivities of the author in question, and then proceed to identify a particularly egregious example of the bias of that position. But, increasingly, both Eberly and DiIulio have moved to buttress their views with arguments from liberal as well as conservative positions. And, simultaneously, the intellectual respect their work has commanded has meant a further moderation in the tone of their critics.

At a recent three-day conference at the University of Pennsylvania that focused centrally on DiIulio's work, for example, principal critics spoke respectfully in both tone and content. Ethnographer Elijah Anderson, author of the sociological classic, *Streetwise*, asserted that the structural economic factors debilitating poverty communities are so severe that policy advances, educational services, and increased employment are needed just as much as is an increase in religious presence. Poverty specialist Kathryn Edin, recalling the participant observation she performed with anthropologist Laura Lein[3] in two faith-based nonprofits that received federal funds, traced the contradictions in service provision faced by the faith-based group as it sought to conform to the guidelines of its governmental grants. And historian Thomas Sugrue, author of the prize-winning study of Detroit, *The Origins of the Urban Crisis*, warned that the current movement seems to focus excessively on the provision of social control and social services, when the provision of social change is sorely required.

Responding to each of these commentators, DiIulio (1988) acknowledged the validity of their major points, indicating that many institutions will have to work successfully, partnerships will need to be fine-tuned, and both "service and justice" will need to be provided and advanced.

From a policy perspective, DiIulio himself supports implementation of the "so-called Charitable Choice provision," first passed by the House of Representatives in 1996 as part of the welfare reform legislation. He explains that this "provision encourages states to use faith-based organizations to provide services for the poor. It allows religious organizations to receive contracts, vouchers, and other government funding on the same basis as other providers while protecting the religious integrity and character of those organizations." As long as certain rules are followed—1) the faith-based service is not the only one in town; 2) the service does not discriminate on the basis of church membership; 3) programs are presented with "secular goals"—DiIulio urged that governmental funds be provided directly to faith-based organizations and not just to their secular service arms.

Pepperdine University political scientist Stephen Monsma seeks to buttress the case for charitable choice by noting that the strings that often are attached to federal funds limit the authority and function of religious organizations. He argues for an approach he calls "positive neutrality," which rests on five major principles (1996: 174–77):

1. protection of the "religious autonomy of religiously based nonprofit organizations"

2. rootedness in "both the free exercise and no-establishment clauses" of the Constitution

3. government "neutrality in regard to all religious beliefs—and between belief and nonbelief"

4. consistency with "history and existing practices"

5. protection of a "just order" and "society as a whole"

The doctrine of positive neutrality, as Monsma develops it, seeks to protect the right of the religious nonprofit to receive governmental funds while it simultaneously follows its own autonomous urges to limit employment to its own members and to mix religious and secular services.[4] Only three forms of conditions could be attached to federal grants under this doctrine: 1) money could not be provided to "activities and programs that are primarily other-worldly in nature," 2) "funds could not go to nonprofits that teach hatred or intolerance or in other ways work to destroy the social fabric fundamental to civil society," and 3) "recipient organizations must be willing to submit to certain limited reviews and licensing standards" (Monsma, 1996: 180–82). These conditions should apply to all governmental grants, Monsma adds, whether given to religious or secular organizations.

A more immediate argument in support of "charitable choice" rests on the failure of the family, school, economy, and government in the low-income minority areas of American cities. This argument claims that the partnership approach between these institutions has failed miserably in serving the needs of ghetto residents, and that, therefore, First Amendment concerns should be set aside to allow for a vigorous religious response to social crisis. Support for "charitable choice" is urged by two of the three reports earlier mentioned (the Council on Civil Society and the National Commission on Civic Renewal) and congressional leaders like Senator John Ashforth (R-MO), who regularly introduces such legislation.

Some who oppose charitable choice support a position more consistent with Monsma's fourth principle: that there be consistency with "history and existing practices." Monsma (1996: 110) asserts the case for this approach:

> As the previous chapter's survey results made clear, many religiously based organizations from almost all religious traditions receive substantial portions of their budgets from governmental sources. And they do so with few perceived problems and limitations. The system—jerry-built and haphazard though it may be—works. Why then rock the boat and risk capsizing a *modus operandi* the American Civil Liberties Union and Americans United for the Separation of Church and State, on the one hand, and the United States Catholic Conference and the National Association of Evangelicals, on the other, find satisfactory?

This traditional approach could involve enhancing philanthropic giving to effective activist ghetto religious groups while sustaining the constitutional separation between church and state, especially at the level of K–12 education. Americans United for Separation of Church and State, a national advocacy organization, urges opposition to "charitable choice" legislation, not only because of its violation of the church-state boundary, but also because it would permit religious institutions receiving governmental funds to discriminate in their employment practices and to violate the religious liberty of program beneficiaries. As Monsma notes, Americans United are joined in this position by a wide range of other nonprofits, including the Baptist Joint Committee on Public Affairs, the Friends Committee on National Legislation, the Jewish Council for Public Affairs, the General Conference of Seventh-Day Adventists, and the National Education Association.

There is a third way to address the relationship between government and faith-based organizations, and it is even more tough-minded than maintaining the existing system of conditional funding. This path urges that really hard questions be asked of faith-based practitioners before they receive funding from any source. Primary among these concerns is the one raised by an obscure European philosopher named Marx 150 years ago: to what degree does religious faith serve to distract individuals and communities from what is really important in day-to-day existence? (In other words, does formal religion actually serve as an "opiate of the people"?) The late social philosopher Zellig Harris put the matter directly in *The Transformation of Capitalist Society:* "People's moralizing and feeling of moral justification can serve to strengthen their disposition to act; but this may simply be a self-justification for controlling others" (p. 55).

The complex and intriguing policy debates surrounding charitable choice raise again the policy issues of advocacy, finance, and partnering dynamics that earlier chapters have seen characterizing the contemporary boundary wars between government and nonprofit organizations. While the religion-led civil rights movement of the 1960s focused on the advocacy of social change rather than the provision of social service, the pragmatic ministers of the 1990s choose to put their greatest emphasis on directly serving the needs they perceive as those of ghetto youths. While the conservatives of the past sought to reduce governmental funding of social programs, new conservatives like Monsma and DiIulio seek to direct increased governmental funding to faith-based organizations. And while such governmental funding has increasingly been won by faith-based service organizations, conservatives now seek to untie many of the strings formerly attached to such grants—creating the possibility for such funding to support programs that combine sacred and secular, and are administered by staff members hired in part on the basis of their ties of faith.

In a curious way, the debates over charitable choice mirror the controversy that surrounded the Istook Amendments of the mid-1990s. Istook, his critics asserted, sought to defund progressive nonprofits by denying funding to organizations that spent any of their non-governmental funding on advocacy and lobbying. Charitable choice supporters, on the other hand, appear set on expanding funding to faith-based nonprofits, even while liberals contend that these organizations should be denied support if they hire and pay staff on their own criteria, even if paid entirely from their own resources. Both conservatives, in the Istook case, and liberals, in the charitable choice instance, seek to remove funding from organizations which show themselves to be unwilling to conform to what are presented as larger principles of acceptable partnership.

However these debates are resolved, and whatever the ranges of autonomy that eventually are provided to nonprofit recipients of public funds, the question "Who advocates change?" will remain. It is that question that the final section of this chapter turns to address.

## Who Advocates Change? Who Speaks for Justice?

It sometimes appears that there is an inexorable movement throughout the third sector from advocacy to service. It's the same old story, an article in a recent issue of the *Philadelphia Inquirer* tells us.[5] A voluntary organization well known for its direct action finds itself under strong pressures to focus on service provision. Membership that numbered millions 70 years ago has shrunk to a few thousand nationally today. But social capital still remains to be built, so "They deliver food baskets to the poor, protest toxic waste dumps, clear litter from highways and have helped a little old lady out of a jam." Echoing, though somewhat weakly, Independent Sector's call for all citizens to volunteer five hours a week, the group urges its members to "take an hour a week and spend it with an elderly person."

What bastion of the third sector is this? Why, none other than The Pennsylvania American Knights of the Ku Klux Klan. What next, one is tempted to ask. Thanksgiving turkeys, wrapped in a big white bow?

Nowhere has the movement from advocacy to service been more pronounced than in the third-sector circles that have moved from anti-poverty action to the provision of food to those in need. In a powerful and well-documented book, sociologist Janet Poppendieck describes the process by which the provision of food to the "hungry" has become a major preoccupation of many volunteers and voluntary agencies. Dealing with the realities of the human suffering occasioned by cuts in federal and state welfare programs, these voluntary programs have grown dramatically in an effort to meet the most dramatic human needs uncovered by new welfare practices.

The problem with this approach is, as one provider of emergency food observes to Poppendieck, that "The math just doesn't work." The Food Stamp program was reduced by $4 billion per year as of 1996, but the value of all of the food that passed through the food banks of Second Harvest amounts to $1 billion a year. Poppendieck (1998: 298) concludes that "No one but a fool would imagine that the charitable food network, already stretched thin, will be able to miraculously stretch again to cover this abyss, and the leaders of the emergency food movement have been saying so, loud and clear."

To sociologist Poppendieck, efforts to replace lost programs of food and income support by voluntary provision inevitably suffer from "seven deadly 'in's'": insufficiency, inappropriateness, nutritional inadequacy, instability, inaccessibility, inefficiency, and indignity. Ultimately, despite "the famous passage from First Corinthians rendered as 'And now abideth faith, hope, charity, these three; but the greatest of these is charity'," Poppendieck (pp. 230–31) quotes anthropologist Mary Douglas: "Though we laud charity as a Christian virtue, we know that it wounds."

Poppendieck (1998: 268–74) documents the pressure that voluntary organizations find applied to their workings to focus attention on the provision of service rather than the exercise of advocacy. Board members are often conservatives unwilling to criticize the neo-conservative powers of the age; constraints of time and energy militate against performing advocacy if it detracts from feeding those in need; donors often prefer to see the problem in "human" rather than "structural" terms; and volunteers "are often less enthusiastic about advocacy than about direct service." These pressures give rise to a challenging paradox: the provision of service to those in need of food attracts resources, but the ultimate mission of the agency is to render that service unnecessary. As anyone knows who has served a meal to a hungry, and grateful, person, it is tempting, on departing from the mission, to catch oneself saying, "I hope to see you next time." But, of course, the aim of the activity is not to see the person next time, to hope that next time they will not need the act of charity.

The cruelest paradox involved in giving food to those in need is that the very act of charity contributes to the development of a larger system—which Poppendieck (pp. 293–94) calls the "emergency food system":

> The United States Department of Agriculture uses it to reduce the accumulation of embarrassing agricultural surpluses. Business uses it to dispose of nonstandard or unwanted product, to protect employee morale and avoid dump fees, and, of course, to accrue tax savings. Celebrities use it for exposure. Universities and hospitals, as well as caterers and restaurants, use it to absorb leftovers. Private schools use it to teach ethics, and public schools use it to instill a sense of civic responsibility. Churches use it to express their concern for the least of their brethren, and synagogues use it to be faithful to the tradition of including the poor at the table. . . .

And so on for courts, environmentalists, penal institutions, youth-serving agencies, and ordinary individuals. Comments Poppendieck, with an irony that may grate a bit harshly (p. 294): "If we didn't have hunger, we'd have to invent it."

One might be tempted to call this anti-hunger machine of society a "post-ideological feeding complex." Indeed, only four of 71 food banks surveyed in one study allocated as much as 2 percent of their budget to lobbying (Bread for the World Institute, cited in Poppendieck, 1998: 271). As Elizabeth Boris has discovered in her research, which covers activities of the entire range of tax-exempt organizations, advocacy plays a minor role in the organizational lives of the third sector:

- Only 5.5% of all nonprofit organizations are categorized as "advocacy" related in their mission and program.

- These organizations tend to be among the smaller, rather than the larger, organizations within the nonprofit sector.

- Among all charitable and educational organizations, less than one one-thousandth (0.1 percent) of all expenses are directed toward lobbying.

The nonprofit choir, Boris's research dramatically demonstrates, sings barely in a whisper when it comes to the advocacy of social or legislative change. No wonder that Poppendieck, in her conclusion, urges that the food banks and feeding stations of America enlist themselves in a movement to eradicate poverty, redirecting their structure and program in a process to "transform themselves from charitable programs to cooperative endeavors," following Harry Boyte's analysis of "free spaces" described above (Chapter 8). "In my most optimistic scenarios," she concludes (1998: 317), "I envision turning our kitchens and pantries into free spaces, places where people can meet and interact across the gulf of social class and the divisions of race and ethnicity, not as givers and receivers in ways that widen the gulf, but as neighbors and fellow citizens in ways that strengthen social bonds." This vision of the third space as places in which the full range of human needs can be advanced is one that ultimately must address the resources we claim by means of work and ownership, topics that form the focus of the following chapter.

# 11

# Social Entrepreneurship and the End of Work

A highly unsettling aspect of the modern political economy involves the withdrawal by both government and business from the roles they achieved a generation ago as near-universal employers and widespread providers of income. How will we learn to cope with a world in which it appears that fewer and fewer people will enjoy the rights and privileges of steady well-paid employment? These and other problematic issues are explored in this chapter.

The future of work has been addressed in an important book by economic analyst Jeremy Rifkin. Entitled *The End of Work: The Decline of the Global Labor Force and the Dawn of the Post-Market Era* (1995), most of the book is about work, and why it has become so hard to find in recent years. Rifkin documents the impact of the new technology revolution brought by automation and microchip-based information processing. This revolution offers a choice between liberation from long work hours, on the one hand, and an increasing social division between the over- and the underemployed, on the other.

Rifkin believes that we are in the process of making the wrong choice, and that future generations will be faced with dwindling prospects for steady employment of any sort. While fortunes are being made by those who own the patents on technological innovations, most members of the middle classes are on their way to dwindling incomes, threats to whatever jobs they are able to secure, and an inadequate financial base to assure a comfortable retirement.

To achieve the goal of sustaining employment in a society facing the end of work, Rifkin (1995: 256–67) proposes that employers, guided by policy makers, move to reduce the conventional work week to as low as 30 hours, earning in the process tax forgiveness and returning to employees a fuller share of the productivity gains involved in the technological revolution of our times. In his scheme, the third sector takes on a significant role as a provider of valued work.

That these issues already weigh heavily on the minds of the citizens of the modern state is readily apparent, as was dramatically brought to the fore by the New Hampshire primary campaign of Republican presidential candidate Patrick Buchanan in 1996. In Rifkin's view, business corporations, which form the mainstay of the modern economy, are beating a hasty retreat from their accustomed role of providing for mass employment. The increasing use of part-time positions, contract hires, temporaries, and outsourced work make this apparent. Rifkin argues that only the most adept 20 percent in society can expect anything resembling full employment in the years ahead, many retained under the terms of what has been called "dejobbed vendor-mindedness."

While the corporation withdraws from its previous commitment to employ, so does its first-sector counterpart, government. The *de facto* freeze on taxation at every level of the federal system assures the steady reduction of governmental payrolls, both for employees and beneficiaries of welfare, healthcare, and retirement programs.

At the same time, the third and the fourth (family, kin, community) sectors, themselves hardly independent of business and governmental support, are also dealt reeling blows. Family disorganization rises with underemployment, and charitable donations of time and money are threatened while the needs claimed by clients of social agencies rise.

Meanwhile the chorus of society's leadership voices continues to sing the same increasingly discordant tune: education is the answer—just become computer literate and prepare yourself for many job changes! As the rate of college graduation in the United States approaches the 40 percent rate, however, the number of good jobs provided by all employers, public and private, decreases. Employment increasingly comes to resemble a game of musical chairs, albeit with fewer seats placed into play with every passing year.

This neo-Darwinist perspective, however attractive it may sound to society's rich and powerful, ignores the fundamental law of American capitalism most prominently discovered by Henry Ford: consumers are as important as providers in a mass economy. Ford sustained employment at his factories in part to assure that his workers could also be purchasers of the vehicles they made. Likewise, Aetna Insurance Executive John Filer never ceased to remind his listeners that a society in chaos could not sustain a viable insurance industry.

Survival of the fittest multi-jobbing part-time workers will not feed all, or even most, families in society in the challenging years ahead. In a society like that of the United States, with its high "civil war potential" (as political scientist Austin Ranney once put it), only disaster waits if only the few have wealth, only a minority have adequately compensated work, and the majority competes for survival at or about the minimum wage. Facing such a future, today's leaders in every institution must join to develop ways of extending the range of employment to those seeking to carry the responsibilities of adult citizens.

To achieve the goal of sustaining employment in a society facing the end of work, Rifkin (1995: 256–67) has proposed the development of the third sector as a locus of increased employment. Specifically, he suggests that third-sector organizations augment their employment roles, supported by public and philanthropic policies providing 1) "a social wage for community service" and 2) "shadow wages for voluntary work." A similar note was echoed in statements by both U.S. presidential candidates, Clinton and Dole, in the 1996 campaign.

A variety of third-sector policy initiatives have been proposed to address the end of work. Rifkin has proposed a "social wage for community service,"[1] a tax deduction for volunteering,[2] and a limit to the work week.[3] Both Clinton and Dole suggested that churches hire an additional staffer. New Jersey requires employees to pump gasoline by forbidding self-service gasoline islands, and Gans has proposed similar schemes as well as widespread job-sharing.[4] And Edgar and Jean Cahn have developed a system of "time dollars" by which individuals in a community can bank their volunteer contributions and draw on that account at a later date by benefiting from the volunteer time of others.[5]

## The End of Work Descends: The Case of Cape Breton Island

There is something about an island that focuses the mind on boundaries. Even if a bridge or ferry connects the island to the mainland at a point or two, the distinctiveness of the island's location invites its examination as an entity on its own.

So it is with one of North America's far-flung islands, Cape Breton. Set at the end of a path of Atlantic lands in Canada's Nova Scotia, Cape Breton is a remote, wild, lovely, and underdeveloped region. Approximately 110 miles long and 90 miles wide, the island is connected by a single causeway, built in 1955, to mainland Nova Scotia. Its 1991 population was 161,686, nearly 10,000 below the figure for 1976.

The decline in population has been fueled by the rapid arrival of the end of work on Cape Breton. Gertrude Anne MacIntyre (1995: 18–19) describes the process:

By 1993, the overall unemployment rate for Cape Breton Island was close to 23 percent with only 46,000 Cape Bretoners employed, compared to 67,000 in 1987; 55,000 in 1988; 53,000 in 1989; and 50,000 in 1992.

The high unemployment rate can be attributed to the decline in the resource industries in Cape Breton. . . . Coal mining and steel production, two major industries on the island, have been in decline since the end of World War II. The coal mines employ 3,000 people, while the steel mill employs only 600. The fishing industry in Cape Breton, as in the rest of the Atlantic Provinces, has shrunk, and forestry is threatened by a variety of forces from environmentalism to government restrictions.

Residents of the island have been long accustomed to unfavorable shifts in the job market, and have responded historically with strategies employing both "exit" and "voice" (to use the classic options described by Hirschman). Exit options have been three: move to the "Boston states," head "down the road" to Toronto, or learn to live on welfare benefits. Each exit option has become more problematic with the passage of time, but all were firmly etched into the culture of the island. As one observer put it: "The wolf of economic collapse has been heralded so often here, over the last 75 years, that many people simply assume that the sheep are really in no long term peril" (John E. deRoche, Blair Riley, and Gerald Smith, quoted in MacIntyre, 1995: 21).

Voice options have traditionally involved a militant stance by labor union activists. Cape Breton has been the venue, MacIntyre observes, for "labor disputes that have broken out in riots and demonstrations" throughout the 20th century. As late as 1992, a bankrupt rope company was thwarted in its plans to sell its equipment to an American company. "Local people blockaded the plant and refused to let the new owner remove the machinery. In due course, the provincial government brought the equipment back from the American purchaser for $350,000 more than he paid for it" (MacIntyre, 1995: 14). Despite the occasional victory for direct labor action, jobs have continued to hemorrhage and "new ventures supported by government grants have not created the expected number" of replacement positions (MacIntyre, 1995: 14). Violence and crime have been noted to be on the increase as jobs and population decline.

## Confronting Work's End:
## The Role of the University College

In the mid-1990s a new actor appeared upon the community economic development scene in Cape Breton, forging a number of partnerships between public, private, and voluntary organizations throughout the island. This actor was the local "university college," personified by its vigorous new president, Jacquelyn Thayer Scott. Scott, a Kansan by birth, had built a successful career in Canada first in public relations, and then as director of continuing education at the prestigious University of Toronto. Armed with a mid-life doctorate in nonprofit organization management from the University of Colorado, she was offered the presidency of one of Canada's weakest and most troubled institutions of higher learning in 1993.

The University College of Cape Breton, the institution that called Scott to its presidency, was founded in 1974 in a merger of two existing institutions, the Sydney campus of St. Francis Xavier University and the Nova Scotia Eastern Institute of Technology. It entered a post-secondary environment in Nova Scotia, a province of less than one million persons, already populated by 12 universities and more than 20 community colleges (Scott, 1998). And it brought into the mid-1990s a record of 20 years of underfunding and some dramatic instances of mismanagement—all housed in a remote and windswept campus composed of a collection of businesses a Canadian newsmagazine is said to have once described as possessing "all the charm of an abandoned suburban light industrial mall."

In the Anglo-American educational tradition, a "university college" refers to a small liberal arts college within a much larger university. Scott poured new wine into that bottle, however, and began to speak of her university college as combining the "community needs" tradition of the land-grant university, the "reflective/critical/ethical" tradition of the liberal arts college, and the "applied hands-on" focus of the community college.

Faced with a culture that was accustomed to cycles of protest and acquiescence, Scott sought to convince her faculty and students that the world had changed, and that they would need to change with it. In a speech that details her experiences at UCCB, she wrote:

> Our biggest challenge is the most fundamental: restructuring our view of learning and matching it to both what we know about the natural world (as a result of quantum mechanics and complexity theory, for example) and what we know from recent years of brain research. That is, we must make our learning more modularized, multi-sensory, interactive and problem-focused, whether that occurs in the classroom or via an internet connection. The learning we offer must become more firmly connected to the experiences and expectations of learners and the communities of which they are a part. Old disciplinary and sequential learning boundaries must further collapse if we are to meet learners' needs. And, surely, if we do not, only the most historically established and well-endowed among us will survive intact, and then principally because we are selling a network

of social connections rather than a post-secondary connection. (Scott, 1998: 4–5)

The contemporary university college, Scott explains:

- is community based;

- values multi- and interdisciplinary perspectives;

- seeks to develop students in the role as individuals in community;

- views learning holistically, interweaving concepts and theories with their applications in the workplace, family, and community;

- places special emphasis on the "second iteration of knowledge creation—its application to the solution of human problems."

Scott set about her presidency of UCCB determined to see it provide intellectual guidance, suitable space, and the development of "inter-sectoral learning" toward the long-term goal of achieving a "better fit between public policy and the private market." She located a source of construction funds on a Friday, available by application by the next Monday, and her team worked all weekend with an eager local architect to design a building that would eventually connect the various outlying campus structures while creating a magnificent core structure for the campus. The price tag of the new building eventually came to $18 million, and the cost was fully covered by ensuing grants and subsidies.

Within the space of the new campus, UCCB proceeded to develop a wide range of partnerships with businesses, public agencies, and nonprofit organizations. Among the major partnerships developed between 1993 and 1998 were:

- a memorandum of Understanding with Enterprise Cape Breton Corporation (federal agency for regional economic development), which has facilitated dozens of university-business partnerships;

- a partnership with the Cape Breton County Regional Economic Development Authority, which includes the province's economic development ministry, the regional municipality, and the aforementioned Enterprise Cape Breton Corporation;

- an alliance with the Strait Regional School Board in both training and economic development activities;

- a linkage with secondary schools and national industry sector councils, in training and industry support activities such as automotive repair, environmental technologies, and tourism and hospitality;

- development of a Cultural and Heritage Advisory Group, which meets monthly with cultural industries in the area;

- an intervention with local governments, school boards, and non-profit organizations to declare Cape Breton a "Smart Region" and to negotiate with central governments for program status provided by this designation;

- a series of contracts with "First Nation" Mi'qmaq aboriginal communities to provide special and regular courses and the development of Mi'qmaq Studies as a discipline, culminating in the establishment of a Mi'qmaq Institute;

- a collaborative venture with municipalities, First Nations, and non-profit organizations to facilitate the establishment of the Bras d'Or Watershed Management Commission, to plan for the health and uses of the island's dramatic inland salt-water sea;

- facilitation of a Technology Advisory Group, which monthly draws 150 entrepreneurs, students, government officials and others interested in fostering the development of technology-based industries in Cape Breton.

The originality and power of the collaborative partnerships developed by the Cape Breton social entrepreneurs is striking, particularly to those familiar with the timidity and isolation of the typical institution of higher learning. In the case of the partnership with Enterprise Cape Breton Corporation, for example, when its executive position became vacant, UCCB successfully proposed that the agency's new director be seconded from the UCCB administration. When the governmental minister responsible for making the appointment appeared with the UCCB president to make the announcement, they not only acknowledged a possible conflict of interest, but declared it to be deliberate, since both organizations shared an "overlapping area of mutual goals and objectives" (Scott, 1998: 8).

The Technology Advisory Group meetings are highly energized, and have proven a decisive force in the growth of the multimedia industry sector on Cape Breton Island. Where no such businesses existed before the development of this activity, more than 60 such enterprises had been developed by 1998. Moreover, in several cases when an enterprise relocated from the island, care was taken by the founding entrepreneur to leave behind as many positions as were being removed from the local economy. The opening of a Technology Enterprise Center on the campus, offering space for incubating high-tech businesses and providing them with business and technical support services, further strengthens the linkages between the college, government, and private-sector venture capital resources.

The University College model developed in Cape Breton has been further extended toward the creation of several university-owned and operated companies, whose profits are shielded from taxation by dint of their being solely owned by the UCCB Foundation. Further, applied research activity has been recognized and applied to decisions involving promotion and tenure, and a new multi-disciplinary structure has been adopted in place of conventional academic departments. UCCB has also involved itself in providing direct services to elementary school students, women leaving abusive relationships, seniors seeking to retain an independence in their lives, and far-flung residents of the region seeking to advance their knowledge by means of distance learning.

Recognition and awards are beginning to be received by the UCCB, including the Conference Board of Canada's national award for Excellence in Business-Education Partnerships. And, surely, this contemporary example of enlightened use of the third space in community development may be compared in its vision and impact with such far-sighted institutions as Chicago's Hull House of the 1920s or the more contemporary development of the community school by leaders of the University of Pennsylvania in the 1990s. It is still too early to tell if the work of Jacquelyn Thayer Scott and her colleagues can reverse the end of work in Cape Breton, but it is clear that a massive and imaginative effort is being launched toward that end. A vital and participative third space is, indeed, under construction in that Atlantic province.

## Something Rather Different: Social and Economic Development in a Suburban Town

It is a long way from Cape Breton Island to Swarthmore, Pennsylvania, both socially and geographically. Swarthmore, a pleasant tree-lined suburban town, is situated eleven miles southwest of Philadelphia. Located on land granted in 1681 by William Penn to British Quakers Henry Maddock and James Kennerly, the Borough of Swarthmore is presently home to about 6,000 residents. Swarthmore College, with its 1,300 students, is the town's principal industry, and easy access to center city Philadelphia is provided by a commuter train line and a recently constructed freeway connection. The town grew up around the college (founded in 1864) and the rail line (opened in 1854 and expanded in the early 1880s).

The poet Auden once spent a term as a visiting faculty member at Swarthmore College, and is remembered in town for his reference to the town as "a pleasant place." Swarthmoreans are proud of their town's designation as a "tree city," and its residents live in a wide variety of comfortable homes, condominiums, dormitories, and apartments. Open space is provided in a number of small town parks, and the surrounding trails penetrate the wilderness of the "College woods" along the twisting path of Crum Creek, which winds below the plateau on which the academic buildings are sited.

Swarthmore residents are highly educated, 33 percent having completed some form of graduate study. Incomes are comfortable, though not outlandish, with a median household income of just below $55,000 reported by the 1990 census. Black population in town declined from 8.5 percent in 1930 to 4.2 percent in 1990, despite a dramatic increase in blacks among the student body of the college, which remained all-white until the late 1950s. By 1990 the college counted 150 blacks among its student body, and another 110 African Americans were resident in the non-college areas of the town. The historically black area of town, a few blocks of modest homes on Bowdoin and surrounding avenues, had become largely integrated by the late 1990s.

The most contentious issues in town involve schools. Swarthmore's own high school was closed in the early 1970s, in a school merger with the larger Wallingford district on the west side of Crum Creek. Public school students continue to attend schools in town through the fifth grade.

Taxes and politics give rise to occasional differences, but at lower levels of intensity than questions of educational home rule. A taxpayers' organization sporadically expresses its concerns, and political patterns have shifted from typically Republican to usually Democratic over the years. But for all practical purposes, the two parties are indistinguishable in their positions on local issues, and the town's mayor is typically elected on a bipartisan ballot.

The high ground in Swarthmore is held by Swarthmore College, and in more than one respect. Not only is the college highly regarded for its intellectual accomplishments and collegiate program, but it also dominates the town physically. Parrish Hall, the college's massive central building, crowns the highest point in town, and tree-lined Magill Walk leads down from Parrish to the picturesque railroad station, now home to the construction business of William Cumby, who also serves as the borough's mayor. On the other side of the railroad tracks, the town's business center angles between the major north-south roadway through town, Chester Road, and the railroad's path toward central Philadelphia. It is a business district without a front door, and its four major block faces can be entered from a variety of residential streets.

In the late 1990s the configuration of the business district of Swarthmore became the focus of intense community interest and concern. A town-gown Strategic Planning Committee was convened by borough

160 GROWING CIVIL SOCIETY

council, and swiftly became the venue for the venting of a set of un-
anticipated citizen suspicions. The committee found itself faced with
a number of intensely interested citizens, eager to speak their mind on
issues of town center development. Letters multiplied in *The Swarthmorean*, the village's widely read community newspaper, and a set of
divisions in opinion began to emerge. A community bulletin board
was provided by town bookseller Patrick Flanigan on the windows of
Booksource, his centrally located enterprise.

Prominent urban developer Christopher Leinberger was invited to
speak to the community by the Strategic Planning Committee in January of 1998. Leinberger, a graduate of the college and a former member
of its Board of Managers, painted an image of a beleaguered village,
faced with the need to change drastically or to run the risk of deterio-
rating, as, he indicated, had recently transpired in nearby Morton,
Ridley, and Landsdowne boroughs. Swarthmore, Leinberger observed, was not located in the "favored quadrant" for metropolitan development, which he observed lay to the northwest of Philadelphia,
and its going commercial rent was viewed as incapable of funding significant renovation.

If Swarthmore were to upgrade its town center, Leinberger advised, it might well consider reforms along the following lines:

- Permit liquor to be served so that top-notch restaurants could be developed. (An historically Quaker town, Swarthmore has been "dry"
since its inception.)

- Provide local accommodations, particularly for families and visitors
to the college. (The town hosts no residential inn, and not even a
bed and breakfast.)

- Double the commercial space of the town center to assure a "critical
mass." (One way of accomplishing this would be by using a strip
of college-owned land facing the present business district.)

- Add parking, possibly in a multi-level structure. (Currently, all
parking in town is street-level, with one small town lot providing
space near the center.)

Leinberger's views were quickly challenged in *The Swarthmorean*
by several town residents, including Ezra Krendel, a retired professor
from the University of Pennsylvania's Wharton School. Krendel characterized Leinberger's preferences as tending toward "upscale shops,
restaurants, a good hotel, coffee houses and the infrastructure for a
night of convivial pub crawling." To support such a district, Krendel
observed, many people bearing money would have to be attracted to
an area that, at present, is decidedly functional rather than upscale.

And these folks would largely come by car. "The resulting traffic in this little town would put our children and older people at an unacceptable risk and would lessen the security of all of us. This grandiose scheme might benefit landowners on either side of Chester Road but could destroy our current business community."

Krendel concluded his letter by noting that he, like other residents of the town, "enjoy the many cultural and recreational amenities made available to us by the college," which he views as "crucial to the quality of life in our town." Nevertheless, he continued, there are "significant" differences between college and town: "If what I heard . . . last week is a serious plan, and the buildup its promulgator got . . . leads me to believe that it is, this is a very significant difference and a threat to the tranquillity if not the existence of Swarthmore as we know it."

Several other letter writers addressed similar themes in the weeks that followed. Several letters addressed the value of the services provided by the variety of current town merchants, from Fred the barber to Mary the launderer. One local professor even put in a good word for neighboring Morton, which for generations has provided Swarthmore students the chance to slake their collegiate thirsts with wholesome, though alcoholic, beverages.

Borough Councilperson Lisa Aaron, chair of the Strategic Planning Committee, pleaded for moderation in the discussion, noting that the next step in the process would be to conduct a market study. Writing to *The Swarthmorean*, Aaron cautioned that "Right now, nothing has happened, nothing has been decided. (And, no, contrary to some rumors floating around, there have been no variances or any other kind of official permission to do anything.) Depending on the results of the market study, the possibilities may be a very large universe indeed. The choices will be ours."

Leinberger, rumored to be a leading candidate to perform the market study, announced that he would not bid on the contract, and the initial peak of community concern began to subside. The Strategic Planning Committee then set about the task of appointing a consultant to lead a rather more expansive community plan, and by late spring, the firm Urban Partners was selected to lead this process. The Strategic Planning Committee was then dissolved, replaced by a committee of 15 citizens appointed by borough council, and identified as the Town Center Task Force. Among the citizens appointed to this task force were several outspoken critics of the original committee, including Ezra Krendel.

The inauguration of the town task force, for which some 45 residents wrote letters offering to serve, gave rise to an initial sustenance of the suspicious participatory energies that characterized the pre-task force days. The planning consultant hired to supervise the process guided the process through a series of initial meetings, and suggested that the convening of a "town meeting" would be a desirable early activity. The town meeting began with the airing of a number of guarded statements, with concerns about increased traffic and the potential location of undesired businesses too close to the homes of residents. But, as the evening proceeded, a tone of greater consensus, laced with good humor, began to emerge. Statements of "not in my back yard" regarding the possible location of an inn, for instance, were followed by the observation of one resident that an inn, if built, should allow for the sale of alcoholic beverages—a controversial contention in a town of Quaker lineage. "Prospective parents visiting Swarthmore College," this townsperson opined, "will need a drink when they learn what their child's education is going to cost them."

Within weeks of its first meeting, the Town Center Task Force found itself no longer at the center of community controversy. Krendel and several other frequent critics found themselves to be part of the establishment, no longer in a position to raise potshots from outside its boundary. The participatory fever returned to normal, and the task force's deliberations, visits to other similar towns, and even its preliminary conclusions found themselves receiving less space, and in more secondary pages, of *The Swarthmorean*. Long-learned lessons of pluralist participation played themselves out as a time of widespread and intense concern became channeled by structures of recognized legitimacy and authority. These structures were not strictly governmental—though the Task Force was appointed by borough council. They occupied precisely the societal space students of civil society have identified as waiting to be created between family, government, and voluntary association. Michael Walzer (1995: 7) identifies the sphere of groups like the Swarthmore Town Center Task Force as "the space of uncoerced human association and also the set of relational networks—formed for the sake of family, faith, interest and ideology—that fills this space." As the new Methodist minister and a psychotherapist took their places as co-chairs of the task force, they were joined by residents of varying occupations, places of residence, ages, genders, races, and religions, including leaders from the college and the business community. Swarthmore showed that it could create, and successfully navigate within its own third space.

## Rich and Poor within Society's Third Space

Still uncertain in its development, in both the Swarthmore and the Cape Breton experiences, was the degree to which even the most civil, participatory, innovative, and best-led processes of third-space development could weigh decisively against the economic forces that continued to reduce employment in Cape Breton, and to limit business income even in a continuingly privileged Swarthmore. Indeed, some of Swarthmore's residents had years before shifted the locus of their voluntary participation to the nearby city of Chester, where poverty and racial discrimination had produced a legacy of urban distress. Retired college professors like former Temple social work dean Will Richan and political scientist Charles E. Gilbert joined active members of several local churches in providing their skills as literacy tutors, mentors, and organizational developers to such Chester missions as the Chester East Side Ministry, a Presbyterian facility, and several other churches. Other townspersons, including one group at the Swarthmore Friends Meeting, provided meals in conjunction with other church groups in Delaware County on a regular basis to persons gathered at the county shelter, just across Cobbs Creek from the City of Philadelphia. These various town-based volunteer activities drew an increasing participation from school-aged participants throughout the 1990s.

In Cape Breton, community development leader Greg MacLeod (quoted in MacIntyre, ed., 1998, ch. 2), priest and philosopher, has observed that the "main actors" in the modern economy, "the ones determining the shape of our society, are large business corporations," and that if society is really to be changed, such organizations must be reshaped to allow for "majority local ownership and control." MacLeod, from his present faculty position at the University College of Cape Breton, works "to institutionalize stewardship in community business corporations." "In our experimenting," he advises, "we must insist that the economy is *for* people and the people are *not for* the economy."

Theodore Lowi (1979: 28ff.) has observed that most voluntary associations, large and small, "have given up their spontaneity for a solid administrative core.... Such groups naturally possess potential political power, but only occasionally are they politicized. The rest of the time they administer." Lester Salamon's research (1993) indicates that only 3 percent of nonprofit agencies primarily engage in advocacy, only one in five report engaging in any advocacy at all, and that four in five "mostly administer." If the Cape Breton lessons are to be learned, however, and if Swarthmore is both to reshape its town center and constructively impact the Chester ghetto that adjoins it to the south, societal space will need to be claimed that allows for both advocacy and administration. If social entrepreneurship is to become a force capable of positively impacting society, it will need both to create jobs and to advance the well-being of those left behind by society's systems of power and inequality.

Institutional building within society's third space requires individuals and groups to confront, surmount, and reconstruct what Edward Carothers (1970) identifies as society's "cruelty systems":

> Cruelty systems cannot be amended by suspended compassion, abstract goodwill, sentimental tenderness. What is required is action designed for the social reorganization of life around a better set of ethical values and purposes. . . . Nothing ever happens as a result of exposure unless action is organized. . . . Individuals acting alone really can't do much to correct or improve social conditions.

The address, and potential redress, of society's cruelty systems does not appear to be an overwhelming preoccupation of its third sector as presently construed. This neglect of pressing need has, indeed, been observed by several national commissions that have reported in recent years. The work of these commissions is reviewed in the ensuing chapter.

# Part Five

---

*Searching for*
*Meaning and Justice*

# 12

# Commission Reports on the Third Sector

When the nonprofit sector emerged as a visible force in American society in the early 1970s, a national commission (which became known as the Filer Commission) was established to review its role and the issues its emergence brought forth. In a time of similar turmoil and change, voices continue to be raised urging the creation of "Filer II" or some similar vehicle for understanding the role of the third sector in American life. Indeed, several commissions have recently been created to represent a variety of ideological positions within the field, typically centrist or neo-conservative. This chapter reviews the landscape of commissions on the sector, and asks if yet more are needed.

## The Filer Commission

Historian Peter Dobkin Hall's work is standard on the Filer process, whose formal title was the Commission on Philanthropy and Public Needs. The Commission emerged from one corner of the political tumult of the 1960s, when Congress sought to tighten restrictions on the activity of foundations by means of the Tax Reform Act of 1969. The philanthropic establishment, led by none other than John D. Rockefeller III, proposed a partnership approach with government. Rockefeller, acting quite independently from other powerful foundation leaders, joined with leadership of the House Ways and Means Committee, Treasury Department officials, and other institutional elites in establishing a series of committees, ultimately to become the Commission. With the appointment of insurance executive John Filer as chairman, the "Citizens' Commission on Private Philanthropy and Public Needs" was announced by Secretary of the Treasury George Shultz and Ways and Means Committee Chair Wilbur Mills in 1973. The Commission's mandate included the examination of matters relating to the well-being "of the whole private nonprofit sector" (Hall, 1992: 75).

The Commission reported in six volumes, published by the Treasury Department in 1976 and 1977. Hall (1992: 78) summarizes its findings:

> This comprehensive multidisciplinary survey of every aspect of charitable tax-exempt organizations described and analyzed the role of nonprofits as employers, as sources of essential health, educational, welfare, and cultural services, and as forces in political life. The work also carefully considered the regulatory and tax issues affecting these organizations' well-being. Most importantly, the work gave substance to what, up to then, had been only an idea: that charitable tax-exempt organizations composed a coherent and cohesive "sector" of American political, economic, and social life. This unified conception of nonprofits as part of a "third," "independent," or "nonprofit"—or, as the commission preferred to call it, "voluntary"—sector lay the groundwork for establishing organizations that could give its common interests unified expression.

The Filer Commission was, as Hall (1992: 247) observes, "relatively speaking, a representative body with an ambitious and apparently open-ended research program. There was no way of predicting what its conclusions might be." It attended with some interest and an often surprising patience to the input of a "Donee Group," established under the leadership of Robert Bothwell to represent the interests of those receiving philanthropic support. But a major goal sought by a majority of its members—to establish a " 'permanent national commission on the nonprofit sector' to collect data on the sector's sources and resources, to explore and propose ways to provide giving and nonprofit activity, to provide a forum for public discussion of issues affecting the nonprofit sector, to study its relationship to government, and to act as an ombudsman in protecting the sector's interests" (ibid.)—was blocked by forces on both the left and right.

Conservatives held that these functions should be provided by an organization that was itself a nonprofit, and left-liberals, led by the Donee Group, feared that "such an agency would quickly become the captive of larger and better organized interests" (ibid.). The political center delivered the final blow, when President Carter's "new treasury secretary, Michael Blumenthal, expressed skepticism about the ability of such a body to simultaneously represent the public interest and defend a private one" (ibid.).

Filer's legacy was found in the significant role it played in, to use

Hall's term, "inventing the nonprofit sector," and the creation of two important organizations that spun off from its work: Independent Sector, which was formed to represent the common interests of nonprofit organizations; and the National Committee for Responsive Philanthropy (NCRP), which continued the advocacy agenda of the Donee Group in representing those "disenfranchised" from the making of philanthropic decisions. Independent Sector proved a sturdy force in restraining the efforts of both the Reagan administration of the 1980s and the Republican congressional majority of the 1990s to limit advocacy by nonprofit organizations. And the NCRP established itself as a continuing voice of vigor and intelligence in asserting that philanthropy has a particular obligation to support organizations "which seek justice for low-income people, racial and ethnic minorities, women and others who are targets of discrimination, and which seek environmental sanity."[1]

## The Possibility of "Filer II"

Twenty years after Filer's first report, the Indiana University Center on Philanthropy, an academic representation of the sector made visible by Filer, convened a conference of influentials in the philanthropic world to review the work of the original commission, and to explore the possibility of establishing a contemporary version of the effort.

By the time this convening was completed, two things had become quite clear. First, the sector had plenty of work to do to restore its public image as a reliable provider of services and advocacy. And, second, the establishment of a "Filer II" was not to be chosen as the way to go about meeting that goal.

As the twelve tables of eight reported their discussions—each balanced among carefully chosen invitees representing givers, foundation staffers, association leaders, and academics—it was clear that the Commission idea would not carry its home precinct. Five tables reported universal opposition, four a mixture of yeas and nays, and three a tepid "Yes, but . . ." response.

In the concluding statements from the floor, the trend became a landslide. The only support for Filer II came from a couple of veteran fund-raisers, eager once more to respond to a bell that had brought Filer $2 million a quarter-century before, though mostly from a single source. One after another, voices addressed an emerging consensus: the sector needs to speak for itself, through its established organizations, and with a clear and powerful voice.

Following on themes raised by Michael Seltzer (Ford Foundation), Mark Rosenman (Union Institute), Peter Goldberg (Family Service America), Sara Melendez (Independent Sector), Bob Bothwell (National Committee for Responsive Philanthropy), and John Simon (Yale University), Adam Yarmolinsky, one of Filer's six lead consultants, set the conference conclusion in his closing statement: We are not in a "pre-Filer situation," he argued. Now, the third sector needs to speak for itself. "Listen to us," he stated. "We, and the people we are trying to help, are in deep trouble."

The challenges identified for the sector were truly staggering: a decline in giving in the face of a coming transfer of wealth; the failure of accountability and regulation in the face of widespread distrust and visible corruption; a continuing uncertainty over tax policy as nonprofits become increasingly commercialized; a challenge to advocacy from the new right that reflects an evident willingness to bargain away the First Amendment; and a need to assure the participation of the young in a society in which civil society is steadily losing ground to privatism.

To some of these challenges arose commitments from the participants. Independent Sector's Melendez, following on a powerful plenary paper by her own vice-president, Virginia Hodgkinson, spoke of her organization's commitment to a national process of issue identification and citizen education; NCRP's Bothwell reminded the group of the need to address the "war on nonprofits" by such means as his organization's recently released work on "Foundations in the Newt Era"; Yale's Simon reminded the group of the power that a quick-response "white paper" series might carry; and fund-raiser George Brakeley described the uses to which a "philanthropic index" might be put by an organization like the NSFRE (National Society for Fund-Raising Executives).

Ultimately, it was a day carried by Washington, the home of the sector-serving organizations, rather than New York, the seat of corporate wealth and foundations. And it was a day that would have pleased Filer, seeing that it was organizations like Independent Sector and the National Committee for Responsive Philanthropy, conceived in the turbulent process of that initial commission, that were now ready to shoulder the load. Rather than requiring the field to wait for the funding, appointment, and functioning of a new commission, with its glacial process and inevitable controversies, the conference organizers had clearly brought the real issues of the day to a clear and searching illumination.

## But the Commissions Continue: 1) A Voice from the Right

If Filer II was not to be, that certainly did not mean that there would not be commissions. In 1997 and 1998 four separate commission enterprises reported to the American public. Each of these ventures had its own set of sponsors and its own angle on the role of voluntary and nonprofit organizations. Each was chaired by a prominent set of leaders, often chosen from persons recently or temporarily removed from elective public service.

Milwaukee's Lynde and Harry Bradley Foundation spent a million dollars establishing and funding its own commission, which it called the "'National Commission' on Philanthropy and Civic Renewal." This group was chaired by long-time presidential hopeful Lamar Alexander, formerly governor of Tennessee and a sometime developer of for-profit educational ventures.

The central message of this commission combined conventional Republican skepticism about government and foundations with a faith in the power of community-based organization that would warm the heart of a 1960s radical. Its major points were four:

1. More giving needs to be effectively directed to the benefit of those most in need.

2. Many of the best charities are local and independent of government.

3. Donors are well advised to become "civic entrepreneurs," strategically involved in the organizations they support.

4. Organized philanthropies often focus too heavily on research and theory, failing to provide simple and direct service solutions to pressing problems.

Of these four points, the first two are rather commonsensical, but hardly original, while the third and fourth imaginatively repackage the traditional right-wing distrust of big, "liberal" foundations and progressive community demands for social change.

The Bradley-Alexander commission sought to go further in its work than these simple assertions. It elaborated its argument so that it opposed a number of policies central to the Clinton-Gore administration: AmeriCorps, governmental-nonprofit partnerships, service-learning in schools, and what Bill Clinton called at the 1997 Presidents' Summit "big citizenship." A critical view of the Commission raised several questions about this aspect of its work (Van Til, 1997b):

> In this effort to make political hay out of its few simple observations, the commission settles itself on a goodly number of painful nettles. Why, for instance, use the expensive device of the foundation-sponsored commission, with 19 commissioned papers, two surveys, and a national profile of organizations, only then to claim that foundations are engaged in "too much study"? Why rail against the evils of "Big

Citizenship" without letting on to what should replace it: "Little citizenship"? Weak democracy? Why claim that careful evaluation should be made of programs while observing that a worthy organization's "purpose and achievements are readily perceived by anyone who visits them"?

The Bradley-Alexander commission created a rather demanding regimen for individuals inclined toward serving as philanthropic donors. Such individuals are advised to become "civic entrepreneurs," "prepared to be as exacting in [their] giving as in other areas of life." The benefactor must also learn to focus, "laser-like," on "actual results." S/he must no longer be content to give in a "haphazard, unplanned, and non-strategic" way, but must make effectiveness a principal criterion (National Commission on Philanthropy and Civic Renewal, 1997: ch. 6).

As the giver learns to become strategic, s/he is advised to apply ten tests before making any contribution. The Commission advises that it "demands the same seriousness as a long-term investment." The givers are informed that before settling on a donation, they must determine that the organization is locally based and operated (national organizations are not viewed as being sufficiently close to those in need). And the beneficiary must also be shown to be "entrepreneurial."

A further test requires that the recipient organization place "strict demands" on the people it helps. Good signs here are dress codes and mandatory attendance requirements. In addition, the organization must show that it provides a "refuge of tranquillity, order and permanence" in an "otherwise chaotic" community. Finally the organization must be "focused"; it must prove itself to depend on "little or no" governmental support; and it should be able to impress the visitor with the efficacy of its mission (pp. 75–76).

The tests devised by the Bradley-Alexander group are complex, vague, and difficult for donors to apply, and some of them seem quite unconvincing. Nonprofit executives can put on persuasive "show and tell" sessions to wow one-time visitors, for example, especially if they place "strict demands" on their employees and clients. And winning highly competitive governmental grants is typically viewed as a reward for productive work, and not a mark of suspicion.

Even more controversial is the insistence of the commission that social needs should be addressed only by the provision of services. They warn against supporting groups that seek to address the "root causes" of problems, and urge that, instead, funders focus on treating the "symptoms" of these problems.[2] By focusing only on the treatment of symptoms, the commission seeks to banish advocacy, protest, and social change—and related efforts to confront business and government with demands that they provide jobs, income, and health care—as inappropriate targets of giving.

Finally, the commission misses the chance to introduce new ideas that might cross traditional ideological divisions. It does remark on the role of faith-based community action in dealing with ghetto problems, but provides no discussion at all about providing public funding for these programs. It presents a long list of technical requirements for the effective funding of community-based organizations, and completely neglects to mention the widespread growth in community foundations, which exist to guide individual giving to such organizations.

The Bradley-Alexander commission manifests the limitations of its host foundation's "democratic capitalist" ideology. The report is openly hostile toward government, foundations, and established nonprofit organizations. By placing nearly all of its hopes for change in the hands of corporations, their owners, and local service organizations, the Bradley-Alexander approach greatly limits the institutional tools that may be put to the task of constructing a better society.

## The Commissions Continue: 2) Voices from the Center

Three additional commission-like reports were released in 1998 on philanthropy and the nonprofit sector. Each of these reports represented a centrist position, seeking to combine liberal and conservative views into an acceptable vision of the role of the third sector at the turn of the millennium.

Each of these efforts was organized as a team effort—seeking, in various ways, to present a new consensus about the role of participation, trust, association, and moral belief in society. Sometimes, as with the American Assembly, the report was only reviewed by its team—"No one was asked to sign it," the Assembly reports, and "not everyone agreed with all of it" (American Assembly, 1998: 5). In the case of the Civil Society report, two full pages are devoted to a reproduction of the very signatures of the team, reminiscent of the Declaration of Independence. (Senator Dan Coats, R-Indiana, takes the opportunity to play "John Hancock" by using a particularly thick pen.) The National Commission on Civic Renewal lists its members, and identifies one issue, that of school choice, on which they failed to find agreement with each other.

1) The American Assembly was, in many respects, a poor man's Filer II. Organized by outgoing Indiana University Center on Philanthropy director Warren Ilchman, it fielded its team from third-sector influentials who met for several days at the new Getty Museum in Los

Angeles. Invited to the event were funders, including Disney's John Cooke and MacArthur's Adele Simmons; nonprofit executives, from City Year's Alan Khazei to Girls Inc.'s Isabel Stewart; and an assortment of scholars who had studied the third sector, largely drawn from the Indiana University faculty. Ilchman was joined by Duke economist Charles Clotfelter and former Indiana University president Thomas Ehrlich in playing the principal roles in the process.

The message of this report was that the future holds good times for the philanthropic/nonprofit world and hard times for society: "The challenge is to exploit the opportunities to best advantage" (p. 7). Society is in trouble because of increasing inequality, emerging demographic tensions, uncertainties accompanying globalization, technological dislocations, and eroding values. But philanthropy can grow because of increased wealth and the potential of increasing contributions and pay-outs. The report concludes with the presentation of a number of relatively unexceptional listings of recommendations to improve philanthropic performance and accountability (e.g., "Philanthropic and Nonprofit Organizations Need to Strive for Operational Efficiency").

2) The Council on Civil Society relied more heavily on public intellectuals in building its smaller team, which included Francis Fukuyama (author of *Trust*), William Galston (author of *Liberal Purposes*), Cornel West (author of *Race Matters*), political scientist James Q. Wilson, and pollster Daniel Yankelovich. Senator Coats's conservative presence was balanced by that of liberal Senator Joseph Lieberman (D-CT).

To this group, "civil society" includes families, communities, and neighborhoods, faith communities, voluntary civic organizations, arts organizations, local government, educational institutions, business-related organizations, and the media. Thirty-five very brief recommendations are provided to revitalize these vast reaches of American society. Of these recommendations, only two pertain to the third sector as it is commonly defined: Senator Coats's well-worn proposal for a $500 tax credit for contributions to poverty-fighting nonprofits, and a call for greater emphasis on "sportsmanship and fair play" within youth organizations.[3]

3) The National Commission on Civic Renewal was chaired by former Senator Sam Nunn (D-GA) and former Secretary of Education William Bennett. Its members included a number of national association leaders (including United Way's Elaine Chao and self-help activist Robert Woodson) and a rather large number of foundation leaders (ranging from outgoing Rockefeller Foundation director Peter Goldmark to Boston Community Foundation leader Anna Faith Jones to the Bradley Foundation's Michael Joyce).

A key staff role was played by William Galston of the University of Maryland, a leading thinker in the communitarian movement and President Clinton's former domestic advisor.[4] No scholars associated with third-sector studies served on the Commission, though on its various advisory panels did serve ARNOVA career awardees Amitai Etzioni and Virginia Hodgkinson, as well as such leading ARNOVA members as Lester Salamon, Robert Putnam, Kathleen McCarthy, and Steven Rathgeb Smith.

This Commission will probably be best known for its Index of National Civic Health, which shows a precipitous decline from 1960's 125 to a present-day score just over 80. This index is built from five components, each weighted at 20 percent: 1) political components of turnout and other activities; 2) trust in others and confidence in the federal government; 3) membership (which includes actual membership, charitable contributions, and local participation); 4) security (which includes youth murder rates, fear of crime, and survey-reported crime rates); and 5) family (which includes divorce and non-marital birth rates).

The Commission also employed a "good news–bad news" approach. The good news involves "the stirrings of a new movement of citizens acting together to solve community problems" (National Commision on Civic Renewal, 1998: 9). The bad news is that "Too many of us have become passive and disengaged," lacking in "confidence in our capacity to make basic moral and civic judgments, to join with our neighbors to do the work of community, to make a difference" (p. 6).

The answer provided by the Commission is to rediscover the idea of "civic liberty," and to rely on "commitment" rather than "expertise." The Commission is less sanguine than the Council on Civil Society about moral renewal. The Commission observes: "Civic renewal does not require moral perfection," and though it does rest on a moral foundation, "it does not require any particular denominational creed. The foundation we need is rather the constitutional faith we share—in the moral principles set forth in the Declaration of Independence, and the public purposes set forth in the Preamble to the Constitution" (p. 12).

Many themes raised in these reports merit the careful attention of those concerned with citizen and voluntary action in modern life: the rising role of faith-based organizations within the third sector; the relative importance of voluntary/nonprofit organizations in relation to the other denizens of the "civil society" (from family to neighborhood to labor union); the place of "moral truth" in the provision of social trust; the links (if any) between social civility and civil society.

The answers provided are typically moderate in tone, centrist in political inclination, and more inclined toward moral than structural reform. They tend to accept current realitiès of political and economic power, with their associated inequalities in wealth, income, and ownership—although the American Assembly group does worry about the increasing "urgency" of this issue. On the whole, however, the message is that what is needed is a more active citizenry, "doing their share, in free association with one another" (National Commission on Civic Renewal, 1998: 20), evincing an "ethic of sacrifice and responsibility" (Council on Civil Society, 1998: 26), while advancing traditional American values of "trust, service, and the common purpose" (American Assembly, 1998: 27). Whether this approach will prove any more helpful than the conservative vision of faith-based localism is certainly subject to debate. But this debate cannot be productively conducted unless a third position is reviewed—one which might be taken by a progressive commission on the third sector, though such a body has yet to be formed or to make its report.

## The Absence of a Voice from the Left

While the right and the center have been busily producing their visions of a reinvigorated civil society, the American left has been strangely silent. In part, this silence reflects the shame Republican politicians have managed to attach to the label "liberal." And, in greater part, it reflects the demise of progressive thought in an era dominated by the demise of communism internationally, and the assumption on the part of many intellectuals that political democracy and economic capitalism are inextricably linked. A final explanation for the absence of a progressive vision is found in the quiet ability donors, particularly foundation leaders, are able to exercise in channeling thinking along lines donees perceive as likely to generate grants. For all of these reasons, progressive thinking on the third sector tends to be confined to a few small think tanks and a number of disparate, and quite poorly funded, community-based organizations.

A progressive vision of the third sector would recognize the impact that structural control of the economy exercises on political, social, and community life. It would define a democratic polity in which the equality of citizenship was backed by an awareness that inequalities in income, wealth, and control can overwhelm the impact of a "one person, one vote" political system. It would view the third sector with a similar awareness of the ways in which giving and volunteering can be used to oppress as well as to liberate disadvantaged individuals.

A progressive vision of the third sector would not preach the gospel of "democratic capitalism," but would rather dissect the dubious links conventional wisdom has sought to construct between these two rather disparate institutional constructs. It would examine the ways in which one person's good fortune, pluck, and prosperity may rest on increasing the misery of the growing ranks of the poor and desperate, both home and abroad. It would seek a more complete understanding of the recurrent headlines of modern life, headlines like: "Stock Market Gains with News of Unemployment's Rise."

In their analysis of social economics, economists Greg and Paul Davidson (1988) analyze the conservative economists' dictum that a "natural rate of unemployment" of about 6 percent is required to sustain workplace discipline and to restrain an unsettling swell in the rate of inflation. Why, they ask, should we all commit ourselves to an uncivil economy, and allow ourselves to celebrate our good fortune when it is itself a direct product of the suffering of others?

The extreme right in American life expends a good deal of effort attempting to convince the rest of us that we need the sufferings of the poor and the unemployed to sustain our own comfort, and that if we only give them a few alms we can rest comfortably in this state of increasing inequality. The Bradley-Alexander commission, for example, speaks glowingly about the merits of treating the symptoms of social problems rather than their "root causes," as though the creation of a happy and well-disciplined army of the poor is the best that we can do.

The "moral middle," best represented by the Council on Civil Society, talks of a "moral economy," by which they mean the need to restrain the market when it provides goods and services of dubious moral value. "Consider just a few obvious examples," the Council (1998: 16) urges, beginning with the "increasingly crude use of sex by corporate advertisers to sell products," continuing with "complacency in the face of jolting new disparities" between the "most successful and the most shattered among us," and eventually arriving at our "tendency to treat other people, and at times even ourselves, primarily as consuming objects who purchase an identity in the market place." These fundamental flaws in the market system, the Council concludes, "are not exempt from the need for moral renewal."

The Council, like the American Assembly, engages in a discourse that has become increasingly common in modern life. I call this phenomenon "secular Marxism." Secular Marxism is like classical Marxism in that it describes serious problems associated with the economic system in terms of their consequences, but it differs from the classical view in its avoidance of any implication that these problems might be caused by anything that is structured into the economic system. Secular Marxists describe problems in terms of "income gaps" between rich and poor, or "excessive consumerism," focusing on values rather than structures in their explanations. They do not choose to explore whatever underlying causes of inequality may be found in the control of material resources like capital, labor, wealth, and property.

The American Right does not espouse secular Marxism. Its view is simply that there remain some poor people in modern society, that some of them should be helped, and that the number of rich and well-off is growing both in number and generosity. The Bradley-Alexander commission puts this position clearly:

> America is the richest, most generous nation on Earth. In no other country do individuals, communities, foundations, corporations, and other private philanthropies give so many billions to such a wide variety of worthy causes and organizations. Yet among all these commendable activities and missions, helping the poor and people in need has always played a special role. For many Americans, it defines the essence of charity. (National Commission on Philanthropy and Civic Renewal, 1998: 11)

Right-wing philanthropies work long and hard to convince Americans that there is nothing wrong with capitalism, and that all would work very much for the best in this very fine world if only government would get out of the way. The Bradley-Alexander report (ibid.) puts it this way:

> Today, however, far too much of the private largesse intended by its donors to improve the condition of the poor is misspent or misdirected. This gap between the generosity and good intentions of Americans and the actual impact of their giving on those in need is the central concern of the National Commission on Philanthropy and Civic Renewal.

A great deal of effort, backed by a great deal of money, is expended to sell the public on the right's message that all we need is a little more direction to our philanthropy. This systematic campaign has been detailed by the National Committee for Responsive Philanthropy (NCRP) in its report, "Moving a Public Policy Agenda: The Strategic Philanthropy of Conservative Foundations" (Covington, 1997). The NCRP finds that a dozen conservative foundations systematically direct their grants to policy specialists who not only justify the "democratic capitalist" ideology, but then seek to "market" those ideological wares as if they were a new model refrigerator or automobile.

The challenge this onslaught from the far right presents to progressives is this: Should they respond in kind to the blitz of dubious research, simplistic solutions, and clever marketing issuing from the well-funded right? Or should they actually try to take research and critical analysis seriously, engaging themselves and the broader citizenry in a real process of examination and problem resolution? And if they make either choice, will anyone support them in that work?

The NCRP puts the dilemma well: "The world of liberal and progressive nonprofits confronts an entirely different funding dynamic. Rather than being rewarded or encouraged for their public policy activism, they are often required to downplay their policy commitments in order to secure foundation support" (p. 47). Right-wing policy development, NCRP reports, is currently attracting four times the amount of funding that is being directed to progressive institutions, and policy magazines they identify as right-wing receive ten times the level of support provided to media on the progressive side.

Indications that a coalition of moderate and progressive foundations are taking the NCRP report to heart give hope to those who see the need to counter the propaganda blitz from far-right foundations and their kept intellectual-marketers. Perhaps the time is coming in which a focused structure will emerge for policy research aimed toward the construction of a truly civil society and economy.

In such an initiative, competent thinkers who understand the third sector directly would address the manifold issues of policy in this field—issues like assessing third-sector–governmental partnerships, evaluating the merits of donee organizations, addressing the role of the third sector in ameliorating the crises of work and welfare, and balancing the contributions of volunteers with paid employees—issues that confront Americans daily in their roles as citizens, givers, volunteers, taxpayers, and employees.

As the third sector emerges as a policy field in its own right, it will be important that strong and independent thinking address the consideration of issues, the shaping of positions, the development of op-eds and white papers, and the placement of these statements in national media. Such a task would require the commitment of outstanding thinkers and writers, the dedication of outstanding leadership, and the mobilization of effective organization.

It seems altogether appropriate to develop an effective way by which serious thought and consideration are given to the role of society's third sector, thought organized on a level playing field, one on which ideas develop, contend, and receive fair consideration, despite the cacophony and simplicity of so much contemporary American public discourse. The following chapter seeks to model such a process, calling upon the ideas of a half-century of leading thinkers about the importance of finding ways of growing civil society in an age of increasing social, economic, political, and cultural incivility.

# 13

# Civil Society and the Escape from Madness

If the voluntary action of individuals and groups is to be regarded as really important, a noticeable effect must be evident in the quality of individual and societal life. Without that effect, the conclusion might be warranted that third-sector actions are real but relatively unimportant, a kind of frill on the margins of what really counts in society.

Until very recently, prevailing treatment of the third sector confirmed the widespread notion of its marginality. The *New York Times*, to take one eminently establishmentarian example, routinely assigned a society reporter to cover stories concerning voluntarism and the third sector. Universities of the first and second rank almost completely ignored work in this arena, while considerably extending their course offerings and degrees addressing the work of business and government. Schools possessed extensive curricula in civics and social studies, but provided few opportunities for their students to learn by doing the work of community service and civil education. And, even in family life, the importance of connecting with larger issues and forms of social organization languished with the coming of television and other forms of mass entertainment.

In the midst of this long-time tendency to marginalize the role of the third sector in American life, the 1990s saw, for the first time, the entrance of books which discussed the role of voluntary and nonprofit organization on the shelves of major bookstores. Widely reviewed and distributed were such titles as *The Spirit of Community* (by Amitai Etzioni, 1993), *Jihad vs. McWorld* (by Benjamin Barber, 1995), *The End of Work* (by Jeremy Rifkin, 1995), *Trust* (by Francis Fukuyama, 1995), *Voice and Equality* (by Sidney Verba et al., 1995), and *Everything for Sale* (by Robert Kuttner, 1997). Two additional books were published in 1998: Barber's *A Place for Us: How to Make Society Civil and Democracy Strong*, and Don E. Eberly's *America's Promise: Civil Society and the Renewal of American Culture*. Joining this list in 2000 was the long-awaited contribution by Harvard's Robert Putnam, *Bowling Alone: Civic Disengagement in America*, whose preceding essays have received extended and extensive consideration by press, policy maker, and influential alike.

The issues joined by Etzioni, Barber, Rifkin, Fukuyama, Verba, Kuttner, Eberly, and Putnam could not have been more central for citizens concerned with the future of their society and the global frame that surrounds it. Not only were their books important, but their authors stood in the first rank of American scholarship.

- Etzioni, a past president of the American Sociological Society, defined the terms and beliefs of the new "communitarian" movement he and other colleagues had founded—a movement based in large part on the potential contributions of third-sector actions and organizations. Earlier, Etzioni had detailed the structure of what he was first to call, in a powerful and evocative term, the "active society" (1968).

- Barber, the nation's preeminent student of democratic theory, described the rise of two social forces destructive of both democracy and civil life: the advance of monopolistic control of capital he called "McWorld" and the rise of collective mania and group racialism he identified as "Jihad." In a later book, he directly addressed issues of civil society (1998).

- Rifkin, a prominent social activist and author, explained, as we have seen in an earlier chapter, a coming crisis in the distribution of compensated employment occasioned by the extraordinary dispersion of a single technological innovation—the microchip.

- Fukuyama, whose work on "the end of history" brought him widespread intellectual celebrity, detailed the increasing loss of trust in political, social, cultural, and interpersonal relationships.

- Verba, a distinguished Harvard political scientist, with his associates Kay Lehman Schlozman and Henry E. Brady, probed for the presence and absence of what they called "civic voluntarism" in American society.

- Kuttner, a prominent economics journalist, detailed the "commodification" of American life, and pointed to the importance of "reclaiming civil society" from the forces of wealth and power that threaten contemporary democracy.

- Eberly, initially known as a neo-conservative protégé of former U.S. Secretary of Education William Bennett, expanded his organizational and intellectual range to include a number of traditionally liberal conceptions on the role of civil society in American life (1998).

- And Putnam, another Harvard political scientist whose work on participation in Italy had become a social science classic, explained what he called "the strange disappearance of civic America" as a complex creation of a society increasingly addicted to the flickering image of the ubiquitous television screen.

With Etzioni's reminder that both rights and responsibilities are important, Fukuyama's demonstration that social capital is a precondition for economic growth, Rifkin's clear call for service as employment, Barber's warnings of the follies of corporate merger and ethnic cleansing, Verba's identification of religion as a bulwark of participation, Kuttner's documentation of the power of private ownership and control, Eberly's reminder that nonprofits often fail to address issues of poverty and need, and Putnam's warnings that true association is increasingly imperiled by familism and mass culture, the contemporary reader was presented with compelling arguments demonstrating the need for a vital and well-constructed third sector.

## Erich Fromm and the Roots of Modern Madness

Like any contemporary analyst of societal realities, Etzioni, Barber, Rifkin, Fukuyama, Verba, Kuttner, Eberly, and Putnam stand on the shoulders of an earlier generation of social theorists as they seek to explain their understandings. Among these intellectual giants is Sigmund Freud, who developed in his classic analysis, *Civilization and Its Discontents,* the conception that societies, as well as individuals, could be seen as mentally ill. Freud wrote of "social" and "collective" neuroses, and foresaw the development of research into the "pathology of civilized communities."

Freud's intellectual descendant, psychoanalyst Erich Fromm, sought to advance in his 1955 book, *The Sane Society,* the research Freud had anticipated. Fromm argued that it follows from the definition of the term "mental health" "that it must be defined in terms of the adjustment of society to the needs of man" (p. 72). Fromm's definition of mental health was presented as

the ability to love and to create, by the emergence from incestuous ties to clan and soil, by a sense of identity based on one's experience of the self as the subject and agent of one's powers, by the grasp of reality inside and outside of ourselves, that is, by the development of objectivity and reason. (p. 69)

Fromm proceeded to examine the "somewhat neglected pathogenic function of society" (p. 77). He begins by asking: "What kind of men ... does our society need?" And he answers: "It needs men who co-operate smoothly in large groups; who want to consume more and more, and whose tastes are standardized and can be easily influenced and anticipated. It needs men who feel free and independent, not subject to any authority, or principle, or conscience—yet willing to be commanded, to do what is expected, to fit into the social machine without friction" (p. 110).

Fromm's book is remarkable not only because he is willing to argue that a contemporary Western society like that of 20th-century America may be mad, but his argument also serves as a template for the work of many social critics who have also examined the social crisis of our times. Time and again these critics have repeated notes Fromm sounded in his symphony of social criticism and reconstruction, published almost a half-century ago. The reader is invited to consider the echoes of Fromm's pioneering tones through the footnotes to this chapter, which display contemporary renditions of those themes.

Those of us who live in modern industrial-urban societies, Fromm observes, share a number of characteristics that clearly do not fit his definition of mental health. We are incapacitated from productive activity in each of society's major institutional sectors.

In *family and community life*, we:

1. believe "that every desire must be satisfied immediately" and that "no wish must be frustrated" (p. 164); moreover, we find ourselves unable to distinguish between "happiness" and "fun" (p. 201).[1]

2. are unable to experience ourselves as "active bearers of our own powers and richness" (p. 124).[2]

3. relate to others as "between two abstractions, two living machines, who use each other" (p. 139).[3]

4. are condemned to live alone, unable to sustain an intimate relationship with a partner, because we are incapable of building a collaborative relationship which adjusts our "behavior to the expressed needs" of another person (p. 199).[4]

5. act as "passive and alienated" consumers (p. 136), consuming things simply in order to "have them" (p. 132) and surrounding ourselves with products "of whose nature and origin we know nothing" (p. 134).[5]

In the *workplace,* we are also incapacitated. Fromm finds that there, we:

1. are alienated from the work we perform and the products we produce by our work (p. 110–13).[6]

2. find that work is becoming "more repetitive and thoughtless as the planners, the micromotionists, and the scientific managers further strip the worker of his right to think and move freely" (J. J. Gillespie, quoted in Fromm, 1955: 125).[7]

3. focus on (abstract) exchange value rather than (concrete) use value of what we are able to create and possess (p. 116).[8]

4. experience work as "an economic atom that dances to the tune of atomistic management" (p. 125), while being manipulated by bureaucratic managers and organizations that treat us "as though they were figures, or things" (p 126).[9]

5. think of ourselves only "as a thing to be employed successfully on the market," not as "an active agent, as the bearer of human powers" (p. 142).[10]

When we relate to *public affairs and governmental life,* those of us in modern society:

1. feel helpless "before the forces which govern us" (p. 137).[11]

2. conform ourselves to an authority that is "anonymous, invisible, and (itself) alienated" (p. 152).[12]

3. are unable to express our political will because we "do not have any will or conviction" of our own (p. 185).[13]

4. "use television to build up political personalities as we use it to build up a soap" (p. 186).[14]

5. are possessed of "a deep sense of powerlessness in political matters (though not necessarily consciously so)" and hence find ourselves reduced "more and more" in "political intelligence" (p. 191).[15]

And, in the *associational life of the society,* we individuals are also thwarted. Instead of finding meaningful contact with our fellow beings, we:

1. find that we cannot relate to the human dimensions of societal problems (p. 119).[16]

2. have a deep sense of powerlessness, for "if one cannot act effectively—one cannot think productively either" (p. 191).[17]

3. value "indiscriminating sociability and lack of individuality" (being "outgoing") and "socially adjusted" in light of the ease with which we and others talk about our "problems" (p. 157).[18]

4. accept a thoroughly secularized religion, in which "we are not concerned with the meaning of life" and "we start out with the conviction that there is no purpose except to invest life successfully and to get it over with without major mishaps." We simply take God "for granted" (p. 176).[19]

5. are unable to perform the positive psychic task of tolerating "insecurity, without panic and undue fear" (p. 196).[20]

## A Template for Social Reform

Faced with this daunting set of socially induced disabilities, what are we to do? Fromm has a number of suggestions, involving radical ("going to the roots"—p. 273) reforms that might be introduced in the structures and processes of all of society's major sectors: "Sanity and mental health can be attained only by simultaneous changes in the sphere of industrial and political organization, of spiritual and philosophical orientation, of character structure, and of cultural activities" (p. 271). In other words, all four sectors need to work well and together in a healthy modern society:

> Trying to advance radically in one sector to the exclusion of others must necessarily lead to the result . . . that the radical demands in one sphere are fulfilled only by a few individuals, while for the majority they become formulae and rituals, serving to cover up the fact that in other spheres nothing has changed. Undoubtedly *one* step of integrated progress in all spheres of life will have more far-reaching and more lasting results for the progress of the human race than a hundred steps preached—and even for a short while lived—in only one isolated sphere. Several thousands of years of failure in "isolated progress" should be a rather convincing lesson. (pp. 272–73)

Solutions that involve either pure capitalism or pure socialism will therefore prove inadequate. "Super capitalism" will only deepen the pathologies he has identified; and "centralized planning can even create a greater degree of regimentation and authoritarianism than is to be found in Capitalism or in Fascism" (pp. 277–78). Rather, Fromm presents a template for social reform, one that has been followed by numerous authors following in his steps. Fromm began with the business sector, offering a number of suggestions for its reform:

1. Work should be reorganized to recognize the fact that both its "technical" and social aspects are important factors in determining

the degree to which it is experienced as "meaningful and attractive" (p. 299).[21]

2. It is critical that all participants in business organizations—owners, employees and managers alike—participate in both "management and decision making" within the corporation (p. 323).[22]

3. There is no substitute for the building of an "independent economic existence" (p. 293), in which one enjoys "the whole fruit of one's labor," is able to "educate oneself," and pursues a "common endeavor within a professional group" (pp. 309–10).[23]

Within the governmental sector, Fromm urges the adoption of three reforms in policy and structure:

1. A guaranteed income should be available to all, for up to a two-year time period, to allow individuals to support themselves and their families even if they have quit their job voluntarily, wish to prepare themselves for other work, "or for any personal reason which prevents . . . earning money" (p. 336).[24]

2. The governing structures of democracy should be reorganized into "relatively small groups . . . comprising not more than . . . five hundred people. In such small groups the issues at stake can be discussed thoroughly, each member can express his ideas, can listen to, and discuss reasonably other arguments" (p. 341).[25]

3. A reflective national process could be established to structure policy debates and record votes; "with the help of the technical devices we have today, it would be very easy to register the over-all result of these votes in a short time" (p. 342). Decisions from the process could then be "channeled into the level of the central government" (p. 343).[26]

Major reforms in third-sector structure and process advocated by Fromm involve:

1. "Doing away with the harmful separation between theoretical and practical knowledge" in our educational system, which should involve significant possibilities for adult education as well as a thorough recasting of approach at the elementary and secondary levels (pp. 345–46).[27]

2. Supporting and extending the creation of "collective art," the processes by which we "respond to the world with our senses in a meaningful, skilled, productive, active, shared way" (p. 347).[28]

3. Welcoming the emergence of a new and "universalistic" religion in the years ahead, a religion which "would embrace the humanistic

teachings common to all great religions . . . [and whose] emphasis would be on the practice of life, rather than doctrinal beliefs" (p. 352).[29]

## From Madness to Civil Society

The path to civil society from societal madness will not be an easy one to build and maintain. But it follows a trail well marked, as the degree of consensus among social critics and reformers as to its general direction is surprisingly high. As civil society is discovered and built, it will be important to specify the role voluntary and nonprofit organizations can and should play in its creation. This task, as well, involves a process of social creation, a trek from nonprofit sector to third space that forms the subject of the final section of this book.

# Part Six

*A Third Space*

# 14

# Beyond the Myths of Sector

The last quarter of the 20th century has seen a dramatic rise in the numbers and visibility of nonprofit organizations in the United States. Seeking to make sense of this organizational growth, both scholars and organization leaders have increasingly come to speak of the rise of a nonprofit "sector." This chapter questions the future viability of the sector concept, and seeks to return dialogue in the field to a quest for understanding the significance of action rather than assaying the weight of organization.

## The Limits of Nonprofit Organization

In a burst of excitement about the role of society's third sector over the past 25 years, both scholars and professionals may have missed noticing a number of limits to the contributions of nonprofit organizations. It may well be only a matter of time, as Yale law professor Henry Hansmann predicted in an important paper written in 1987, until many nonprofits will choose financial viability over maintenance of mission. And those choices will inevitably have implications for the several types of tax exemption enjoyed by most nonprofit organizations. Hansmann (1987b: 25) put it as follows:

> The really important issue facing the nonprofit sector is the future treatment, not of nonprofits' unrelated business activities, but rather of their primary or "related" activities. . . . How . . . does one defend tax exemption for nonprofit hospitals, nursing homes, health care agencies, publishers and all the other types of nonprofit firms that

provide services that are similar to, and in competition with, business firms? If a satisfactory answer to this question cannot be given—and I believe that an answer is not easy to find—then these organizations may ultimately have their tax exemption and other privileges withdrawn.

In his more recent study of *The Ownership of Enterprise,* Hansmann (1996: 245) notes that the nonprofit form provides only one of a number of ways in which organizations may be non-investor-owned. It is also possible to organize ownership cooperatively, through such forms as worker ownership, cooperatives of many sorts (agricultural, retail, or wholesale), associations or clubs, condominiums, or mutual banks or insurance companies. Differences between such producer- and consumer-owned firms and the nonprofit, Hansmann observes, tend to be very small. Indeed, he adds, "As owner-control becomes increasingly attenuated in a formally owned firm, the difference between such a firm and one that is formally unowned (that is, nonprofit) tends to vanish." At the same time, Hansmann observes, in most of the important areas of health care, the nonprofit form has become "increasingly anachronistic."

As Hansmann told me in a recent interview, the issue remains a salient one today. Most nonprofit colleges and universities, and most public ones as well, have become nearly indistinguishable from the emerging for-profit universities, he observed, selling their degrees on a course-by-course basis. Support for their programs has moved from the supply side (scholarships, for example) to the support of demand (vouchers from employers or governments). A similar process has transformed health care nonprofits into commercial institutions, which have become heavily dependent on third-party public and insurance payments to support the demand for their offerings.

In Britain, a similar process of sectoral transformation has also elicited concern. Policy analyst Barry Knight observed in a controversial report that much of his country's voluntary sector is filled with "para-state" organizations, and the Independent Commission on the Future of the Voluntary Sector, chaired by social administration scholar Nicholas Deakin, observed that British charity law misplaces such institutions as its "public" schools, religious institutions, and party-related think tanks under the rubric of its "voluntary sector."

As the German historian Rudolph Bauer has succinctly put it, in a capitalistic society all organizations are capitalistic. Or, perhaps, almost all. Certainly a major function of government, at every level, is to sustain the routine workings of the economy, and to protect its profits and employment levels from severe dislocations. At the same time, nonprofit organizations face a financial bottom line as harsh as that of any business. Granted that many are able to supplement their fee income with charitable contributions or labor contributed in the form of voluntary time, but a good number of the nearly 1.5 million exempt organizations function as tax-free businesses, producing the same kinds of products as their cousins in the for-profit sector—jobs and services. The jobs and services provided by such "commercial nonprofits" are often only remotely connected to any charitable, educational, or other redeeming social purpose. As Teresa Odendahl (1987: 16) has documented in her work on giving, "a key motive for philanthropy is the desire to maintain control over the disposition of money."

## Does the Nonprofit Sector Really Exist?

Foremost among the researchers who have employed the concept of the nonprofit sector has been Johns Hopkins University's Lester Salamon. A tireless organizer of research activity in the field, Salamon convened, directed, and secured funding for a 13-country Comparative Nonprofit Sector Project, the major study of its sort. In a variety of publications from the project, Salamon and his associates have trumpeted the role of this new societal force.

Salamon's principal assertions about the significance of the nonprofit sector are the following:

- SOCIAL AND ECONOMIC POWER: The nonprofit sector is a "major social and economic force," with "substantial and growing employment and a significant share of the responsibility for responding to public needs" (Salamon and Anheier, 1994: 113). Its size in 22 countries examined in one study amounts to a "$1.1 trillion industry," equivalent in size to the "world's eighth largest economy" (Salamon, Anheier, et al., 1998: 4).

- CITIZEN ACTIVITY: This sector is "preeminently the 'citizen's sector'" (Salamon and Anheier, 1994: 98). "Indeed, a veritable 'global associational revolution' appears to be underway, a massive upsurge of organized private, voluntary activity in literally every corner of the world" (Salamon, Anheier, et al., 1998: 2; cf. also Salamon, 1994).

- POLITICAL SIGNIFICANCE: "The rise of the nonprofit sector may well prove to be as significant a development of the latter twentieth century as the rise of the nation-state was of the latter nineteenth century" (Salamon, 1994: 111).

- STRONG STAYING POWER: "In fact . . . assertions about the demise of the nonprofit sector deserve the same response that American humorist Mark Twain gave to rumors about his untimely death. 'These reports,' remarked Twain, 'have been greatly exaggerated'" (Salamon and Anheier, 1994: 23). Nonetheless, the "nonprofit sector remains the 'lost continent' on the social landscape of modern society, invisible to most policymakers, business leaders, and the press, and even to many people within the sector itself" (Salamon, Anheier, et al., 1998: 2).

Countering these contentions are a number of assertions, which, interestingly enough, have been made by the same Lester Salamon:

- NONPROFIT ORGANIZATIONS ARE BECOMING INCREASINGLY "MARKETIZED." Salamon (1995: 213) anticipates that as the nonprofit sector grows, "this growth will occur through greater integration of the voluntary sector into the market economy." His research shows how heavily supported the nonprofit sector has become by fees and governmental contracts. In the aggregate, nonprofits in the United States receive 57 percent of their support from fees, and 30 percent of their support from governmental sources, and both these percentages are growing (Salamon, Anheier, et al., 1998: 11). Moreover, the often claimed "independence" of the nonprofit sector is rather misleading, as the role of the nonprofit sector has become "interdependent" with government, and more recently, business (Cf. Salamon and Anheier, 1997: 293). Salamon advises (1999: 177): "A sector whose mythology celebrates independence must now come to terms with the need for close working relationships with business and government to solve pressing public problems."

- CITIZEN INFLUENCE IS LARGELY ABSENT FROM A LARGE PORTION OF THE NONPROFIT SECTOR. Less than one-sixth of the nonprofit sector addresses issues of broad citizen concern using structures that directly involve citizens in the governance and workings of the organization itself. Fully 82 percent of the sector involves health care institutions, schools and colleges, and business organizations—few of which involve active citizen participation in their governance or widespread use of volunteers in their provision of service.[1]

- THE NONPROFIT SECTOR MAY ITSELF BE A MAJOR CONTRIBUTOR TO POLICY BIAS, INSTABILITY, AND STALEMATE. When nonprofit organizations address issues of public policy, they do so from a variety of ideological and/or practical perspectives. As Salamon (1993) puts it, the relationship between the nonprofit sector and democracy "may be highly problematic," depending on a series of characteristics of governmental, for-profit, and nonprofit organizations alike:

1. "Where the State is exercising overweening power and challenging the existence of any autonomous social space, the nonprofit sector can be a *prerequisite* for democracy.
2. "Where private groups, whether based on economic interest, ethnicity, or some other basis, have destroyed any real sense of common purpose and strained the bonds of 'citizenship,' the nonprofit sector can be a serious *barrier* to democracy.
3. "Where agencies shy away from advocacy activities and pursue a narrow conception of their role, nonprofit organizations can become largely *irrelevant* to democracy."

- NONPROFIT ORGANIZATIONS RECEIVE INADEQUATE AND DECLINING LEVELS OF PHILANTHROPIC SUPPORT. While nearly three-fifths of the support for nonprofit organizations come from fees, the proportion of support provided by charitable or philanthropic contributions is rapidly declining. Studies by Salamon (Salamon and Anheier, 1994: 61; Salamon, Anheier, et al., 1998: 11) find this level dropping from 19 to 13 percent between 1990 and 1995. Ten percent has conventionally been viewed as providing a minimal financial base for a healthy nonprofit sector.

Salamon (1995: 44–48) anticipated this decline in philanthropic support in his analysis of four dimensions of "voluntary failure" that confront modern societies: philanthropic insufficiency, philanthropic particularism, philanthropic paternalism, and philanthropic amateurism. On philanthropic insufficiency, Salamon observed that "The central failing of the voluntary system as a provider of collective goods has been its inability to generate resources on a scale that is both adequate enough and reliable enough to cope with the human service problems of an advanced industrial society."

In recent work, Salamon writes of a "civil society sector" in place of the "nonprofit sector" concept (Salamon and Anheier, 1997), and his current title at Johns Hopkins has become Director of the "Center for Civil Society Studies." In an article on the "civil society sector," he notes that if only voluntary and nonprofit organizations are counted as being within the civil society sector, "it has the unfortunate effect of relegating the other sectors to the status of being 'uncivil.' More importantly, it overlooks the extent to which the 'civil society sector' relies on the other sectors to survive" (Salamon and Anheier, 1997: 65).

Writing with his long-time colleague Helmut Anheier, Salamon suggests that a "true 'civil society'" may well be "one in which there are three more or less distinct sectors—government, business, and nonprofit—that nevertheless find ways to work together in responding to public needs. So conceived, the term 'civil society' would not apply to a particular sector, but to a *relationship* among the sectors, one in which a high level of cooperation and mutual support prevailed. This is the conclusion that seems to emerge from our data" (Salamon and Anheier, 1997: 65).

Other scholars who have come to find the nonprofit sector a dubious concept include Peter Dobkin Hall, Perri 6, Ralph Kramer, and Don E. Eberly:

- Hall (1992: 1) analyzes the nonprofit sector as an "invented concept," predicting that the "sanitized language that renders the terms *nonprofit* and *nonprofit sector* so suitable as a basis for political accommodation also, in its essential ambiguity, assures future conflict."

- Perri 6, a British scholar, asked in a 1994 essay if "anyone will talk about 'the third sector' in ten years time?" He concluded that the "undermining of the claim of sectoral distinctiveness probably also reflects a real historical process by which social welfare industries and market conditions in them have changed, which may have had the effect of eroding the distinctiveness of the behaviour of organisational forms" (6 and Vidal, 1994: 407).

- Kramer (1998), in an exhaustive review of the nonprofit and social welfare literature, asks of nonprofit organizations in the 21st century: "Will sector matter?"

- Eberly (1998: 67–69), reviewing findings from the Salamon-Anheier research, emphasizes the considerable degree to which nonprofit organizations do not address the needs of the poor, and do not direct volunteer solutions to meet needs of social service.

## Sweating Down the Nonprofit Sector

Salamon (1995: 261–64) has argued that the myths of "pure virtue" and "voluntarism" are "dysfunctional" for defining and understanding the contemporary nonprofit sector. But why not go further with the same logic, and contemplate the possibility that the very idea of a nonprofit sector may itself be mythic, carrying its own burdens of deception and dysfunctionality?

Consider the following argument: Unlikely as its implementation may be, is it not possible that its consideration would sharpen attention to the need to cultivate civil society, to nourish its third space?

- Many of the nearly 1.5 million tax-exempt organizations in the United States essentially behave as though they were tax-free businesses, distinguishable only from other businesses by the non-distribution constraint, which requires that their assets not be divided among owners upon the dissolution of the organization, but rather be donated to other nonprofit entities.

- Among those organizations that most nearly behave as tax-exempt businesses are almost all major nonprofit health-related entities (e.g., hospitals, nursing homes, home health care providers, suppliers), most "private" colleges and universities, some social service agencies, many "arts and culture" organizations, and the largest number of influential trade and professional organizations.

- What remains in the tax-exempt sector are a (relatively large number) of small health-related organizations, a range of community-funded primary and secondary schools largely of religious nature, a wide range of social service organizations that reflect community concerns and widely employ volunteer labor, an increasingly diverse and muscular set of churches and other faith-based organizations, a range of foundations with varying goals and purposes, a (rather large and often religiously grounded) group of development organizations, a very wide mixture of arts and culture organizations (many operating as small businesses), and a range of (typically) smaller civic, advocacy, and environmental organizations organized on a scale that varies from the local to the national.

- Assume now, for the sake of illustration, that the operating expenses of nonprofit social service organizations and nonprofit arts and culture organizations are evenly divided between essentially business functions and those infused with a voluntary commitment. Further grant Hansmann's assumption that only one-fifth of nonprofit schools and colleges act differently from the business model.

Now the following table may be derived, based on data provided from the various reports of the Johns Hopkins researchers.[2] Table 1 examines the operating expenditures of organizations typically counted as members of the U.S. nonprofit sector, dividing these organizations into two major groups. On the left side are organizations that may plausibly be seen as operating essentially as tax-exempt businesses, that is, largely supported by fees. On the right side are the operating expenses of organizations more fully characterized by voluntary and citizen-directed missions and processes.

Recasting the numbers in Table 1 as percentages of total full-time-equivalent employment with the organizations of the nonprofit sector,

Table 1. Operating Expenses of Two Major Categories of Nonprofit
Organizations

| ESSENTIALLY OPERATING AS TAX-EXEMPT BUSINESSES IN STRUCTURE AND PROCESS | SUBSTANTIALLY VOLUNTARY AND CITIZEN DRIVEN IN MISSION AND PROCESS |
| --- | --- |
| Hospitals, nursing homes, health care providers and suppliers (49%) | |
| Most private colleges and universities; other research and training (16%) | Community and faith-based primary and secondary schools (1%); one-fifth of private colleges and research institutes (4%) |
| | Churches and other faith-based institutions (8%) |
| Social service/development and housing organizations, often providing services funded by governmental grants and contracts (6%) | Social service/development and housing organizations, providing services with strong community and volunteer-based support (6%) |
| Business and professional organizations, including trade associations and unions (5%) | A few professional organizations |
| Arts, culture, and recreation organizations, supported by fees (1.5%) | Arts, culture, and recreation organizations, supported by contributions and governmental grants (1.5%) |
| | Civic/advocacy/environmental/ international organizations (1%) |
| | Foundations (0.4%) |
| **TOTAL IN CATEGORY (77.5%)** | **TOTAL IN CATEGORY (21.9%)** |

including volunteers, Table 2 provides the estimate that two-thirds of
the nonprofit sector, as conventionally understood, consists of work
largely indistinguishable from that provided by a business, or governmental, employer.[3]

Only when the deployment of private charitable giving is considered do we find a plurality in the right column. Table 3 shows that
two-thirds of all giving goes to the non-commercial part of the sector,
with two-thirds of that sum going to religious institutions. The nearly
$140 billion donated annually by individuals (85%), foundations (9%),

Table 2. Employment (Including Volunteers) of Two Major Categories of
Nonprofit Organizations

| ESSENTIALLY OPERATING AS TAX-EXEMPT BUSINESSES IN STRUCTURE AND PROCESS | SUBSTANTIALLY VOLUNTARY AND CITIZEN DRIVEN IN MISSION AND PROCESS |
|---|---|
| Hospitals, nursing homes, health care providers and suppliers (31%) | |
| Most private colleges and universities; other research and training (13%) | Community- and faith-based primary and secondary schools (1%); some private colleges and research institutes (3%) |
| | Churches and other faith-based institutions (10%) |
| Social service/development and housing organizations, often providing services funded by governmental grants and contracts (12%) | Social service/development and housing organizations, providing services with strong community and volunteer-based support (12%) |
| Business and professional organizations, including trade associations and unions (3.5%) | A few professional organizations |
| Arts, culture, and recreation organizations, supported by fees (4%) | Arts, culture, and recreation organizations, supported by contributions and governmental grants (4%) |
| | Civic/advocacy/environmental/ international organizations (3%) |
| | Foundations (0.9%) |
| **TOTAL IN CATEGORY (63.5%)** | **TOTAL IN CATEGORY (33.9%)** |

and corporations (6%) is directed in three portions: one-third to essentially commercial institutions (mainly public and private colleges and universities), one-half to religious institutions, and one-sixth to the citizen- and voluntary-directed organizations of the sector.[4]

Now perform the following social transformation, and open an exit from the nonprofit sector for those organizations that choose commercialism over mission. If such organizations were provided an orderly pathway toward their recognition as businesses, and were no longer granted eligibility for tax and other public benefits, the privi-

Table 3. Charitable Donations to Two Major Categories of Nonprofit Organizations

| ESSENTIALLY OPERATING AS TAX-EXEMPT BUSINESSES IN STRUCTURE AND PROCESS | SUBSTANTIALLY VOLUNTARY AND CITIZEN DRIVEN IN MISSION AND PROCESS |
|---|---|
| Hospitals, nursing homes, health care providers and suppliers (8%) | |
| Most private colleges and universities; other research and training (9%)<br><br>Public colleges and universities (7%) | Community- and faith-based primary and secondary schools and some public and private colleges and research institutes (4%) |
| | Churches and other faith-based institutions (48%) |
| Social service/development and housing organizations, often providing services funded by governmental grants and contracts (3.5%) | Social service/development and housing organizations, providing services with strong community and volunteer-based support (3.5%) |
| Business and professional organizations, including trade associations and unions, and other nonprofit organizations (4%) | A few professional organizations |
| Arts, culture, and recreation organizations, supported by fees (1.5%) | Arts, culture, and recreation organizations, supported by contributions and governmental grants (1.5%) |
| | Civic/advocacy/environmental/ international organizations (4.5%) |
| | Foundations (6%) |
| **TOTAL IN CATEGORY (33%)** | **TOTAL IN CATEGORY (67.5%)** |

leges of tax exemption could then be focused upon those organizations that would be chosen to continue to enjoy those privileges.

A process of organizational review might be used to identify those organizations undeserving of privileges of tax exemption. Among the tests that might be used to remove such organizations are four recently suggested by Joseph Galaskiewicz:[5]

1. To what degree does the organization place the quest for achievement of mission above the search for private gain?

2. To what degree does the organization avoid "chiseling" in the quality of service it provides when its income dwindles?

3. To what degree does the organization seek to avoid "dumping" unprofitable but appropriate clients in favor of those with the ability to pay?

4. To what degree does the organization treat its employees, both paid and volunteer, with appropriate respect to their commitment and contributions?

Consideration might be given as well to several elements, properly modified, of Pennsylvania's HUP test, as discussed above (p. 35):

5. To what degree does the organization advance an appropriate charitable or philanthropic purpose?

6. To what degree does the organization donate or render freely a sufficient portion of its services?

7. To what degree does the organization benefit a substantial class of persons who are legitimate subjects of charity?

8. To what degree does the organization relieve the government of the obligation of providing a particular program or set of services?

Additional criteria may be drawn from concepts that have figured importantly in this work. It would be utopian to expect every tax-exempt organization to meet all of these goals, but demonstrating that they are being advanced by the organization should surely assist in its quest to merit standing at the core of the nation's third space:

9. To what degree does the organization build and maintain social capital in society?

10. To what degree does the organization provide voice to a particular segment of the population, thereby enhancing the pluralist structure of society?

11. To what degree does the organization contribute by structure and process to the building of a communitarian society, fostering both a sense of right and a sense of responsibility?

12. To what degree does the organization address the material needs of its members—enhancing their employment opportunities,

helping them build a social economy, developing new ventures along lines of social entrepreneurship?

If such tests were developed, refined, and applied, organizations in the large institutional categories of the nonprofit sector—colleges, hospitals, churches—could sort themselves out. Those that were found to be essentially commercial could be distinguished from those continuing to serve a voluntary or charitable purpose. The organizational world that would result would be one in which the third space was given greater recognition. Its main categories would be the following:

- tax-exempt nonprofit organizations whose current missions and practice substantially meet criteria for organizational tax exemption, including, where appropriate, eligibility to receive tax-deductible contributions;

- non-exempt nonprofit organizations, receiving no special tax consideration other than coverage by the nondistribution constraint (including those hospitals, schools, and colleges not able to demonstrate a mission beyond the sale of their services, as well as most membership, professional, and commercial nonprofit organizations); and

- for-profit organizations.

The third sector, by this redefinition, could thereby be sweated down to a much smaller universe of organizations than the present hodgepodge of 1.5 million member- and public-serving organizations that includes social clubs, churches, labor unions, business associations, service providers, and political parties. A third space of vital and productive action could thus replace a statistical nonprofit sector, which at present includes many organizations only incidentally connected to the advance of human welfare.

This "statistical nonprofit sector," consisting of organizations vastly disparate in purpose, structure, and mission, has taken the form of a societal "Roach Motel," into which organizations stream to check in, but few if any ever check out.[6] Would it not make better sense, in terms of both research and law, to allow those among them who begin with a third-sector mission, but have then become essentially commercial or governmental, to be shown to a decent but firm exit from the sector?

What remained would be a true third sector, consisting of organizations advancing missions of service and advocacy—and adhering to the principle of providing means: blind service in a context of abundant voluntarism and charitable support. Both member-serving and public-serving organizations would continue to be among those awarded special tax consideration, but the crucial tests would lie in the actual activities of the organization.

Those organizations that would remain in a sweated-down sector would benefit from the focused application of tax exemption and deductibility. Indeed, a smaller sector would make a strong claim for increased levels of tax deductions for their donors, as the flow from the charitable "tax expenditure" budget would be blocked from reaching essentially commercial establishments like hospitals and fee-driven private schools, colleges, and universities.

The largest change here would involve the loss of deductibility of contributions to many educational institutions at the college and university level, now supported on grounds of a long-held tradition that sees these organizations as worthy of unquestioned public support. My suggestion would require these organizations to earn that support, not simply by providing a service they label as "education," but also by meeting the tests suggested above. Supplemental support of essentially commercial educational institutions perceived to play an important public role could be provided, in addition, by public subsidies in the form of vouchers and other demand-side forms of assistance.[7]

A lean third sector, consisting only of organizations true to principles of voluntary citizen-driven service and advocacy, would merit both the public privileges and the reputation it must continue to earn. Quality would thus prevail over quantity, and appropriate recognition would be given to the basic organizational fact, underwritten by 300 years of American history, that organizational missions and structures shift over time, regularly crossing the boundaries between institutional sectors. Surely the time has come to let organizations exit as well as enter the space that is the usually vital, often vibrant, and always shifting ground of America's third sector.

# 15

# Growing Civil Society, Using the Third Space

If Erich Fromm has been the 20th century's quintessential societal analyst, Vaclav Havel may be seen to stand as its foremost visionary of what voluntary action may contribute to the building of civil society and the productive filling of society's third space. Widely known for the plays he has written, the dissent he expressed in his nation's struggle for freedom, and the dignity and good humor with which he has served as president of the Czech Republic, Havel is also a searching social thinker, whose work provides the outlines for a powerful theory of the third space.

## Living within the Third Space

Havel came of age as a dissident intellectual in what he now calls a "post-totalitarian" society, the repressive but largely non-violent Czechoslovakia of the post–World War II era. While neither permitted to attend university nor trained as a social scientist, Havel nonetheless came to articulate a powerful and persuasive theory of society in which voluntarism stands at the very core.

In his essay "The Power of the Powerless," Havel (1990: 42–44) identifies the role of ideology in a totalitarian society: "It acts as a kind of bridge between the regime and the people, across which the regime approaches the people and the people approach the regime." Ideology creates a "bridge of excuses between the system and the individual," which "spans the abyss between the aims of the system and the aims of life." In such a system, everyone is involved and enslaved, "not only the greengrocers but also the prime ministers. . . . Both . . . are unfree, each merely in a somewhat different way."

The human spirit can only survive in the face of so stark a social reality by "living within the truth," by which Havel (1990: 59–60) indicates "any means by which a person or a group revolts against manipulation: anything from a letter by intellectuals to a workers' strike, from a rock concert to a student demonstration, from refusing to vote in the farcical elections to making an open speech at some official congress, or even a hunger strike."

Living within the truth means that an individual comes to recognize the depth of society's moral crisis, the degree to which his time and place has drifted from the bounds of sanity. And this task faces us in the "free" societies of the West as well as the post-totalitarian societies of Central Europe:

> A person who has been seduced by the consumer value system, whose identity is dissolved in an amalgam of the accoutrements of mass civilization, and who has no roots in the order of being, no sense of responsibility for anything higher than his or her own personal survival, is a *demoralized* person. The system depends on this demoralization, deepens it, is in fact a projection of it into society. (Havel, 1990: 62)

But consciousness alone will not suffice; it is necessary to develop as well what Havel calls a "hidden sphere" (p. 66) in society, a place safe from political control. This space includes "everything from self-education and thinking about the world, through free creative activity and its communication to others, to the most varied free, civic attitudes, including instances of independent social self-organization" (p. 85). This hidden sphere forms "an area where a different life can be lived, a life that is in harmony with its own aims" (p. 102) and which begins to impact and change the "power structure" of society (p. 105).

In the post-totalitarian society, state-dominated associations begin to disintegrate under the pressure of student and youth organizations, which represent "genuine expressions of the tendency of society to organize itself" (p. 108). And in Western societies, a similar process of liberation from the manipulations of big governments and big corporations is also required. Indeed, in the Western "democracies," "People are manipulated in ways that are infinitely more subtle and refined than the brutal methods used in the post-totalitarian societies" (pp. 115–16). They may enjoy personal freedoms and securities, "but in the end [these freedoms] do them no good, for they too are ultimately victims of the same automatism, and are incapable of defending their concerns about their own identity or preventing their own superficialization" (ibid.).

"What then is to be done?" Havel's answer involves the "moral reconstitution of society" (p. 117). "I believe in structures . . . that are open, dynamic and small; beyond a certain point, human ties like personal trust and personal responsibility cannot work." Havel concludes his essay by describing the spontaneous model of organization that emerged in the Czech third space in 1989, and identifies this process as a model from which all who value democracy may learn.

Timothy Garton Ash (1990: 147) observed Havel as he put his theories into practice during ten historic days in Prague in 1989. Garton Ash observes that

> A concept that played a central role in opposition thinking in the 1980s was that of "civil society." 1989 was the springtime of societies aspiring to be civil. Ordinary men and women's rudimentary notion of what it meant to build a civil society might not satisfy the political theorist. But some such notion was there, and it contained several basic demands. There should be forms of association, national, regional, local, professional, which would be voluntary, authentic, democratic, and, first and last, not controlled or manipulated by the Party or the Party-state. People should be "civil": that is, polite, tolerant, and, above all, non-violent. Civil and civilian. The idea of citizenship had to be taken seriously.

Civil society exists where people create and/or find spaces to come together to meet with each other, share feelings, thoughts, and observations, and then follow those considerations with action, when they should so choose. Such space must at once exist on levels psychological, social, political, economic, cultural, and physical. That is, it requires individuals entering it to be motivated to interact with others, possessed of the skills required to join in mutual consideration, permitted to gather by legal authority, comfortable enough to devote time and energy to the process, able to transcend cultural diversities through interaction, and possessed of an actual place to gather.

Such third spaces are problematic in every time and place.[1] They may be perceived as potentially revolutionary, and therefore in need of governmental regulation, as in France. Or they may be seen as detracting from the higher business use of property, as in shopping malls, and therefore in need of prohibition. But where they can be found and sustained, such third spaces contain the chance that people can gather, and, in ways small but important and, sometimes, great and significant, make the world a better place.

Havel's vision of the third space involves places where people come together to do the important work of finding themselves by building a just and humane social order. We have seen in previous chapters that this space is no respecter of sector: it may be in a commercial establishment like Swarthmore's Booksource, a public milieu like the University College of Cape Breton, or a nonprofit venue like Chester's Eastside Ministry or Camden's Shalom Baptist Church. What is centrally important about the third space is not where it is located, but how it comes that people decide to congregate there to do their work.

David Riesman and Nathan Glazer (1950), in a classic article, explained the quality of work citizens must perform if their societies are to be healthy and productive. Such work, they found, takes the form of "involvement" in ways that individuals invest with both "affect" and "competence." Five specific criteria for such involved, competent, and engaged action in social affairs were presented, and stand yet today as criteria for the productive development of human activity within society's third space. In such space, activity is generated that:

1. is more directly concerned with achieving human ends than it is with securing institutional means;

2. is more directly concerned with what has been or can be personally experienced than with more remote interests;

3. expresses a concern with the welfare of self and others rather than exclusively with self or exclusively with others;

4. addresses trends and elements that are not necessarily in the focus of attention of the mass media rather than issues exclusively drawn from events currently in the media's eye;

5. shows people exercising a critical or independent view of authority, rather than evincing an unquestioning acceptance or rejection of the claims of any particular authority.

## Locating Society's Third Space

If the third space of society is where society's members gather as whole individuals to address matters of common concern, then where do we find "first" and "second" spaces? Here I would suggest we recall Walter Adamson's suggestion that civil society occupies "the public space between large-scale bureaucratic structures of state and economy on the one hand, and the private sphere of family, friendships, personality, and intimacy on the other" (quoted in Walzer, ed., 1995: 44). The first space, thus, can be seen as the private sphere of family, kin, and neighborhood, while the second space is occupied by the large-scale structures of governmental, corporate, and many large nonprofit organizations. What distinguishes the third space is not the formal characteristics of its organization, but the quality of its process and the scope of its ambition. It is in the third space that whole persons come together to reflect and act upon what they need as members of a broader community and world. That space can exist within organizations of any time, as well as in the interstices between them.

The third space is not independent from society's major institutions: government at all levels, businesses large and small, nonprofit organizations directed toward member or public benefit, schools, religious organizations, families, communities, neighborhoods, and the like. Rather, the third space exists in dynamic interdependence with, and within, these basic societal institutions, linking individuals in their home bases of family and community to the larger governmental and economic structures within which all citizens, workers, and consumers must necessarily learn to seek their way in contemporary society.

Returning to the PECTS schema introduced earlier in this book, it now becomes possible to restructure it as follows. In the *first space:*

C = those organizations that represent the essential structures of society: families; kin groups; neighborhoods; primary gatherings within churches and other faith-based institutions; school networks of students, parents, and teachers; and other face-to-face groups through which people make sense of the world they live in and values are shared, built, and communicated. These linkages may, in a modern society, be more or less insulated from control by, and support of, public or market modalities. What transpires in this sphere forms the basic character of a society, but also fuels the nature of its "culture wars." In the contemporary United States, these culture wars focus on such issues as abortion and the right to life, the privacy of choice of sexual partners, public support of school vouchers and their links to religious expression, and public access to television, radio, and other mass media.[2]

In the *second space,* several sets of institutional realms, including:

P = those institutions that emerge from a democratic polity: government at all levels and a plethora of non-governmental organizations chartered and funded by public action. Included here are many nonprofit social service agencies, largely funded from governmental sources. These organizations may appropriately be identified as forming a governmental sector.

E (economic), N (nonprofit) = those organizations designed to provide gainful employment or profit for their workers and owners, including both for-profit businesses and corporations and not-for-profit enterprises offering services, largely for fee, to their clients/consumers/members. Included here are most nonprofit hospitals, nursing homes, colleges and universities, museums and other cultural organizations, business/professional/labor union organizations. These organizations may appropriately be identified as forming a "private" sector.

And, not to forget, Religion (faith-based organizations) and Education (schools, colleges, and universities)—each with their own traditions, professional identities, bases in university curricula, and institutional autonomies and privileges. Some might want to place them in P, E, and N, as above, but to most actors within these spheres, theirs are separate and distinct organizational realms of action.

In the *third space:*

TS = the third space of society, located within the interstices of its politics, economics, and culture. Included in this space are those voluntary, nonprofit organizations which represent (to use Gamwell's [1984] felicitous term) the "teleologically prior" concerns of such action—advocacy for social change and justice, service to the poor and despised, articulation of concerns for community and quality of life in the context of social responsibility. Also included in this space are individual and collective acts of reflection and action that extend beyond the formal limits of their duties and responsibilities within governmental, corporate, family, religious, educational, media, or other established organizations. This space is driven by individuals acting as organizers of their communities and entrepreneurs of its social, economic, and political enterprises, acting beyond their normal roles as functionaries of these organizations and institutions. Plausible members in this version of what David Morris (1999) calls the "independent sector" include small farms, community pharmacies, independent booksellers, and community cooperative enterprises. Excluded would be those para-political, para-social, and para-economic clubs and cabals that seek to work outside the realm of law in society; they would remain subject to both the rule of law and exclusion from a legitimate role in the third space.

The third space is a normative concept, one that requires a quality of outcome, and simply the assumption of a particular organizational form. Third space cannot be produced by the simple transmutation of an excess corporate profit into a charitable "gift": tainted money remains suspect unless it is transformed by a self-conscious philanthropic effort.[3] What is teleologically prior about voluntary action is the coming together of individuals to address issues of significant personal, community, and social concern—and their efforts to somehow improve the world as a result of that dialogue.

Included in the third space are some, but certainly not all, of the member-focused "grassroots organizations" that David Horton Smith (June and September 1997) has persistently reminded us are central to the voluntary sector. Such organizations hold great potential in the third space, but often confine themselves to limited, consummatory goals and activities, rather than serving to link individuals to broader societal concerns and structures. As Robert Putnam observes (2000), there is a wide and important difference between participatory processes that bring people together across the social chasms of class, race, gender, ethnicity, and the like, and those that wall people off from such diversity in their own clubs, neighborhoods, religious institutions, schools, and communities.[4]

The process by which the third space is built often begins with a single step—the thoughtful and humane action of an individual, seeking to join with others in advancing the impact of that action. Such steps may, or may not, originate or continue to be located within the confines of any of society's "sectors." It is highly likely, however, that the action will not be moved solely by the quest for either economic profit or governmental coercion. But it may be motivated in part by such economic or political constraints, as long as it is also infused by criteria such as those recounted by Riesman and Glazer.

The work that can be done within the third space is manifold. As Hammack and Young (1993: 404–405) have shown, it may include:

- the provision and production of services
- advocacy for causes
- building of consensus for change
- promotion of innovation
- support for the basic functioning of democracy and markets
- promotion and protection of key societal values
- provision of knowledge

These important societal tasks are not only advanced by formal tax-exempt organizations within the third sector. They can also be accomplished by the enlightened efforts of for-profit businesses and corporations, attuned to social purpose and community need as well as the expansion of the bottom line. And they can be secured as well by governmental actions, at the national as well as the local levels, which are inspired by legislators and administrators committed to the intelligent use of democratic powers.

## Ten Steps for Building, Preserving, and Extending Society's Third Space

In concluding this final chapter, let me speak very plainly. The commercialization of nearly everything in American life, in combination with the privatization, isolation, and trivialization of so much of contemporary politics, media, and family life, severely threatens important traditions of common concern and action in our society. William Galston (1998: 11) has expressed this dilemma powerfully:

> When Americans say (as they have repeatedly in opinion surveys over the past decade) that the United States is in the grip of a moral crisis, they mean in part that key formative institutions—families, neighborhoods, public schools, voluntary organizations, religious institutions, and governmental structures—are weaker than they once were. They also mean that newer social forces, particularly the mass media, are stronger than they should be and tend to foster traits of character—greed, violence, lust, misogyny, disrespect, heedlessness, passivity—at odds with true virtue.

There are a number of things we, in our various roles as persons and citizens and organizational members, employees, and leaders, might choose to do, faced with these challenges. Each of these actions will bring us into contact with entrenched interests, often backed by formidable financial and organizational resources. On the side of the third space, there stands the power of ideas and organized individuals. Contests between such forces are often uneven, but not wholly foreordained. There are a variety of actions that might be taken, and I will suggest a list of ten:

1.  RECOGNIZE THAT THIRD SPACE HAS A WORTH ABOVE JEWELS. Without the possibility of acting with others in a space in which complaints are heard, injuries recognized, and injustices righted, the individual is really no more than a cog in a gigantic organizational machine. Being able to respond critically and effectively to the many needs for understanding and change that living with others provides is as close to an invaluable skill as life provides any of us.

2.  LET THE BUSINESS-LIKE NONPROFITS BE, BUT ONLY SUBSIDIZE THOSE THAT MERIT SUPPORT. Big government, big business, commercial nonprofit organizations—each is important in providing for the many needs of a modern society. But these mass organizations should not be celebrated for gifts they do not provide. If they are service organizations, by all means let them serve. If some of them want to indulge in a bit of puffery or boosterism about belonging to "the nonprofit sector," let them have their harmless fun. But there is no need to enshrine that or any other organizational sector in society. Rather, society's top-heavy organizations might be recognized for what they really are—largely commercial establishments exempt, in some cases, from some taxation, and often providing what some people need and want, though almost always at a price. Without processes of internal citizenship

and control (third space within them!), these large organizations can get out of control—manipulating their consumers, voters, members. Such organizations, whether large or small, fully deserve a response from the third space, ranging from action from within to boycotts and other demonstrations from without.

3. HOLD A CONTEST TO VALIDATE A NAME FOR SOCIETY'S THIRD SPACE. A wide range of names have been applied to society's third space, and most have proved inadequate to the task. It is not an entirely "voluntary" sector, because paid staffers play crucial roles in many of its organizations. Neither "tax-exempt" nor "nonprofit" captures any but the driest legalisms, and hardly inspires enthusiasm. "Independent sector" flies in the face of the "interdependence" of these organizations, and stands as a rather silly oxymoron in the field. "Communitarianism" has meaning, but fails to trip off the tongue in any persuasive fashion. "Points of Light" provides a nice image, but suffers from an excessive individualism as well as the hand of laissez-faire ideology. "Charitable" as a modifier carries the same limitation. "Third sector" is a rather intriguing term, but the very presence of a "sector" can be challenged, as seen in the previous chapter. "Civil society" is a hopelessly murky and polysemic (one term, many meanings) concept, which can be molded into almost any shape. "Third space" is my effort to prompt a reconsideration of name. "Active society" is surely what I would like to see created, and may still be the most accurate and inspiring term yet created (cf. Etzioni, 1968). Why not call a national contest to name what it is that we can identify and value, but have yet to signify with an evocative and accurate identity?

4. INVENTORY THIRD SPACE IN COMMUNITIES—LOCAL, REGIONAL, NATIONAL AND GLOBAL. This is a challenge for the researchers among the readership of this book, but individuals can make their own impressionistic assessments as well: every neighborhood, town, or region needs to nurture its third space. A census is recommended: Where can and do people actually get together to talk and explore? In churches, coffee shops, bookstores, and city halls? How much space is available, and with what ease? How can this space be expanded in terms of its visibility and accessibility? And, on the national and global levels, how can third space become a virtual creation, linking individuals and groups electronically across the limits of distance?

5. BE A JOINER OF THIRD SPACE. One can be led to third space, but what does it take to enter and participate there? Here the message needs repetition: "Come on in—the water's fine!" And the oldest law of voluntary action still applies: people will volunteer to

participate if they are asked to do so by someone they know and trust. Whether it be a discussion group, a voluntary service providing organization, a community-oriented church or other faith-based group, a local theater or arts center, a social change organization or movement, a political party, a block association, a union, a parents' association, a seniors' or youth group (and so on and on), it will provide a chance to join with others in linking to a broader world of meaning and purpose. This chance is usually worth taking, and, unless the group that is joined is really a coercive messianic movement, it is always possible to excuse oneself early or not return for a second session.

6. PROVIDE FINANCIAL SUPPORT TO ORGANIZATIONS YOU KNOW, NOT THOSE THAT ONLY PROMOTE THEMSELVES WELL AND ADVERTISE EFFECTIVELY. The fund-raiser's call is to the nonprofit as the catalog is to the corporate marketer. In both cases, let the buyer beware! The best rule, of course, is to give to organizations which you know by dint of your own personal acquaintance, such as organizations for which you volunteer or are a member. There are, of course, compelling reasons to support organizations that work nationally or internationally, and scale in itself should not dissuade giving. But givers should be as certain as they can that the organizations they support are valid and vital, and that they really need one's individual gift.[5]

7. BE A CREATOR OF THIRD SPACE, WHEREVER AND WHEN-EVER. The best of physical spaces, designed in the built environment, will not suffice to produce valued interaction. Somebody has to take the first step, dream the dream, and take the risk of suggesting a conversation, a meeting, a process, an action. Such individuals are the true social entrepreneurs of society, for the risks they take involve the use and creation of social capital.

8. TRACK AND TRUMPET THE ACCOMPLISHMENTS WON IN THIRD SPACE. When something happens, it is vital to let other folks know about it. This is where the community press can make its most important contribution. When a campaign is underway, get the word out. When it completes its tasks, let people know what has been done, and what has been won (or lost). Academic researchers and teachers: among your most significant professional contributions are studies of what works (and what does not) and why, in the third space, and your involving students in that empirical search.

9. STRUGGLE VIGOROUSLY AGAINST THE COMMERCIALIZA-TION OF NEARLY EVERYTHING. As nearly everything is now for sale in these United States, it becomes an ever more important

struggle to sustain community- and volunteer-based organizations. The consumer can, however, buy from cooperatives where available, and pay the few extra cents that the local pharmacist or grocer needs to charge to remain financially afloat. Moneys saved by not purchasing unneeded goods are also productively contributed to the many vital organizations working effectively throughout society's third space. A world in which only commercial space existed would steadily erode the quality of any society's common and private lives.

10. BE EVER ALERT TO THE NEED FOR MORE. Social capital tends to wither when it isn't used. A working definition of an activist is "one who remains alive," or, as Erich Fromm might put it, "one who seeks to remain sane in a very difficult world." Bringing people together to make things happen is a very human and often intensely gratifying way to live.

## A Final Observation

In the final analysis, what really counts is the informed, voluntary, and self-actualizing activity of individuals, joined with others in a search to build a better, fairer, and more productive society. Organizations and institutions often, but certainly not always, provide for such worthy endeavors. But the test of a society like ours does not ultimately inhere in form or structure. Rather, its worth should be judged by the content of the actions and outcomes these structures generate and assure. Only some of what goes on in each sector meets the criteria for effective action within society's third space. But it is what happens in that space that most surely indicates the value of a society's accomplishment.

How successful are we at the turn of a millennium? How vital is our democracy? How much in control are we of our economic future? How optimistic should we be for our children's lives? Take a close look at what's changing in the Swarthmore Town Center, at what's happening to work on Cape Breton Island, at what the kids are doing when they leave Chester's East Side Ministries summer program. Assess these spaces, and others within your ken. The future will begin to emerge in clearer view.

# NOTES

### 1. Building Blocks for the Third Sector

1. William Van Til presents his autobiography, including the story of his mother's early life in Gananoque, in *My Way of Looking at It* (1996).

2. Among the 19th-century associationalists identified by Hirst are Robert Owen, Pierre-Joseph Proudhon, F. W. Maitland, John Neville Figgis, Otto von Gierke, G. D. H. Cole, Harold Laski, and Emile Durkheim.

3. "The Responsive Community Platform: Rights and Responsibilities," pp. 251–67 in Amitai Etzioni, *The Spirit of Community* (New York: Crown Publishers, 1993).

4. A related analysis by William Julius Wilson focuses particularly on the low-income black community. See *When Work Disappears: The World of the New Urban Poor* (New York: Knopf, 1996).

5. For a full description of the time dollar approach, see Cahn and Rowe (1992).

6. "What Does It Take to Be a 'Social Entrepreneur?'"

7. My suggestion to the serious reader is to begin a consideration of the "civil society" concept with two readers, one edited by John Burbidge (1998), the other by Michael Walzer (1995).

### 2. Mapping the Boundaries

1. Two-sector maps see the third sector simply as a residual organizational category, lacking both the clarity and the power of the two primary sectors of state and market. Belgian economist Sybille Mertens (1998) describes such renditions as belonging to the "old scheme of things," and maps the third sector as simply serving as background to the first two sectors.

2. This ordering has been presented by Bruce Hopkins in his influential book *Law of Tax-Exempt Organizations* (1997).

3. For a number of other visual representations of the sectors, see Kramer (1998), Appendix.

4. Economic definitions of the third sector are based on the concept of exchange (cf. Dewey, 1927). Among the most influential economic approaches are those of Mancur Olson (1971), Kenneth Boulding (1973), Henry Hansmann (1987a), and Burton Weisbrod (1988). Olson defines the problem of the "free rider" as endemic to voluntary organization; Boulding posits the existence of a "grants economy"; Hansmann posits market failure as a basic force

behind voluntary organization development; and Weisbrod brings these elements together in an integrated theory. A weakness of the economic perspective, which lends itself well to the charting of national accounts of productivity, involves the underestimation of voluntary action. Much of what third-sector organizations do is not easily or appropriately valued in dollars (cf. Hodgkinson et al., 1992).

5. Nonprofits caught Tocqueville's eye as he looked at America because he was looking at democracy. In a sense, the third sector exists in relation to the concept of democracy in a society (cf. Bellah et al., 1985). More recently, Jennifer Wolch (1990) argues that one of the most significant roles of nonprofits involves advocacy, social innovation, and to "watch government." If nonprofits are perceived as intermediaries in society, then it is in their capacity as mediators that nonprofits act as advocates for the values, issues, and rights that are part of the interests of the sector. More importantly, they are a voice for the common good. They come to serve as a non-governmental way of expressing the power of the people. Etzioni (1993; cf. also Etzioni 1976) proposes that the political role of voluntary organizations be extended to provide a forum where the community vision can develop. He sees voluntary associations functioning as agents to build a sense of "common good," rather than as representatives of special interests in the political debate.

6. In *The Law of Tax-Exempt Organizations* (1997), Bruce Hopkins proposes a methodology for "defining" charitable organizations, which resembles the child's game: "I will tell you what it is not, you guess what it is." According to Hopkins, the best way to understand is to contrast. Not surprisingly, a negative definition of nonprofits surfaces. One positive factor for inclusion in the sector is, however, provided. According to Hopkins, the "private inurement" doctrine is currently the substantial dividing line adhered to in many recent tax court decisions. Clearly a "nonprofit" is fundamentally not meant to enrich anyone.

7. David Billis (1993) writes that organization theory has been insufficiently applied to understanding the managerial and organizational issues in the third sector. He formulates a third-sector definition from the organizational perspective. On the organizational culture of these public and private worlds, Billis reminds us that these organizations develop clearly understood rules of the game, bureaucratic structures, managerial command systems, membership and voting structures, and are based on ideas of commitment, love, and affection. In examining organizations this way, Billis raises the question of how third-sector organizations represent or advocate the interests of their stakeholders and members.

## 3. The Third Sector as a Political Force

1. For the clearest and fullest descriptions of this tradition, cf. Hall (1992) and Salamon (1997).

2. The preceding paragraphs have been drawn from Jon Van Til, "NCRP: A Qualitative Assessment," paper presented to ARNOVA, November 1999. Robert Smucker and I authored the section presented here, and I am grateful to him for his research and colleagueship.

## 4. National Service in Theory and Practice

1.  Data informing this chapter have been collected as part of a national study of AmeriCorps designed, conducted, and administered by the George H. Gallup International Institute, and funded by the Robert R. McCormick Tribune Foundation. The support of that foundation is gratefully acknowledged, though the author is solely responsible for the interpretations drawn in this book.

The first phase of the study consisted of a national opinion survey of AmeriCorps, conducted in August 1995 by the Gallup Institute. Gallup conducted 1,027 interviews, creating a weighted base of 1,624 interviews, ensuring a random sample of the national population.

The second phase involved a qualitative study of the field workings of AmeriCorps, conducted between January and May 1997. Three field sites were selected for these observations, assuring a wide range of community variation: the predominantly white, middle-class, and middle-sized Western city of Colorado Springs; the predominantly minority, poor, and small Eastern city of Camden (New Jersey); and that quintessential metropolitan city, Chicago. The Camden focus groups contained representatives from programs throughout the southern portion of New Jersey, including Atlantic City.

In each of the cities selected for the field research, three sets of interviews were conducted: 1) in-depth interviews were conducted with 16 selected community leaders, focusing on their perception and opinions of the AmeriCorps programs in their locales; 2) focus group interviews were conducted with 10–12 participants in AmeriCorps programs in these locales; and 3) focus group interviews were conducted with 10–12 nonprofit organization managers who served as "employers" of AmeriCorps participants in the three cities.

2.  Most of the AmeriCorps members interviewed in the focus groups served in the core program, AmeriCorps*State and National. Two members of the Colorado Springs group were drawn from AmeriCorps*VISTA.

3.  A second set of findings show that black and lower-income respondents value the instrumental gains of national service more highly than do white and upper-income respondents. No surprise there. But blacks and lower-income respondents also value the symbolic gains of national service more highly. These findings are supportive of Christopher Lasch's view of the "revolt of the elites" in American society. Blacks and low-income respondents report more enthusiasm, excitement, and outright patriotism than do those in more advantaged societal positions.

## 5. The Emerging Field of Nonprofit Policy Study

1.  For an analysis by a leading scholar who also served as a delegate to the Summit, see Brudney (1999).

## 6. Making Money, Wielding Power, and Other Temptations of Nonprofit Life

1.  John Glaser (1994: 76) sees Aramony as a "human service entrepreneur." Such people, he writes, "have the ability to take a simple idea and mold it into something that can be visualized and implemented. Their enthusiasm

is highly contagious, and they can provide an organization with a sense of mission, excitement, and momentum. However, a darker side to Aramony's entrepreneurial personality gradually emerged that created major problems."

### 7. The Art and Business of Nonprofit Organization Management

1. Journalists and reformers can also try to apply the "sweat test." Computer billionaire Bill Gates was taken to task early in the nonprofit literature for charitable stinginess. However many billions he donates never seem to be enough to his critics. Whether Gates breaks out in a sweat about this has not yet been determined.

2. See Van Til et al. (1990) for further consideration of these variations in historical and contemporary philanthropic practice.

3. A particularly useful discussion of these concerns occurred at the May 1999 meeting of the annual "Nonprofit Management Regional Research Forum," held in Philadelphia under the sponsorship of LaSalle University's Nonprofit Management Development Center.

### 8. When the Business of Nonprofits Is Increasingly Business

1. Another argument along similar lines is made by David Starkweather in his chapter "Profit Making by Nonprofit Hospitals," in Hammack and Young (1993: 105–37).

2. More recent data published in the NPT, however, does indicate that the situation seems to have reversed for day care, with the vigorous expansion of programs offered by the YWCAs of America.

3. Ian Zack, "We Want U! How Madison Avenue Educated the American University," *New York Times*, August 5, 1998, p. B8.

4. Cedric Jennings is the subject of a book by Ron Suskind, *A Hope in the Unseen: An American Odyssey from the Inner City to the Ivy League* (New York: Broadway Books, 1998).

5. See, in particular, Ralph M. Kramer, *Voluntary Agencies in the Welfare State* (Berkeley: University of California Press, 1981).

6. Evans and Boyte (1992: 18) elaborate upon their usage. "We have used the terms 'space' and 'social space' to suggest the lived, daily character of those networks and relationships that form the primary base of social movements. The concept of social space grows from traditions of social geography, ethnology, and phenomenology. It suggests strongly an 'objective,' physical dimension—the ways in which places are organized and connected, fragmented, and so forth; and a subjective dimension, space as understood, perceived, and lived—what seems customary, familiar, part of daily experience."

### 9. Civil Education: Moving to Define an Ambiguous Tradition

1. John Dewey, *Education Today* (New York: Greenwood Press, 1940), quoted in Robelen, p. 1.

2. Quoted in Robelen, 1998, p. 3.

3. Quoted in ibid., p. 4.

4. Quoted in ibid.

5. Among faculty members offering courses involving "academically

based community service" are linguist William Labov, anthropologist Peggy Sanday, and natural scientist Robert Giegengack.

6. Cf. Center for Community Partnerships, "Summary of Penn–West Philadelphia Public Schools Initiatives." Philadelphia: University of Pennsylvania Office of the Vice President for Government, Community, and Public Affairs, April 22, 1998.

7. For further consideration of the Commission's report, see below, Chapter 13. The Commission also makes a number of recommendations for schools that do not pertain to citizen education: developing a "basic curriculum"; testing teachers; developing a voluntary national testing system for students; and expanding school choice. *A Nation of Spectators: How Civic Disengagement Weakens America and What We Can Do about It.* Final Report of the National Commission on Civic Renewal. College Park, Md., 1998, pp. 14–15.

8. Edward J. Bloustein, "Community Service: A New Requirement for the Educated Person," pp. 462–65 in Benjamin R. Barber and Richard M. Battistoni, *Education for Democracy* (Dubuque, Iowa: Kendall-Hunt, 1993).

9. "Rethinking the Purpose of Education," *Educational Leadership.*

## 10. On the Contemporary Hope for Faith and Charity

1. The Commission adds: "Today, because we remain a strongly religious nation, faithful citizens and faith-based institutions are pivotal to any American movement for civic renewal. . . . Leading scholars have called for the development of new local and regional nonprofit grant-making entities that would assist corporations, foundations, and individuals in identifying and supporting worthy faith-based youth and community-building efforts. We agree completely."

2. A fuller consideration of the report of this commission, and the two preceding, will be found in Chapter 13.

3. Their book is *Making Ends Meet* (New York: Russell Sage, 1997).

4. A principal goal of Monsma's effort is to extend the realm of religion-related service organizations to include K–12 schools, which have largely been excluded from receiving such assistance by a series of Supreme Court decisions, which have distinguished school services of the young from social services provided more mature clients.

5. Niki Kapsambelis, "Numbers Falling, Klan Tries to Remake Itself," *Philadelphia Inquirer,* 19 November 1998, p. R3.

## 11. Social Entrepreneurship and the End of Work

1. "The government should also award grants to nonprofit organizations to help them recruit and train the poor for jobs in their organizations. Providing a social wage—as an alternative to welfare—for millions of the nation's poor, in return for working in the nonprofit sector, would help not only the recipients but also the communities in which their labor is put to use." Rifkin, 1995, p. 258.

2. "Providing tax deductions for persons donating their time to volunteer efforts would ensure greater involvement in a range of social issues that need to be addressed." Ibid., p. 257.

3. "Regardless of the particular approaches used to shorten the work week, the nations of the world will have no choice but to downshift the number of hours worked in coming decades to accommodate the spectacular productivity gains resulting from new labor- and time-saving technologies." Ibid., p. 233.

4. "[P]rivate enterprise and government should aim to stimulate the most promising labor-intensive economic activities and stop encouraging new technology that will further destroy jobs—reviving, for example, the practice of making cars and appliances partly by hand. A parallel policy would tax companies for their use of labor-saving technology; the revenues from this tax would pay for alternative jobs for people in occupations that technology renders obsolete. This idea makes good business as well as social sense: human workers are needed as customers for the goods that machines now produce." Also: "In the long run, if the cancer of joblessness spreads more widely among the population, large numbers of the present middle class will have to adapt to the reality that eventually most workers may no longer be employed full time. . . . Worksharing would most likely be based on a 24-hour week. . . . At that point, everyone would in fact be working part-time by today's standards, and new ways to maintain standards of living would have to be found." Herbert J. Gans, "Fitting the poor into the economy," *Technology Review* 98, no. 7 (October 1995), pp. 72–73.

5. "Time Dollars are service credits that reward people—with purchasing power as well as an affirmation of self-worth—for helping others. . . . Time Dollars [also] help knit neighbors into community." Edgar Cahn, "When Money Is Time," *New York Times* op-ed, January 9, 1993.

### 12. Commission Reports on the Third Sector

1. See National Committee for Responsive Philanthropy, "The Mission." Washington, D.C., 1997.

2. The Commission's full quote is remarkable: "Established philanthropy prefers the grand theory—and abstract cause—over the simple solution to a tangible problem. Many philanthropies and foundations suffer from hubris. By targeting deep-seated and intractable (and sometimes irrelevant) sources of problems, and turning up their noses at immediate actions that would both ameliorate today's problems and address yesterday's causes, they often overlook local organizations whose immediate goals are to provide for the direct needs of real people in specific communities. Like government policy makers, many of these organizations try to address broad social conditions, often referred to as 'root causes'—poverty, crime, inequality—rather than treat the manifestations, or 'symptoms,' of these conditions—such as welfare dependency, teen pregnancy, abuse, hunger, or addiction—with direct action in pursuit of rapidly observable results." National Commission on Philanthropy and Civic Renewal, 1997: 18.

3. The Council's central interest lies in the elaboration of what it calls "transmittable moral truth," and it is described above (p. 142).

4. Galston, with two other communitarian leaders, Jean Bethke Elshtain and Mary Ann Glendon, served both on the Commission and the Council on

Civil Society—the only other overlapping membership among the three groups was that held by Disney Company Executive V-P John Cooke, who participated on the Commission and attended the American Assembly conference.

### 13. Civil Society and the Escape from Madness

1. Don E. Eberly (1998: 80) identifies two forms of individualism: "The older form . . . was tied to social obligation and moral norms, while the new is a wholly private and autonomous form that is unprecedented in the American experience."

2. Benjamin Barber observes (1995: 117): "Television is unlikely to enhance learning: it is better at annihilating than at nurturing the critical facilities." Eberly (1998: 118) adds that "The real issue is [the] displacement of core social institutions with an omnipresent entertainment and information media conglomerate."

3. Amitai Etzioni (1993: 27) observes that "Marriage for many has become a *disposable* relationship. It is all too often entered into like a rental agreement—with an escape clause that if it does not suit the parties involved, they may look for another apartment." Eberly explains (1998: 47) that "there are many reasons people feel distant from each other . . . including the uprooting effects of our increasingly fast-paced and anonymous society."

4. Again Etzioni (1993: 27): "We are no longer clear if and when we ought to marry. . . . And if we beget children, it is unclear what we owe them." Francis Fukuyama (1995: 308–309) adds: "The most noticeable deterioration in community life is the breakdown of the family, with the steady rise of the rates of divorce and single-parent families since the late 1960s."

5. Jeremy Rifkin (1995: 19–20) notes that in the early decades of the 1900s, "The American business community set out to radically change the psychology that had built a nation—to turn American workers from investors in the future to spenders in the present."

6. Etzioni (1993: 27) reports that "Almost half of Americans surveyed report chronic malingering at work and calling in sick when they are not sick; one-sixth admit that they have abused drugs or alcohol while at work."

7. Rifkin (1995: 105) notes that "Corporate re-engineering is only in its infancy, and already unemployment is rising, consumer purchasing power is dropping, and domestic economies are reeling from the aftershocks of flattening corporate bureaucracies. All of these problems are likely to accelerate dramatically in the years ahead. . . ." Fukuyama (1995: 316) adds: "While proponents of the Internet have argued that the computer opens up broad new possibilities for 'virtual communities' not dependent on geographic proximity, it would appear that many technological innovations since World War II have had a privatizing effect." Rifkin's book, of course, details the profound capacities of the microchip to disemploy individuals.

8. Eberly (1998: 138) observes that "Chiseled over the entrance to the Social Science Building at the University of Chicago, which gave the United States so many Nobel Laureates in economics, is [the] statement: 'When you cannot measure it, when you cannot express it in numbers, your knowledge

is of a meager and unsatisfactory kind.'" However, he continues: "Often, the most important things in society cannot be captured in numbers or predicted by economic formulae."

9. Fukuyama (1995: 317) makes the telling observation that "many American managers still have not comprehended the ethical bargain that is at the root of lean production and a communally oriented workplace. When they look at Japan, they see a country with weak labor unions, a docile workforce, and substantial managerial autonomy. They often miss the other half of the equation: paternalistic companies that guarantee their workers job security, training, and a relatively high level of benefits in return for loyalty, hard work and above all flexibility." More recently, it has been observed that Japanese managers are beginning to be subject to the same blindness.

10. Rifkin (1995: 195) writes that psychologist Thomas Cottle "has observed that the hard-core unemployed experience symptoms of pathology similar to dying patients. . . . Cottle recalls the sentiments of one of the workers he interviewed, a forty-seven-year-old named George Wilkinson, who was once a manager of a small tool company. He told Cottle: 'There's only two worlds: either you work every day in a normal nine-to-five job with a couple of weeks vacation or you're dead! There's no in-between. . . . Working is breathing. . . .' Cottle reports that a year after making these remarks, Wilkinson killed himself with a shotgun."

11. Barber writes vividly here (1995: 231): "Jefferson's warning that merchants have no country has become a literal truth for the multinational corporations of McWorld. And the markets they ply nowadays are more anonymous still. . . . In order to confront Jihad, to whom does one write? And in what tone? 'Dear nuclear terrorist, perhaps-covertly-supported-by-Iran, perhaps-training-in-Ireland (or is it Libya?), probably-buying-in-Russia-or-Ukraine, possibly-associated-with-Hamas, but then again maybe not . . . ? Please cease and desist or we will. . . .' Then there remains the embarrassing question of what exactly it is we can or will do."

12. Again, Barber (1995: 231): "There does not finally seem to be much hope for traditional international institutions as saviors of democracy on a transnational scale in an era poised between Jihad and McWorld."

13. Sidney Verba et al. (1995: 530) observe: "Citizens complain that politicians are out of touch and unresponsive. And they complain that politicians are unfair, paying attention to some parts of the public—especially, to special interests—rather than to ordinary folks. In short they complain of inadequate voice and unequal voice. Unfortunately, these two ideals—effective voice and equal voice—do not necessarily reinforce each other. Indeed, there may be a tradeoff between them."

14. Robert Putnam (1996: 48) observes that "heavy television watching may well increase pessimism about human nature" and "induce passivity."

15. Barber (1995: 245) notes that "We get the goods but not the lives we want; prosperity for some, but despair for many and dignity for none."

16. Fukuyama (1995: 309) observes that "communities of shared values, whose members are willing to subordinate their private interests for the sake of larger goals of the community as such, have become rarer. And it is these moral communities alone that can generate the kind of social trust that is criti-

cal to organizational efficiency." Eberly (1998: 81) attributes a decline in community to the structures of suburban neighborhoods, which "often reinforce the modern values of separation, individualism, and private choice."

17. Etzioni (1993: 27) presents the chilling data that "Six out of ten [surveyed Americans—59 percent] admit to having used physical force against another person—and fewer than half [45 percent] regret it. Twenty-five percent of Americans say they would abandon their families for money, and 7 percent admit freely that they would kill someone if paid enough."

18. Bertram Gross (1980: 317) finds almost ten million Americans engaged in some sort of psychological "therapy": "the therapists, sometimes consciously and with the immediate interests of their individual patients at heart, accept the realities of a mad society—and provide the escape valves required for its acceptance by their patients."

19. Benjamin Barber (1995: 82–83) observes that religion in the modern world has become "infotainment," and that televangelists, for example, find their success measured "by dollar donations rather than souls saved." Nighttime television celebrity David Letterman regularly presented in 1998 a section of "The Late Show" that explains and then implements the "infotainment" concept.

20. Rifkin (1995: 210–13) sees a large part of America transforming itself into an "outlaw culture." Sociologist Elijah Anderson (1999) has documented the formalization of this culture into a "code of the streets." And Eberly (1998: 171) finds that the way in which the law is applied and enforced contributes to "the steady shrinking of public space": "The space that is truly voluntary and consensual, where people of intelligence and goodwill can join together in rational deliberation, disappears. Meanwhile, the spheres of society where decisions are made on the basis of regulation and power expand."

21. The reorganization of work is a central theme in Rifkin (1995, Part V) and Fukuyama (1995: 356).

22. Cf. Gross (1980), Chapter 20.

23. Rifkin (1995) presents a comprehensive and (I would also assert) compelling vision of a transformed social economy.

24. Etzioni (1993: 264) states that "individuals have a responsibility for the material and moral well-being of others, for ensuring the basic needs of all who genuinely cannot provide for themselves."

25. Cf. Robert Kuttner (1997: 348–51) for a useful discussion on "Renewing Political Life." Cf. also Etzioni (1993: 255–56).

26. Kuttner (1997: 351) describes the promise of the "policy jury" as a model for civic education and participation as part of a useful discussion on "Renewing Political Life."

27. Etzioni (1993: 259), to take one example from the contemporary reform literature, notes that "Education must be reorganized to achieve a better integration between work and schooling."

28. Fukuyama (1995: 351) notes that "modernity and tradition can coexist in a stable equilibrium for extended periods of time" and that "democracy and capitalism work best when they are leavened with cultural traditions."

29. Eberly (1998: 194) observes that "Protestant hegemony over culture is gone forever, thanks both to the rise of secularism and the emergence of newly

influential religious minorities. The search is now on for a framework that draws persons of all faiths into a common understanding of morality and common public language." Verba et al. (1995: 519) identify a further advantage to religious participation: "[B]ecause churches serve as a locus for attempts at citizen recruitment to politics and provide chances to practice politically relevant skills, religious activity has the potential to act as a compensatory factor for participation, partially offsetting the impact of socioeconomic advantage."

### 14. Beyond the Myths of Sector

1. Salamon's data may be summarized with the observation that health and educational organizations amount to two-thirds of paid employment within the nonprofit sector, but only provide one-fifth of its volunteers.

2. Salamon, Anheier, et al., 1998, p. 5; Salamon and Anheier, 1997, Table 6.6; Salamon, 1992; Salamon and Anheier, 1997, Table 11.2.

3. Drawn from Salamon, Anheier, et al., 1998, Appendix, Table 2, and p. 5.

4. Table 3 has been constructed from data presented in Salamon, 1999: 25.

5. Presentation to Independent Sector Spring Research Forum, Washington, D.C., April 1999.

6. The reference is to a commercial advertisement for an insecticide, which entraps and kills household roaches within a box-like container. Hence the name "Roach Motel" and the slogan—paraphrased in the sentence.

7. Such a change is hardly likely, given the power of universities in American life. But I challenge the reader to perform the "mental experiment" involved in such a change, if only to see whether the vision of a more rationally constructed voluntary sector appears to make sense. A similar experiment might also be conducted that separated the tax blessings enjoyed by religious institutions into essentially private (sacramental) and essentially public (advocacy and service) realms. Imagine the political controversy such a proposal might arouse! But contemplate as well the impact of increasing the charitable deduction for the remaining third-space organizations and activities.

### 15. Growing Civil Society, Using the Third Space

1. For a fuller consideration of these aspects of social space, see the work of Richard Sennett, and particularly *The Uses of Disorder* (New York: Random House, 1970), *The Fall of Public Man* (New York: Knopf, 1977), and *Palais-Royal* (New York: Knopf, 1986).

2. Among the most insightful analyses of contemporary culture wars, see Alan Wolfe, "Neither Politics Nor Economics," pp. 241–49 in Walzer, ed. (1995); and James Davison Hunter, *Culture Wars: The Struggle to Define America* (New York: Basic Books, 1991).

3. Teresa Odendahl (1990) most clearly makes this point in her analysis of the ways in which many givers seek to advance their own interests through their philanthropy. The most interesting contemporary case in the transmutation of dubious profit into philanthropy involves the wealth Charles Feeney has amassed from his ownership of a number of duty-free airport stores,

wealth protected from U.S. taxation by being held in a Bermuda-based corporation. Sizable contributions have been directed from this wealth to a variety of liberal third-sector organizations through the modality of a for-profit consulting firm, Atlantic Philanthropic Services. In effect, Feeney has created a foundation entirely insulated from the practice guidelines for progressive philanthropy developed by such organizations as the National Committee for Responsive Philanthropy. Particularly excruciating for those who accept Feeney's largesse is his insistence that they desist from any recognition of the funds. For many of his donees, the reporting of support from "Anonymous" stands out, however, as a clear signal of the source of their support. For further reading on this case, see my *NonProfit Times* article of March 1997, "Unmasking Generosity: Foundations Are Not for Anonymous Giving"; and the lead article in the February 6, 1997, *Chronicle of Philanthropy*, "A Donor's Obsession with Secrecy: Charles Feeney's Private Generosity Prompts Charity Leaders to Weigh the Merits of Anonymous Giving."

4. Contrast Putnam's view on the differences in qualities of participation with the more sterile dialogue between Smith and Lester Salamon as to which form of voluntary or nonprofit organization, "paid staff" or "volunteer-led," consists of unrecognized "dark matter" or overrecognized "bright matter" in the scholarly literature and the world of nonprofit practice (*Nonprofit and Voluntary Sector Quarterly* 27, no. 1 [March 1998], pp. 88–94). Clearly both forms of organization are important, and yet what is most important is what is created by an organization, not how brilliantly it is made to appear.

5. Some nonprofit organizations (the Shriners are the classic example) collect far more money from their campaigns than they are able to use in their work. "Elite" colleges and universities often receive gifts from donors who might productively rethink their own patterns of support, to assure that a need for their giving is really present. On the problem of imbalanced donation, cf. Milofsky and Blades (1991).

# REFERENCES

Abdelrahman, Maha M. 1998. "Civil Society . . . Second Best Option." Paper presented to the Third International Conference of the International Society for Third Sector Research, Geneva, July.

Alexander, George A. 1998. *Swarthmore by the Numbers.* Swarthmore, Pa.: Mind-Meetings Press.

Alexander, Lamar, et al. 1997. *Giving Better, Giving Smarter: The Report of the National Commission on Philanthropy and Civic Renewal.*

American Assembly. 1998. *Trust, Service, and the Common Purpose: Philanthropy and the Nonprofit Sector in a Changing America.* Indianapolis: Indiana University Center on Philanthropy.

Anderson, Elijah. 1999. *Code of the Street.* New York: W. W. Norton.

Anthony, Robert, and David Young. 1988. "The Role of the Nonprofit Sector." In David Gies, J. Steven Ott, and Jay M. Shafritz, eds., *Nonprofit Organization: Essential Readings.* Pacific Grove, Calif.: Brooks/Cole.

Barber, Benjamin R. 1984. *Strong Democracy: Participatory Politics for a New Age.* Berkeley: University of California Press.

———. 1995. *Jihad vs. McWorld.* New York: Random House.

———. 1998. *A Place for Us: How to Make Society Civil and Democracy Strong.* New York: Hill and Wang.

Barber, Benjamin R., and Richard M. Battistoni. 1993. *Education for Democracy: Citizenship, Community, Service.* Dubuque, Iowa: Kendall-Hunt.

Bates, Stephen. 1996. *National Service: Getting Things Done?* Chicago: Cantigny Conference Report, Robert McCormick Tribune Foundation.

Bauer, Rudolph. 1993. Plenary presentation at CIES Conference, Barcelona, June.

———. 1998. "Intermediarity: A Theoretical Paradigm for Third Sector Research." Paper presented to the Third International Conference of the International Society for Third Sector Research, Geneva, July.

Bellah, Robert N., Richard Madsen, Steven M. Tipton, William M. Sullivan, and Ann Swindler. 1985. *Habits of the Heart: Individualism and Commitment in American Life.* New York: Harper and Row.

Bennett, James T., and Thomas J. DiLorenzo. 1989. *Unfair Competition: The Profits of Nonprofits.* Lanham, Md.: Hamilton Press.

Bennett, William J., and Senator Sam Nunn. 1998. *A Nation of Spectators: How Civic Disengagement Weakens America and What We Can Do about It.* College Park, Md.: National Commission on Civic Renewal.

Berger, Peter L., and Richard J. Neuhaus. 1977. *To Empower People: The Role of Mediating Structures in Public Policy.* Washington, D.C.: American Enterprise Institute for Public Policy Research.

Beveridge, Lord. 1948. *Voluntary Action: A Report on Methods of Social Advance.* London: Allen and Unwin.

Billis, David. 1992. "Sector Blurring and Nonprofit Centres: The Case of the UK." A Paper prepared for Presentation to the Annual Meeting of ARNOVA. Yale University; New Haven.

——. 1993. *Organising Public and Voluntary Agencies.* London: Routledge.

Boris, Elizabeth T. 1998. "Myths about the Nonprofit Sector." *Charting Civil Society,* no. 4 (July). Washington, D.C.: The Urban Institute Center on Nonprofits and Philanthropy.

Boris, Elizabeth, and Rachel Mosher-Williams. 1998. "Nonprofit Advocacy Organizations: Assessing the Definitions, Classifications, and Data." *Nonprofit and Voluntary Sector Quarterly* 27, no. 4 (December), 488–506.

Boschee, Jerr. N.d. "What Does It Take to be a 'Social Entrepreneur?'" Minneapolis: National Center for Social Entrepreneurs.

Boulding, Kenneth. 1973. *The Economy of Love and Fear.* Belmont, Calif.: Wadsworth.

Bradley, Bill. 1996. *Time Present, Time Past: A Memoir.* New York: A. A. Knopf.

Bramson, Leon. 1961. *The Political Context of Sociology.* Princeton: Princeton University Press.

Brudney, Jeffrey L. 1999. "The Perils of Practice: Reaching the Summit." *Nonprofit Management and Leadership* 9, no. 4 (Summer), 385–98.

Buckley, William F. 1990. *Gratitude: Reflections on What We Owe to Our Country.* New York: Random House.

Burbidge, John, ed. 1998. *Beyond Prince and Merchant: Citizen Participation and the Rise of Civil Society.* New York: PACT Publications.

Cahn, Edgar, and Jonathan Rowe. 1992. *Time Dollars: The New Currency That Enables Americans to Turn Their Hidden Resource—Time—into Personal Security and Community Renewal.* Emmaus, Pa.: Rodale Press.

Canino, Maria Josefa, and Eugenia R. Echols. 1996. "Latinos and Community Based Nonprofit Organizations: A New Jersey Needs Assessment." Paper presented to the *Nonprofit Management Education 1996 Conference,* Berkeley, Calif. (University of San Francisco).

Carothers, Edward. 1970. *The Churches and Cruelty Systems.* New York: Friendship Press.

Carter, Stephen L. 1998. *Civility: Manners, Morals, and the Etiquette of Democracy.* New York: Basic Books.

Cnaan, Ram A., with Robert J. Wineburg and Stephanie C. Boddie. 1999. *The Newer Deal.* New York: Columbia University Press.

Coleman, James S. 1994. *Foundations of Social Theory.* Cambridge: Harvard University Press.

Connolly, William E. 1995. *The Ethos of Pluralization.* Minneapolis: University of Minnesota Press.

Corporation for National Service. 1997. *Strategic Plan.* Washington, D.C.

Council on Civil Society. 1998. *A Call to Civil Society: Why Democracy Needs Moral Truths.* New York: Institute for American Values.

Countryman, Matthew, and Lisa Sullivan. 1993. "National Service: 'Don't Do For, Do With.'" *Social Policy* (Fall), 29–34.

Covington, Sally. 1997. *Moving a Public Policy Agenda: The Strategic Philanthropy of Conservative Foundations.* Washington, D.C.: National Committee for Responsive Philanthropy.

Cunningham, Jill K. 1993. "Adrift in Utopia: Summer of Service Takes on Baltimore." *Philanthropy, Culture and Society* (November), 1ff.

Dahrendorf, Ralf. 1997. *After 1989: Morals, Revolution and Civil Society.* New York: St. Martin's Press.

Davidson, Greg, and Paul Davidson. 1988. *Economics for a Civilized Society.* Basingstoke: Macmillan.

DeMott, Benjamin. 1995. *The Trouble with Friendship: Why Americans Can't Think Straight about Race.* New York: Atlantic Monthly Press.

De Oliviera, Miguel Darcy, and Rajesh Tandon. 1994. *Citizens: Strengthening Global Civil Society.* Washington, D.C.: CIVICUS.

Dewey, John. 1927. *The Public and Its Problems.* New York: Swallow.

DiIulio, John J., Jr. 1998. "Beyond Ideology: Have Faith in Inner-City Youth." *Penn Arts and Sciences,* University of Pennsylvania (Fall), 7.

DiMaggio, Paul J., and Walter W. Powell. 1983. "The Iron Cage Revisited: Institutional Isomorphism and Collective Rationality in Organizational Fields." *American Sociological Review* 48, 147–60.

Duhl, Leonard. 1990. *The Social Entrepreneurship of Change.* New York: Pace University Press.

Dundjerski, Marina, and Susan Gray. 1998. "A Lesson in Mandatory Service." *Chronicle of Philanthropy* (September 10).

Eberly, Don E. 1998. *America's Promise: Civil Society and the Renewal of American Culture.* Lanham, Md.: Rowman and Littlefield.

Eberly, Don E., ed. 1994. *Building a Community of Citizens: Civil Society in the 21st Century.* Lanham, Md.: University Press of America.

Eberly, Donald J. 1988. *National Service: A Promise to Keep.* Rochester, N.Y.: John Alden Books.

——. 1991. *National Youth Service: A Democratic Institution for the 21st Century.* Washington, D.C.: National Service Secretariat.

Eberly, Donald J., ed. 1992. *National Youth Service: A Global Perspective.* Washington, D.C.: National Service Secretariat.

Ethiel, Nancy, ed. 1993. *Building a Consensus on National Service.* Wheaton, Ill.: Robert R. McCormick Tribune Foundations.

——. 1997. *National Service: Getting It Right.* Wheaton, Ill.: Robert R. McCormick Tribune Foundations.

Etzioni, Amitai. 1968. *The Active Society.* New York: Free Press.

——. 1976. *Social Problems.* New York: Free Press.

——. 1991. *A Responsive Society: Collected Essays on Guiding Deliberate Social Change.* San Francisco: Jossey-Bass.

——. 1993. *The Spirit of Community: Rights, Responsibilities and the Communitarian Agenda.* New York: Crown.

Evans, Sara M., and Harry C. Boyte. 1992. *Free Spaces: The Sources of Democratic Change in America.* Chicago: University of Chicago Press.

Evers, Adalbert. 1995. "Part of the Welfare Mix: The Third Sector as an Intermediate Area between Market Economy, State and Community." *Voluntas* 6, no. 2, 159–82.

Ferris, James M. 1998. "The Role of the Nonprofit Sector in a Self-Governing Society: A View from the United States." *Voluntas* 9 (June), 137–52.

Freud, Sigmund. 1930. *Civilization and Its Discontents.* New York: J. Cape and H. Smith.

Friedmann, John. 1987. *Planning in the Public Domain: From Knowledge to Action.* Princeton: Princeton University Press.

Fromm, Erich. 1955. *The Sane Society.* New York: Holt, Rinehart, and Winston.

Fukuyama, Francis. 1995. *Trust: The Social Virtues and the Creation of Prosperity.* New York: The Free Press.

Galston, William. 1998. "Political Economy and the Politics of Virtue: U.S. Public Philosophy at Century's End." *The Good Society: A PEGS Journal* 8, no. 1 (Winter), 1ff.

Gamwell, Franklin I. 1984. *Beyond Preference: Liberal Theories of Independent Association.* Chicago: University of Chicago Press.

Gardner, Deborah S. 1997. *A Family Foundation: Looking to the Future, Honoring the Past.* New York: The Nathan Cummings Foundation.

Gartner, Audrey, and Frank Riessman. 1993. "Making Sure Helping Helps." *Social Policy* (Fall), 35–36.

Garton Ash, Timothy. 1990. *The Magic Lantern: The Revolution of '89 Witnessed in Warsaw, Budapest, Berlin, and Prague.* New York: Random House.

Gaul, Gilbert M., and Neill A. Borowski. 1993. *Free Ride: The Tax-Exempt Economy.* Kansas City: Andrews and McMeel.

George H. Gallup International Institute. 1993a. *America's Youth in the 1990s.* Princeton, N.J.: Gallup Institute.

———. 1993b. *Perspectives on National Service.* 2 vols. Princeton, N.J.: Gallup Institute.

Gilder, George. 1981. *Wealth and Poverty.* New York: Basic Books.

Glaser, John S. 1994. *The United Way Scandal: An Insider's Account of What Went Wrong and Why.* New York: Wiley.

Gross, Bertram. 1980. *Friendly Fascism: The New Face of Power in America.* Boston: South End Press.

Hall, Peter Dobkin. 1992. *Inventing the Nonprofit Sector and Other Essays on Philanthropy, Voluntarism and Nonprofit Organizations.* Baltimore: Johns Hopkins University Press.

Hammack, David C., and Dennis R. Young, eds. 1993. *Nonprofit Organizations in a Market Economy: Understanding New Roles, Issues, and Trends.* San Francisco: Jossey-Bass.

Hansmann, Henry. 1987a. "Economic Theories of Nonprofit Organization." In W. W. Powell, ed., *The Nonprofit Sector: A Research Handbook.* New Haven: Yale University Press.

———. 1987b. "The Evolution of the Law of Nonprofit Organizations." Paper presented to Spring Research Forum of Independent Sector, March.

———. 1996. *The Ownership of Enterprise.* Cambridge, Mass.: Harvard University Press.

Harbeson, John, Raymond Hopkins, and David G. Smith, eds. 1994. *Responsible Governance: The Global Challenge. Essays in Honor of Charles E. Gilbert.* Lanham, Md.: University Press of America.

Harris, Zellig S. 1997. *The Transformation of Capitalist Society.* Lanham, Md.: Rowman and Littlefield.

Havel, Vaclav. 1990. *Disturbing the Peace: A Conversation with Karel Hvizdala.* Translated from the Czech and with an introduction by Paul Wilson. New York: Knopf.

Haynes, Charles C., ed. 1996. *Finding Common Ground: A First Amendment Guide to Religion and Public Education.* Nashville: Vanderbilt University.

Hirschman, Albert. 1970. *Exit, Voice, and Loyalty.* Cambridge, Mass.: Harvard University Press.

Hirst, Paul. 1994. *Associative Democracy: New Forms of Economic and Social Governance.* Amherst: University of Massachusetts Press.

Hodgkinson, Virginia Ann, Richard W. Lyman, et al., eds. 1989. *The Future of the Nonprofit Sector: Challenges, Changes, and Policy Considerations.* San Francisco: Jossey-Bass.

Hodgkinson, Virginia A., Murray S. Weitzman, Christopher M. Toppe, and Stephen M. Noga. 1992. *The Nonprofit Almanac, 1992–1993: Dimensions of the Independent Sector.* San Francisco: Jossey-Bass.

Hoefer, Richard. N.d. "Nonprofit Group Influence on Social Welfare Program Regulation." Washington, D.C.: Aspen Institute Nonprofit Sector Research Fund.

Hopkins, Bruce R. 1997. *The Law of Tax-Exempt Organizations*. 7th ed. New York: Wiley.

Horwitz, Claudia. 1993. "What Is Wrong with National Service." *Social Policy* (Fall), 37–44.

Hyden, Goran. 1997. "Building Civil Society at the Turn of the Millennium." In John Burbidge, ed., *Beyond Prince and Merchant: Citizen Participation and the Rise of Civil Society*, 17–46. New York: PACT Publications.

James, William. 1968. "The Moral Equivalent of War" (1910). In *The Writings of William James*, ed. John J. McDermott. New York: Modern Library.

Jeavons, Thomas H. 1994. *When the Bottom Line Is Faithfulness: Management of Christian Service Organizations*. Bloomington: Indiana University Press.

———. 1998. "Is Friends' Faith Reflected in Their Economic Lives?" Philadelphia: PYM News, January–February, 2.

Kallick, David. 1993. "National Service: How to Make It Work." *Social Policy* (Fall), 2–7.

Kendall, Jane C., et al. 1990. *Combining Service and Learning: A Resource Book for Community and Public Service*. 2 vols. Raleigh, N.C.: National Society for Internships and Experiential Education.

Kramer, Ralph M. 1981. *Voluntary Agencies in the Welfare State*. Berkeley: University of California Press.

———. 1998. "Nonprofit Organizations in the 21st Century: Will Sector Matter?" Working Paper Series of the Nonprofit Sector Research Fund. Washington, D.C.: The Aspen Institute.

Kuhnle, Stein, and Per Selle, eds. 1992. *Government and Voluntary Organizations*. Aldershot: Avebury.

Kuttner, Robert. 1997. *Everything for Sale: The Virtues and Limits of Markets*. New York: Knopf.

Leland, Pamela. 1996. "Emerging Challenges to Tax-Exempt Status: Responding to a Challenge at the State or Local Level." Chapter 34-A in Tracy Connors, ed., *The Nonprofit Management Handbook*. New York: Wiley.

Levitt, Theodore. 1973. *The Third Sector: New Tactics for a Responsive Society*. New York: Amacom.

Lippitt, Ronald, and Jon Van Til. 1980. "Can We Achieve a Collaborative Community? Issues, Imperatives, Potentials." *Journal of Voluntary Action Research* 10, nos. 3–4, 7–17.

Lohmann, Roger. 1992. *The Commons: New Perspectives on Nonprofit Organizations and Voluntary Action*. San Francisco: Jossey-Bass.

Long, Robert F., and Joel J. Orosz. 1997. "Preparing Future Social Enterprise Leaders." Second Underwood Lecture at the University of Houston, April 23.

Lowi, Theodore. 1979. *The End of Liberalism: The Second Republic of the United States*. New York: Norton.

MacIntyre, Gertrude Anne. 1995. *Active Partners: Education and Local Development*. Sydney, Nova Scotia: University of Cape Breton Press.

MacIntyre, Gertrude Anne, ed. 1998. *Perspectives on Communities: A Community Economic Development Roundtable*. Sydney, Nova Scotia: University of Cape Breton Press.

McLaughlin, Thomas A. 1999. "Social Enterprise: Everyone Can and Should Learn from It." *The NonProfit Times* (February), 18.

Madison, G. B. 1998. *The Political Economy of Civil Society and Human Rights*. London: Routledge.

Magat, Richard. 1988. *Prospective Views of Research on Philanthropy and the Voluntary Sector*. New York: The Foundation Center.

Mannheim, Karl. 1949a. *Ideology and Utopia*. New York: Harcourt, Brace. (Originally published in 1929.)

——. 1949b. *Man and Society in an Age of Transformation*. New York: Harcourt, Brace. (Originally published in 1940.)

Margalit, Avishai. 1996. *The Decent Society*. Cambridge, Mass.: Harvard University Press.

Mertens, Sybille. 1998. "Nonprofit Organizations and Social Economy: Variations on a Same Theme." Paper presented to the Third International Conference of the International Society for Third Sector Research, Geneva, July.

Milofsky, Carl, and Stephen Blades. 1991. "Issues of Accountability in Health Charities: A Case Study of Accountability Problems among Nonprofit Organizations." *Nonprofit and Voluntary Sector Quarterly* 20, 371–93.

Monsma, Stephen V. 1996. *When Sacred and Secular Mix: Religious Nonprofit Organizations and Public Money*. Lanham, Md.: Rowman and Littlefield.

Morris, David. 1999. "Rooted Business." *Co-Op America Quarterly* (Summer), 11.

Moskos, Charles C. 1988. *A Call to Civic Service: National Service for Country and Community*. New York: Free Press.

National Commission on Civic Renewal. 1998. *A Nation of Spectators: How Civic Disengagement Weakens America and What We Can Do about It*. College Park, Md.: University of Maryland.

National Commission on Philanthropy and Civic Renewal. 1997. *Living Better, Giving Smarter*.

Nonprofit Sector Research Fund. 1997. *Competing Visions: The Nonprofit Sector in the Twenty-first Century*. Washington, D.C.: The Aspen Institute.

Odendahl, Teresa Jean. 1990. *Charity Begins at Home: Generosity and Self-Interest among the Philanthropic Elite*. New York: Basic Books.

Odendahl, Teresa Jean, ed. 1987. *America's Wealthy and the Future of Foundations*. New York: The Foundation Center.

Olson, Mancur. 1971. *The Logic of Collective Action*. Cambridge: Harvard University Press.

O'Neill, Michael. 1989. *The Third America: The Emergence of the Nonprofit Sector in the United States*. San Francisco: Jossey-Bass.

O'Neill, Michael, and Dennis R. Young. 1988. *Educating Managers of Nonprofit Organizations*. New York: Praeger.

Osborne, David, and Ted Gaebler. 1993. *Reinventing Government: How the Entrepreneurial Spirit is Transforming the Public Sector*. New York: Penguin.

Ostrander, Susan, Stuart Langton, and Jon Van Til, eds. 1987. *Shifting the Debate: Public/Private Sector Relations in the Modern Welfare State*. New Brunswick, N.J.: Transaction Press.

Parsons, Talcott. 1966. "On the Concept of Political Power." In R. Bendix and S. M. Lipset, eds., *Class, Status and Power*, 2nd ed., 1240–65. New York: Free Press.

Partnering Initiative on Education and Civil Society. 1998. "Declaration: Weaving a Seamless Web between School and Community." Washington, D.C.

Paton, Rob. 1991. "The Social Economy: Value-Based Organizations in the Wider Society." In Julian Batsleer et al., eds., *Issues in Voluntary and Non-Profit Management*, Chapter 1. Wokingham (U.K.): Addison-Wesley.

Payton, Robert. 1984. "Major Challenges to Philanthropy." In the proceedings of the 1984 Independent Sector Meeting and Spring Forum, ed. Virginia Hodgkinson. New York: Independent Sector.

——. 1988. *Philanthropy: Voluntary Action for the Public Good*. New York: American Council on Education, Macmillan Press.

Pestoff, Victor. 1991. "Cooperatization of Social Services—An Alternative to Privatization?" Paper presented at 10th EGOS Colloquium on "Societal Change between Market and Organization," Vienna. Summarized in Ivan Svetlik, "The Voluntary Sector in a Post-Communist Country: The Case of Slovenia," in Kuhnle and Selle, 1992, p. 200, and Kramer, 1998.

Polanyi, Karl. 1957. *The Great Transformation.* Boston: Beacon Press. (Originally published in 1944.)

Poppendieck, Janet. 1998. *Sweet Charity? Emergency Food and the End of Entitlement.* New York: Viking.

Putnam, Robert D. 1993. "The Prosperous Community: Social Capital and Public Life." *The American Prospect,* no. 13 (Spring), 35–42.

———. 1996. "The Strange Disappearance of Civic America." *The American Prospect* (Winter), 34–48.

———. 2000. *Bowling Alone: Civic Disengagement in America.* New York: Simon and Schuster.

Putnam, Robert D., with Robert Leonardi and Raffaella Y. Nanetti. 1993. *Making Democracy Work: Civic Traditions in Modern Italy.* Princeton: Princeton University Press.

Riesman, David, and Nathan Glazer. 1950. "Criteria for Political Apathy." In Alvin Gouldner, ed., *Studies in Leadership: Leadership and Democratic Action,* 505–59. New York: Harper and Brothers.

Rifkin, Jeremy. 1995. *The End of Work: The Decline of the Global Labor Force and the Dawn of the Post-Market Era.* New York: Tarcher/Putnam.

Robelen, Erik W. 1998. "Reengaging Young People." *Infobrief: An Information Brief.* Washington, D.C.: Association for Supervision and Curriculum Development, 13 (June).

Salamon, Lester M. 1992. *America's Nonprofit Sector: A Primer.* New York: The Foundation Center.

———. 1993. "The Nonprofit Sector and Democracy: Prerequisite, Impediment, or Irrelevance?" Paper presented to the Aspen Institute Nonprofit Sector Research Fund Symposium, Wye, Md.

———. 1994. "The Rise of the Nonprofit Sector." *Foreign Affairs* 74, no. 3 (July/August).

———. 1995. *Partners in Public Service: Government-Nonprofit Relations in the Modern Welfare State.* Baltimore: Johns Hopkins University Press.

———. 1997. *Holding the Center: America's Nonprofit Sector at a Crossroads.* New York: The Nathan Cummings Foundation.

———. 1999. *America's Nonprofit Sector: A Primer.* 2nd ed. New York: The Foundation Center.

Salamon, Lester M., and Helmut K. Anheier. 1992. "In Search of the Nonprofit Sector; I: The Question of Definition." *Voluntas, The International Journal of Voluntary and Non-Profit Organizations* (March).

———. 1994. *The Emerging Sector: An Overview.* Baltimore: Johns Hopkins University Press.

———. 1997. *Defining the Nonprofit Sector: A Cross-National Analysis.* Manchester: Manchester University Press.

Salamon, Lester M., Helmut K. Anheier, et al. 1998. "The Emerging Sector Revisited: A Summary." Baltimore: Johns Hopkins University Press.

Schattschneider, E. E. 1960. *The Semisovereign People: A Realist's View of Democracy in America.* New York: Holt, Rinehart, and Winston.

Schene, Patricia. 1992. "Accountability in Nonprofit Organizations: A Framework for Addressing the Public Interest." Thesis submitted to the Graduate School of Public Affairs, University of Colorado, Denver.

Schiff, Jerald. 1990. *Charitable Giving and Government Policy: An Economic Analysis.* Westport, Conn.: Greenwood Press.

Schudson, Michael. 1998. *The Good Citizen: A History of American Civic Life.* New York: The Free Press.

Schumpeter, Joseph Alois. 1947. *Capitalism, Socialism, and Democracy.* 2nd ed. New York and London: Harper and Brothers.

Schuppert, G. F. 1991. "State, Market, Third Sector: Problems of Organizational Choice in the Delivery of Public Services." *Nonprofit and Voluntary Sector Quarterly* 20, 123–36.

Scott, Jacquelyn Thayer. 1992. "Voluntary Sector in Crisis: Canada's Changing Public Philosophy of the State and Its Impact on Voluntary, Charitable Organizations." Thesis submitted to the Graduate School of Public Affairs, University of Colorado, Denver.

———. 1998. "Leveraging the Future: A Case Example of University-Community Collaboration When Hope and Resources Are Constrained." Sydney, Nova Scotia: Office of the President of the University College of Cape Breton.

Sherraden, Michael, and Donald Eberly. 1982. *National Service: Social, Economic, and Military Impacts.* New York, Pergamon.

Shils, Edward. 1997. *The Virtue of Civility: Selected Essays on Liberalism, Tradition, and Civil Society.* Indianapolis: Liberty Fund.

Smith, David Horton. 1973. "The Impact of the Voluntary Sector on Society." In David Horton Smith, ed., *Voluntary Action Research: 1973,* 387–400. Lexington, Mass.: D. C. Heath.

———. 1991. "Four Sectors or Five? Retaining the Member-Benefit Sector." *Nonprofit and Voluntary Sector Quarterly* 20, no. 2, 137–50.

———. 1997a. "The Rest of the Nonprofit Sector: Grassroots Associations and the Dark Matter Ignored in Prevailing 'Flat Earth' Maps of the Sector." *Nonprofit and Voluntary Sector Quarterly* 26, no. 2 (June), 114–31.

———. 1997b. "Grassroots Associations Are Important: Some Theory and a Review of the Impact Literature." *Nonprofit and Voluntary Sector Quarterly* 26, no. 3 (September), 269–306.

Smith, David Horton, Richard Reddy, and Bert Baldwin, eds. 1972. *Voluntary Action Research 1972.* Lexington, Mass.: D. C. Heath.

Stone, Robert. 1998. *Damascus Gate.* Boston: Houghton Mifflin.

Sumariwalla, Russy. 1983. "Preliminary Observations in Scope, Size and Classification of the Sector." In Virginia Hodgkinson, ed., *Working Papers for the Spring Research Forum: Since the Filer Commission,* 433–49. Washington, D.C.: Independent Sector, 1983.

Thompson, Ann Marie, and James L. Perry. 1998. "Can AmeriCorps Build Communities?" *Nonprofit and Voluntary Sector Quarterly* 27, no. 4 (December), 399–420.

Turner, Jonathan H., and Charles E. Starnes. 1976. *Inequality: Privilege and Poverty in America.* Pacific Palisades, Calif.: Goodyear Publishing Co.

Van Til, Jon. 1988. *Mapping the Third Sector: Voluntarism in a Changing Social Economy.* New York: The Foundation Center.

———. 1993. "Here Comes National Service." In Benjamin R. Barber and Richard M. Battistoni, *Education for Democracy: Citizenship, Community, Service,* 184–86. Dubuque, Iowa: Kendall-Hunt.

———. 1994. "Toward Responsible Volunteerism: An Exploration of Operative Doctrines." In Harbeson, Hopkins, and Smith, 1994, 433–49.

———. 1996a. "In the Third Space: On Civil Society and Other Popular Buzzwords." *NonProfit Times* (March).

——. 1996b. "So Many Answers, So Few Solutions." *NonProfit Times* (October).

——. 1997a. "Of America's Promise: Summit Was Grand, but Issues Remain." *NonProfit Times* (June), 20.

——. 1997b. "Making Their Commission." *The American Benefactor* (Fall), 11–12.

——. 1999. "NCRP: A Qualitative Assessment." Paper presented to ARNOVA, November.

Van Til, Jon, et al. 1990. *Critical Issues in Philanthropy.* San Francisco: Jossey-Bass.

Van Til, William. 1996. *My Way of Looking at It.* 2nd ed. San Francisco: Caddo Gap Press.

Verba, Sidney, Kay L. Schlozman, and Henry E. Brady. 1995. *Voice and Equality: Civic Voluntarism in American Politics.* Cambridge, Mass.: Harvard University Press.

Waldman, Steven. 1995. *The Bill: How the Adventures of Clinton's National Service Bill Reveal What Is Corrupt, Comic, Cynical—and Noble—about Washington.* New York: Viking.

Walzer, Michael. 1983. *Spheres of Justice: A Defense of Pluralism and Equality.* New York: Basic Books.

Walzer, Michael, ed. 1995. *Toward a Global Society.* Providence, R.I.: Bergham.

Weisbrod, Burton. 1988. *The Nonprofit Economy.* Cambridge, Mass.: Harvard University Press.

Wernet, Stephen P., and Sandra A. Jones. 1992. "Merger and Acquisition Activity between Nonprofit Social Service Organizations: A Case Study." *Nonprofit and Voluntary Sector Quarterly* 21, no. 4 (Winter), 367–80.

Wilson, William Julius. 1996. *When Work Disappears: The World of the New Urban Poor.* New York: Knopf.

Wish, Naomi B., and Roseanne M. Mirabella. 1998. "Nonprofit Management Education: Current Offerings and Practices in University-Based Programs." In *Nonprofit Management Education: U.S. and World Perspectives,* ed. Michael O'Neill and Kathleen Fletcher. Westport, Conn.: Praeger.

Wolch, Jennifer R. 1990. *The Shadow State: Government and Voluntary Sector in Transition.* New York: The Foundation Center.

Wolf, Maura. 1993. "Involving the Community in National Service." *Social Policy* (Fall), 14–20.

Wolf, T. 1984. *The Nonprofit Organization.* Englewood Cliffs, N.J.: Prentice-Hall.

Young, Dennis R. 1988. "The Nonprofit Sector as the First Sector: Policy Implications." Part 2, no. 3 of *Looking Forward to the Year 2000: Public Policy and Philanthropy.* Spring Research Forum Working Papers. Washington, D.C.: Independent Sector.

6, Perri, and Victor Pestoff. 1993. Plenary presentation at CIES Conference, Barcelona, June.

6, Perri, and Isabel Vidal, eds. 1994. *Delivering Welfare: Repositioning Non-profit and Co-operative Action in Western European Welfare States.* Barcelona: CIES.

# INDEX

JON VAN TIL is Professor of Urban Studies and Community Planning at Rutgers University, Camden. Currently he directs his department's program in citizenship and service education. His books include *Critical Issues in Philanthropy* (1990), *Mapping the Third Sector: Voluntarism in a Changing Social Economy* (1988), *Nonprofit Boards of Directors* (co-edited with Robert Herman, 1988), and *Shifting the Debate: Public/Private Sector Relations in the Modern Welfare State* (co-edited with Susan Ostrander and Stuart Langton, 1987). Earlier books include *Leaders and Followers: Challenges for the Future* (co-edited with Trudy Heller and Louis Zurcher, 1986), *Living with Energy Shortfall* (1982), *International Perspectives on Voluntary Action Research* (1981), and *Privilege in America: An End to Inequality?* (1973).

Van Til served as editor-in-chief of *Nonprofit and Voluntary Sector Quarterly* (formerly the *Journal of Voluntary Action Research*) from 1978 through 1992. He was twice elected president of the Association of Voluntary Action Scholars, and is the founding board chair of the Center for Nonprofit Corporations (Trenton). Van Til currently serves as a trustee of the George H. Gallup International Institute.

Van Til writes a regular column in the *NonProfit Times*, the major trade magazine for the nonprofit sector, and has published in a variety of scholarly journals including *Social Work, Transaction/Society,* and the *Urban Affairs Quarterly*. In 1994 he received the Career Award for Distinguished Research and Service from ARNOVA (Association for Research on Nonprofit Organizations and Voluntary Action).